PATENT DRAWING RULES

United States Patent and Trademark Office
and the World Intellectual Property Organization
Domestic, PCT and Hague Agreement Rules

Second Edition

Studio 94 ^{S.M.}
PUBLISHING

Written & Illustrated by Murray H. Henderson
Edited by Meredith C. Prock

Dedication

I dedicate this book to my favorite policeman, my son, Detective Allen James Henderson 1953 - 2015.

ACKNOWLEDGMENTS
I would like to thank the following people for their assistance, suggestions, remarks and reviews on this book: Meredith C. Prock, editor; the various staff members from the USPTO and WIPO; Macs in Law Offices (MILO); and of special interest during my research – The Oppedahl Patent Law Firm LLC. sponsors of email discussion groups for practitioners in trademarks, patents, copyrights, Patent Cooperation Treaty, Madrid Protocol, and industrial designs. (I am a fly on the wall observing attorney problem areas); and to all those creative people I have had the gratification of assisting with their inventions, from something as simple as a new type of paper clip to the technology that helped get us to the moon.

The author is not affiliated with, nor is he endorsed by, the United States Patent and Trademark Office (USPTO) or by the World Intellectual Property Organization (WIPO).

About the Author

Murray Henderson is a graduate of Cooper School of Art, and attended Cleveland State University, Hawaii Pacific University and the University of Hawaii.

Henderson served eight years in the U.S. Navy Reserve as an Aircraft Torpedoman. He is a retired Technical Illustrator. He has worked for the NASA John Glenn Research Center, Cleveland, Ohio; NASA Langley Research Center, Virginia; Borg Warner and its Research Center, Chicago; Studio 94 Designing Woman Ltd. (his own graphic design studio in Honolulu operated with his wife, the late Evelyn Ryder Henderson).

Past President of Technology Enhancement Ltd. Hawaii; and Past President of The Inventors Connection of Greater Cleveland, a nonprofit corporation assisting independent inventors.

He has more than five decades of experience in patent and trademark drawings along with the graphics needed for business startups for inventors and intellectual property attorneys.

Henderson held a U.S. Government Secret Clearance from 1953 through 1974.

CONTENTS

CONTENTS

CONTENTS

CONTENTS

CONTENTS

CONTENTS

INTRODUCTION

This second edition titled, *Patent Drawing Rules*, was written to replace the first edition titled, *Illustrated Patent Drawing Standards.* This book is a complete rewrite that incorporates the United States Patent and Trademark Office's new rules, laws and standards that are required by the America Invents Act and the Hague Agreement Concerning International Registration of Industrial Designs, and how it affects patent drawings directly and indirectly.

The Leahy-Smith America Invents Act is a major rewrite of the patent laws of the USPTO, mainly by changing a "first to invent" to a "first to file" system to harmonize with patent systems of other countries. All of the AIA rules affect the legal applications that patent attorneys and agents will use, but I am only covering the parts that I feel will affect the patent drawings relative to first to file, affecting how you do drawings for Provisional Application for Patents, prior art, pre- and post-grant publication, and filing in other countries.

> The Hague Agreement Concerning International Registration of Industrial Designs is an agreement to harmonize all the various standards that protect Industrial Designs and Design Patents and bring them into one International Registration similar to the PCT.

Patent Drawing Rules is a concise *desk reference manual* that incorporates areas covered in various USPTO manuals and is the result of the author's many years of experience working with attorneys, agents, engineers, inventors, scientists and entrepreneurs by illustrating their inventions, trademarks and their business startup items such as business cards, letterhead, envelopes, company logos, technical manuals and illustrations for grant programs.

The author takes you through each step of the USPTO and PCT drawing requirements along with illustrations of a related patent drawing. He also covers how patent drawings are made, drawing corrections, and how to submit patent drawing sheets for paper and electronic applications to the USPTO, WIPO PCT and WIPO Hague.

> The only changes the author made to the USPTO and WIPO Drawing Rules are where the text type was changed from regular to **bold** and/or boxed-in to emphasize a point where patent illustrators or attorneys have had questions and attention is needed.

This illustrated book is not intended to be a how-to-draw-book; I assume the readers already know how to draw. This book was created to assist those new to patent drawing and intellectual property professionals in understanding the Patent Drawing Rules that are different from Commercial Drawing Standards. I quote from the USPTO:

"The drawing must show every feature of the invention specified in the claims, and is required by the Office rules to be in a particular form. The Office specifies the size of the sheet on which the drawing is made, the type of paper, the margins, and other details relating to the making of the drawing. The reason for specifying the standards in detail is that the drawings are printed and published in a uniform style when the patent issues, and the drawings must also be such that they can be readily understood by persons using the patent descriptions." From Title 37– Code of Federal Regulations (37 CFR 1.83).

USPTO drawings must illustrate only the description and claims of the patent application in a standard form, as opposed to commercial drawings that are created for competition in marketing, construction, financial, etc., and which usually have an agenda that requires the drawing to stand out from its competitors.

NOTHING IS CAST IN STONE

Everything I have written in this book is a result of my experience as noted on the previous page. There still are a lot of variables with so many patent examiners, attorneys and others in the chain of a patent application. You need to be adaptable to the changes required to complete the task.

There are fundamental differences in what the patent examiners are looking for in application drawings for either nonprovisional applications or design patent applications. The nonprovisional drawings are examined for compliance with all the various technical standards, whereas design patents are examined for their ability to illustrate the ornamental design features of the invention. Design examinations are more subjective and nonprovisional examinations are more functional. But both need to pass the same requirements for suitability for publishing both electronically or on paper.

As of FY2015 there were 8,977 Utility Patent Examiners and 184 Design Examiners at the USPTO. With all these different variables you will likely have a different experience than I did, but if you produce clean, legible drawings using the 37 CFR 1.84 Standards you should be successful.

> Most patent applications will require some changes in the description, claims and drawings; it is the nature of the process. Fortunately, at the present time, most all patent application work is done on a computer and corrections are generally a simple task. (See Chapter Five, Drawing Corrections).

Chapter One

Filing patent drawings with USPTO & WIPO:

Section 1 – Where to find the patent drawing rules

Section 2 – How patent drawings are made

Section 3:

(A) Files to be Submitted – Naming PDF Files

(B) Indexing of EFS-Web Submission

(C) EFS-Web PDF Guidelines

(D) USPTO Electronic Filing System for Patent Applications; WIPO PCT and WIPO Hague eFiling

(E) Modernization of Electronic Patent Application Process

Read Me First

The drawing and reproduction rules are from:

The United States Patent and Trademark Office (USPTO);
USPTO's provisional, nonprovisional (utility), and design patents.

The World Intellectual Property Organization (WIPO);
WIPO's Patent Cooperation Treaty (PCT)
and the Hague Agreement
on the Registration of Industrial Designs.

AUTHOR'S COMMENTS

Because of the likelihood of rule changes after this book is published,
where at all possible, I have referenced the source where the reader
can check on the Internet for possible rule changes and updates.

CHAPTER ONE
INTRODUCTION

Chapter One is divided into three patent drawing subjects:
1) Where to find the patent drawing rules
2) How patent drawings are made
3) Drawing-image naming, indexing, EFS-Web Guidelines, USPTO EFS-Web system for patent applications; WIPO PCT and WIPO Hague eFiling

I start out with "where to find the patent drawing rules" so that the reader can check if there are updated rules since publication of this book.

"Technology has the shelf life of a banana."
An adaption of a Bill Gates quote by Scott McNealy

To simplify the descriptive language used in this book, I am using the word "Rules" to cover the USPTO's various use of: code, laws, regulations and standards used with **patent drawings.** The descriptive word Rules also works with WIPO's Drawing Rules and Administrative Instructions.

GLOSSARY OF TERMS USED

PATENT DRAWING RULE
USPTO: Rule, Standard, 35 USC 113 and 37 CFR 1.84
WIPO PCT: Drawing Rule, Rule 7, 8, 11 and 49
WIPO Hague: Reproduction (Drawing) Rule 9, Administrative Instructions Part 4

DRAWING
USPTO Utility Patent – Line drawing, black & white or color photograph, computer-generated line drawing, grayscale or color modeling image. (Color used only with petition)
WIPO PCT Utility Patent – Black & white line drawings and under limited allowable black & white photographs
USPTO Design under Hague – Line drawing, black & white or color photograph, computer generated line drawing, grayscale or color modeling images

REPRODUCTION
WIPO Hague – Reproduction (drawing); line drawing, black & white or color photograph, computer-generated line drawing, grayscale or color modeling image

NOTE: The **Manual of Patent Examining Procedure** (MPEP) contains most all drawing rules listed in this book. The rules cover patent applications through the USPTO as Receiving Office. (See page 9, Simulated USPTO Home Screen to MPEP.)

How Incorrect Patent Drawings Hold Up an Application
Patent Process Flow Chart

- Conducts formalities reviews, notifies applicant of informalities and issues an Official Filing Receipt
- Assigns Class/Subclass
- Assigned to a Technology Center
- Technology Center dockets case to examiner
- **Publishes the application under 35 USC 122(b)** (for exceptions see MPEP 1120)
- Examiner processes cases in their docket in filing date order
- **Conducts substantive examination of the application (sooner depending on Technology Center or if applying under Accelerated Examination)**
- Examiner notifies applicant via Office Action, First Action Interview
- Examiner considers response from applicant
- Determination to allow or issue final rejection of the application
- Check application status

When filing a United States nonprovisional (utility) patent application along with the required drawings, the application goes through three main processing steps (see chart: The U.S. Patent Process on following page): 1) the Pre-Examination, 2) the Examination, and 3) the Post-Examination. Along with these three processing steps there are two additional examination areas that affect drawings: 1) the 18-month publication of patent applications, and 2) the Quality Review. The total U.S. Patent Process has five examination areas where the patent drawings need to be correct to drawing and reproduction rules to accomplish these three main goals; 1) describe the invention, 2) illustrate the claims, and 3) reproduce clearly.

If the incorrect drawings are rejected in the initial "Formalities Review," it can hold up the "Examination Process." If the drawings do not "reproduce clearly," the application will not be sent to the "18-Month Publication" or if they are published it can cause problems later in "Examiner's First Office Action" and/or in the "Quality Review."

"It is easier to do the job right than to explain why you didn't."
Martin Van Buren

See: Chapter Five, Drawing Corrections.

The U.S. Patent Process

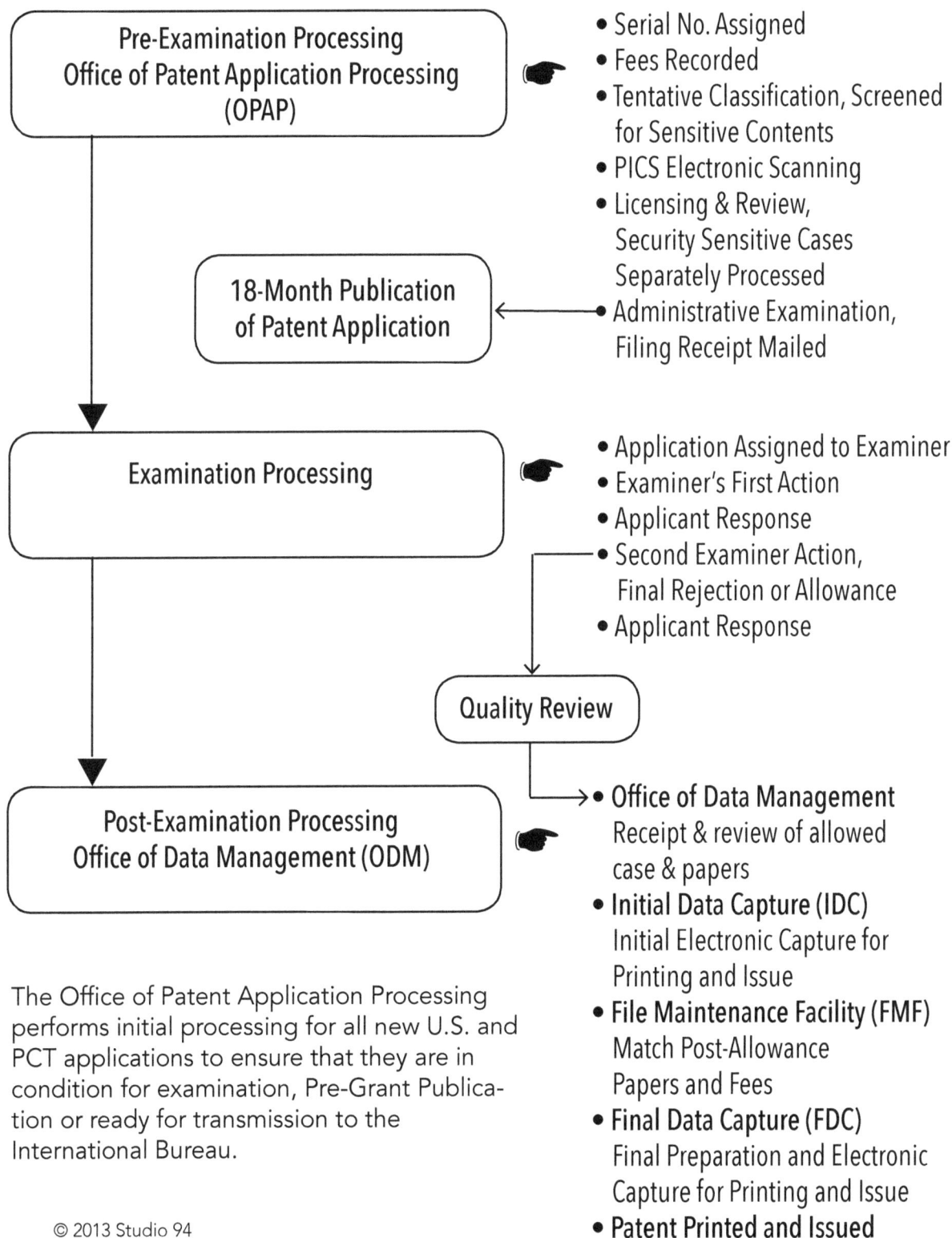

Pre-Examination Processing
Office of Patent Application Processing
(OPAP)

- Serial No. Assigned
- Fees Recorded
- Tentative Classification, Screened for Sensitive Contents
- PICS Electronic Scanning
- Licensing & Review, Security Sensitive Cases Separately Processed
- Administrative Examination, Filing Receipt Mailed

18-Month Publication of Patent Application

Examination Processing

- Application Assigned to Examiner
- Examiner's First Action
- Applicant Response
- Second Examiner Action, Final Rejection or Allowance
- Applicant Response

Quality Review

Post-Examination Processing
Office of Data Management (ODM)

- **Office of Data Management**
  Receipt & review of allowed case & papers
- **Initial Data Capture (IDC)**
  Initial Electronic Capture for Printing and Issue
- **File Maintenance Facility (FMF)**
  Match Post-Allowance Papers and Fees
- **Final Data Capture (FDC)**
  Final Preparation and Electronic Capture for Printing and Issue
- **Patent Printed and Issued**

The Office of Patent Application Processing performs initial processing for all new U.S. and PCT applications to ensure that they are in condition for examination, Pre-Grant Publication or ready for transmission to the International Bureau.

Chapter One
Section 1
Where to find the Patent Drawing Rules

> http://www.uspto.gov

> http://www.wipo.int/portal/en/

USPTO Website

If you are filing via the United States Patent and Trademark Office (USPTO)
as Receiving Office (USPTO RO), the drawing rules published in the
Manual of Patent Examining Procedure (MPEP)
cover provisional, nonprovisional, design, plant,
PCT and Hague Agreement applications.

See the Simulated USPTO Home Screen on the following page.

AUTHOR'S COMMENTS
Why do I use the Manual of Patent Examining Procedure
in reference to most Patent Drawing Rules
when there are other reference guides?
Mainly because the MPEP is what the Patent Examiners
will be using to examine your drawings for compliance
of the Patent Drawing Rules!

---

uspto UNITED STATES
PATENT AND TRADEMARK OFFICE

About Us Careers Contact Us

Search uspto.gov Q

[3] Opens Search Page.

[4] Click to open MPEP index

[2] Type in [MPEP]

MPEP   ✕ Q

Manual of Patent Examining Procedure (**MPEP**)

www.uspto.gov/web/offices/pac/mpep/index.html

Manual of Patent Examining Procedure (**MPEP**) Ninth Edition, Revision 07.2015, Last Revised
November 2015 The USPTO continues to offer an online ...

NOTE:
[1] - USPTO Web address
[2] - Type [MPEP] in search box
[3] - Opens search page
[4] - Click on top line to open current version of MPEP
         http://www.uspto.gov/web/offices/pac/mpep/index.html

[4]

Manual of Patent Examining Procedure (MPEP)

Ninth Edition, Revision 07.2015, Last Revised November 2015

The USPTO continues to offer an online discussion tool for commenting on
selected chapters of the Manual. To participate in the discussion and to
contribute your ideas go to: **http://uspto-mpep.ideascale.com**.

Note: **For current fees, refer to the Current USPTO Fee Schedule.**

Consolidated Laws - The patent laws in effect as of July 31, 2015.

Consolidated Rules - The patent rules in effect as of November 30, 2015.

MPEP Archives (1948 - 2015)

SEE: Following page for MPEP Roadmap to Patent Drawing Rules

Current MPEP:

The documents updated in the Ninth Edition, Revision 07.2015 of the MPEP, whether dated November 2015 or
October 2015, include changes that became effective in July 2015 or earlier.

Searchable MPEP

● **See the user manual or quick reference guide** for help with search features (e.g., default
     operators, proximity searches, and wild cards) and navigation.

Simulated USPTO Home Screen to MPEP

MPEP Roadmap to Patent Drawing Rules
(Manual of Patent Examining Procedure November 2015)

PROCESS
APPLICATION
(100-600)
Chapter 600 - Parts, Form and Content of Application
601 - Content of Provisional and Nonprovisional Applications
608.02 - Drawings (608.02(a) -->(z)

EXAMINATION & PROSECUTION
(700-1400)
Chapter 1400 - Corrections of Patents
1413 - Drawings (37 CFR 1.73)

PCT & OTHERS
SPECIALIZED AREAS
(1500-2000)
Chapter 1500 - Design Patents
1503.02 Design Drawings
Chapter 1600 - Plant Patents
1606 - Drawings
Chapter 1800 - Patent Cooperation Treaty (PCT)
1825 - Drawings

HEAVY DUTY REFERENCE MATERIALS
PATENTABILITY, REEXAMINATION, INTERFERENCE AND OTHER
(2100-2900)
Chapter 2900 - International Design Applications
2909.01 - Official Form
2909.02 - Reproductions (Drawings)
(Hague Rule 9 Administration Instructions 401)

LAWS, RULES & INDEX
APPENDIXES
Appendix L - Patent Laws
Appendix R - Patent Rules
37 CFR 1.84(a) -->(w)
Appendix T - Patent Cooperation Treaty
Article 7 - The Drawings (7.1 -->11.14)
Appendix AI - Administrative Instructions Under the PCT
102 - Use of Forms
410 - Numbering of Sheets for International Publication

37 CFR 1.84 Standards for Drawings

       37 CFR 1.84 is the USPTO's basic set of rules for Patent Drawings that covers most all aspects of what is required.

       The following page has a reference chart showing all parts of 37 CFR 1.84 from (a) through (w). In addition, I have attached two columns (WIPO PCT Rule & WIPO PCT Paragraph) as a reference between USPTO & WIPO PCT Rules.

       The Standards for Drawings can be located in:

MPEP Ninth Edition
Appendix R: Patent Rules
37 CFR 1.84 Standards for Drawings

See Chapter Three
Drawing Rules for Nonprovisional (Utility) Patents
for
Step-by-step details of
37 CFR 1.84(a) through 37 CFR 1.84(w)
Standards for Drawings
and
Details of PCT Rules

USPTO Code of Federal Regulations:	UTILITY PATENT DRAWING RULES: SUBJECT:	WIPO PCT RULE:	WIPO PCT Paragraph:
37 CFR 1.84(a)	Drawings	7.1, 11.10	5.128
37 CFR 1.84(a)(1)	Black ink (black line)	11.13(a)	
37 CFR 1.84(a)(2)	Color	No	
37 CFR 1.84(b)	Photographs		
37 CFR 1.84(b)(1)	Black & white (grayscale)	10.11(e)	5.159
37 CFR 1.84(b)(2)	Color	No	No
37 CFR 1.84(c)	Identification of drawings (paper filing)	11.6(t)	
37 CFR 1.84(d)	Graphic forms in drawings	11.9(b), 11.10	5.107, 8
37 CFR 1.84(e)	Type of paper	11.2, 3, 5	5.133
37 CFR 1.84(f)	Size of paper (sheets)	11.5	5.133
37 CFR 1.84(f)(1)	DIN Size A4	11.2(a)	5.133
37 CFR 1.84(f)(2)	Letter 8-1/2 x 11 inches	No	No
37 CFR 1.84(g)	Margins	11.6(c)	5.133
37 CFR 1.84(g)(1)	DIN Size A4	11.2(a)	5.133
37 CFR 1.84(g)(2)	Letter 8-1/2 x 11 inches	No	No
37 CFR 1.84(h)	Views (plan, elevation or perspective)	7.1	
37 CFR 1.84(h)(1)	Exploded views	7.1	5.129
37 CFR 1.84(h)(2)	Partial views		
37 CFR 1.84(h)(3)	Sectional views	7.1, 11.13(b)	5.129, 5.147
37 CFR 1.84(h)(4)	Alternate position		
37 CFR 1.84(h)(5)	Modified forms		
37 CFR 1.84(i)	Arrangement of views	11.10(d)	5.134, 5
37 CFR 1.84(j)	Front-page view (abstract)	3.3(a), 8.2	5.170, 1, 2
37 CFR 1.84(k)	Scale	11.13(c)(g)	5.150
37 CFR 1.84(l)	Character of lines, numbers and letters	11.13(e)	5.143
37 CFR 1.84(m)	Shading	10.1	5.158
37 CFR 1.84(n)	Symbols	10.1(d)(e)	5.157
37 CFR 1.84(o)	Legends (text matter)	11.11	5.156
37 CFR 1.84(p)	Numbers, letters and reference characters	11.13(e)(h)	5.152
37 CFR 1.84(q)	Lead lines	11.13	5.145
37 CFR 1.84(r)	Arrows	11.13	5.146
37 CFR 1.84(s)	Copyright or Mask Work Notice		
37 CFR 1.84(t)	Numbering of sheets of drawings	11.7(a)	5.140
37 CFR 1.84(u)	Numbering of views	11.13(k)	
37 CFR 1.84(v)	Security markings		
37 CFR 1.84(w)	Corrections (also see Chapter Five) and §1.85	91	5.161
37 CFR 1.58	Tables	11.10(c)(d)	5.109
	List of reference signs	11.13(n)	5.160

Reference table: 37 CFR 1.84 Drawing Rules to WIPO PCT Drawing Rules

WIPO Website

If you are filing via the United States Patent and Trademark Office (USPTO)
as Receiving Office (USPTO RO)
the drawing rules published in the Manual of Patent Examining Procedure (MPEP)
should be adequate for filing PCT and Hague Agreement applications.

NOTE:
I have included the World Intellectual Property Organization (WIPO)
Website information on the following page so that you can
locate complete details on their drawing rules if needed.

[1] http://www.wipo.int/portal/en/

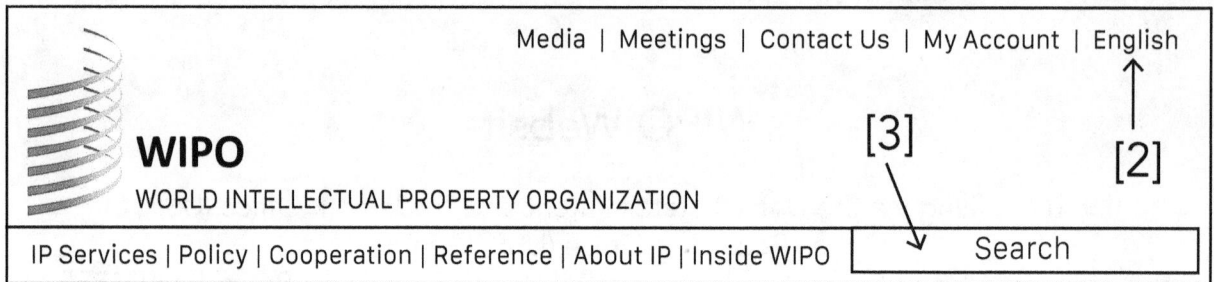

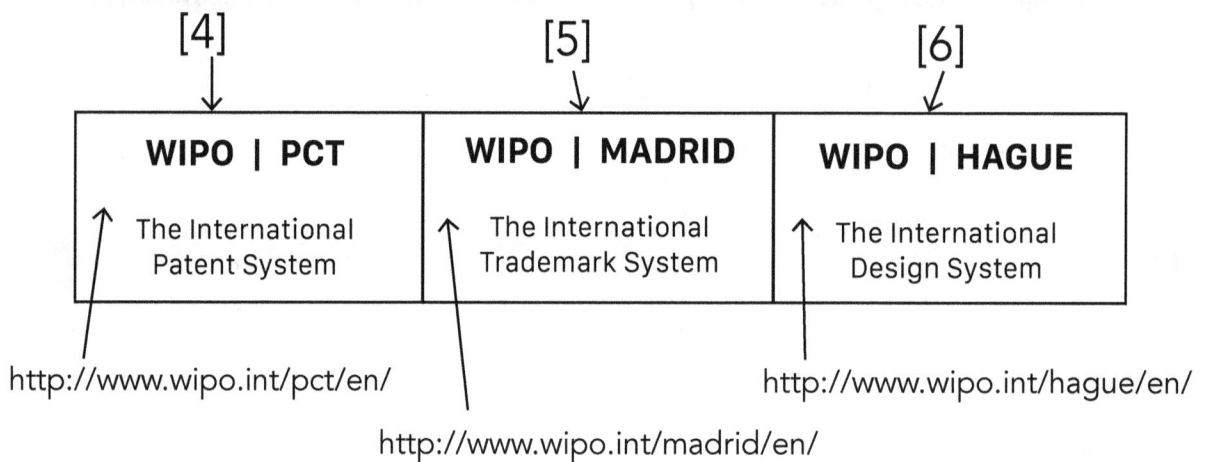

Media | Meetings | Contact Us | My Account | English

WIPO
WORLD INTELLECTUAL PROPERTY ORGANIZATION

[3]

[2]

IP Services | Policy | Cooperation | Reference | About IP | Inside WIPO

Search

[4]

[5]

[6]

WIPO | PCT

The International
Patent System

WIPO | MADRID

The International
Trademark System

WIPO | HAGUE

The International
Design System

http://www.wipo.int/pct/en/

http://www.wipo.int/madrid/en/

http://www.wipo.int/hague/en/

NOTE:
[1] - Start with WIPOs Website at www.wipo or as noted above
[2] - Select your language
[3] - Use quick search such as: [PCT Drawing Rules]
[4] - WIPO PCT Box for complete PCT selections and Drawing Rules
[5] - WIPO MADRID for information on Trademark Drawings and Reproduction Rules
[6] - WIPO HAGUE for Industrial Design Registration Reproduction (Drawing) Rules

Source: Simulated WIPO Home screen by Studio 94 Publishing
WIPO Logo image and web addresses are the property of the World Intellectual Property Organization

Simulated WIPO Home Screen.

The Drawings

PCT Rule 7
The Drawings

7.1. Flow Sheets and Diagrams
Flow sheets and diagrams are considered drawings.

7.2 Time Limit
The time limit referred to in Article 7(2)(ii) shall be reasonable under the circumstances of the case and shall, in no case, be shorter than two months from the date of the written invitation requiring the filing of drawings or additional drawings under the said provision.

PCT Rule 11
Physical Requirements of the International Application

11.5 Size of Sheets
The size of the sheets shall be A4 (29.7 cm x 21 cm). However, any receiving Office may accept international applications on sheets of other sizes provided that the record copy, as transmitted to the International Bureau, and, if the competent International Searching Authority so desires, the search copy, shall be of A4 size.
  [Author's comment: USE A4 period.]

11.11 Words in Drawings
(a) The drawings shall not contain text matter, except a single word or words, when absolutely indispensable, such as "water," "steam," "open," "closed," "section on AB," and, in the case of electric circuits and block schematic or flow sheet diagrams, a few short catchwords indispensable for understanding.

(b) Any words used shall be so placed that, if translated, they may be pasted over without interfering with any lines of the drawings. (See Chapter Three)

Author: "Words In Drawings." The use of text in drawings in filing PCT applications should be concise to facilitate translation into other languages; also if XML is used where the text is linked to the drawings, it will make it easier for the translators.

Additionally see: WIPO/PCT: *How to indicate the text matter in drawings in PCT-SAFE. February 2013* [See: Drawing Details Screen; how to indicate the text matter of the figure for publication, if the figure contains reference labels, if the figure does not contain reference labels. Formatting; Text formatting: Formulae and text containing special characters and where to get help.]

11.13 Special Requirements for Drawings

(a) Drawings shall be executed in durable, black, sufficiently dense and dark, uniformly thick and well-defined lines and strokes without colorings.

(b) Cross-sections shall be indicated by oblique hatching which should not impede the clear reading of the reference signs and leading lines.

(c) The scale of the drawings and the distinctness of their graphical execution shall be such that a photographic reproduction with a linear reduction in size to two-thirds would enable all details to be distinguished without difficulty.

(d) When, in exceptional cases, the scale is given on a drawing, it shall be represented graphically.

(e) All numbers, letters and reference lines, appearing on the drawings, shall be simple and clear. Brackets, circles or inverted commas shall not be used in association with numbers and letters.

(f) All lines in the drawings shall, ordinarily, be drawn with the aid of drafting instruments.

(g) Each element of each figure shall be in proper proportion to each of the other elements in the figure, except where the use of a different proportion is indispensable for the clarity of the figure.

(h) The height of the numbers and letters shall not be less than 0.32 cm. For the lettering of drawings, the Latin and, where customary, the Greek alphabets shall be used.

(i) The same sheet of drawings may contain several figures. Where figures on two or more sheets form, in effect, a single complete figure, the figures on the several sheets shall be so arranged that the complete figure can be assembled without concealing any part of any of the figures appearing on the various sheets.

(j) The different figures shall be arranged on a sheet or sheets without wasting space, preferably in an upright position, clearly separated from one another. Where the figures are not arranged in an upright position, they shall be presented sideways with the top of the figures at the left side of the sheet.

(k) The different figures shall be numbered in Arabic numerals consecutively and independently of the numbering of the sheets.

(l) Reference signs not mentioned in the description shall not appear in the drawings, and vice versa.

(m) The same features, when denoted by reference signs, shall, throughout the international application, be denoted by the same signs.

(n) If the drawings contain a large number of reference signs, it is strongly recommended to attach a separate sheet listing all reference signs and the features denoted by them. (**End of PCT Rule 11.13**)

The international application must contain drawings when they are necessary for the understanding of the invention. Moreover, where, without drawings being actually necessary for the understanding of the invention, its nature admits of illustration by drawings, the applicant may include such drawings and any designated Office may require the applicant to file such drawings during the national phase. Flow sheets and diagrams are considered drawings. (**PCT Article 7**)

Drawings must be presented on one or more separate sheets. They may not be included in the description, the claims or the abstract. They may not contain text matter, except a single word or words when absolutely indispensable. Note that if the drawings contain text matter not in English but in a language accepted under **PCT Rule 12.1(a)** by the International Bureau as a Receiving Office, the international application will be transmitted to the International Bureau for processing in its capacity as a Receiving Office. **See 37 CFR 1.412(c)(6)(ii).** If the drawings contain text matter not in a language accepted under PCT Rule 12.1(a) by the International Bureau as a Receiving Office, the application will be denied an international filing date.

All lines in the drawings must, ordinarily, be drawn with the aid of a drafting instrument and must be executed in black uniformly thick and well-defined lines. Color drawings are not acceptable. **PCT Rules 11.10 to 11.13** contain detailed requirements as to further physical requirements of drawings. Drawings newly executed according to national standards may not be required during the national phase if the drawings filed with the international application comply with **PCT Rule 11**. The examiner may require new drawings where the drawings that were accepted during the international phase did not comply with **PCT Rule 11**. A file reference may be indicated in the upper left corner on each sheet of the drawings.

All of the figures constituting the drawings must be grouped together on a sheet or sheets without waste of space, preferably in an upright position and clearly separated from each other. Where the drawings cannot be presented satisfactorily in an upright position, they may be placed sideways, with the tops of the drawings on the left-hand side of the sheet.

The usable surface of sheets (which must be of A4 size) must not exceed 26.2 cm x 17.0 cm. The sheets must not contain frames around the usable surface. The minimum margins that must be observed are: top and left side: 2.5 cm; right side: 1.5 cm; bottom: 1.0 cm. (**See A4 Layout Sheet**)

All sheets of drawings must be numbered in the center of either the top or the bottom of each sheet but not in the margin in numbers larger than those used as reference signs in order to avoid confusion with the latter. For drawings, a separate series of page numbers is to be used. The number of each sheet of the drawings must consist of two Arabic numerals separated by an oblique stroke, the first being the sheet number and the second being the total number of sheets of drawings. For example, "2/5" would be used for the second sheet of drawings where there are five in all.

Different figures on the sheets of drawings must be numbered in Arabic numerals consecutively and independently of the numbering of the sheets and, if possible, in the order in which they appear. This numbering should be preceded by the expression "Fig."

The PCT makes no provision for photographs. Nevertheless, they are allowed by the International Bureau where it is impossible to present in a drawing what is to be shown (for instance, crystalline structures). Where, exceptionally, photographs are submitted, they must be on sheets of A4 size, they must be black and white, and they must respect the minimum margins and admit of direct reproduction. **Color photographs are not accepted.**

The procedure for rectification of obvious mistakes in the drawings is explained in **MPEP § 1836.** The omission of an entire sheet of drawings cannot be rectified without affecting the international filing date, except in applications filed on or after April 1, 2007, where, if the application on its initial receipt date, contained a priority claim and a proper incorporation by reference statement, the original international filing date may be retained if the submitted correction was completely contained in the earlier application. **See PCT Rules 4.18 and 20.6.** Rectifications of obvious mistakes are not considered to be amendments.

The drawings can be amended during the international phase only if the applicant files a Demand for international preliminary examination. The drawings can also be amended during the national phase. The amendment shall not go beyond the disclosure in the international application as filed. **See PCT Article 34(2)(b).**

If drawings are referred to in an international application and are not found in the search copy file, the examiner should refer the application to a Quality Assurance Specialist in his or her Technology Center or a PCT Special Program Examiner. **See Administrative Instructions Section 310.**

21.0 cm (8 - 1/4 inch)

I.D. Area
5.0 cm x 1.5 cm

Top Margin 2.5 cm (1 inch)

Used only for Paper Filing.

Sight or Image Area:
17.0 cm (6 - 11/16 inch) Width
26.2 cm (10 - 5/16 inch) Height

Left Margin 2.5 cm (1 inch)

Right Margin 1.5 cm (5/8 inch)

29.7 cm (11-11/16 inch)

NOTE:
See Chapters Three and Four on the
USPTO, PCT and Hague rules for
drawing (image) placement and
separation of images in the
sight or image area.

Bottom Margin 1.0 cm (3/8 inch)

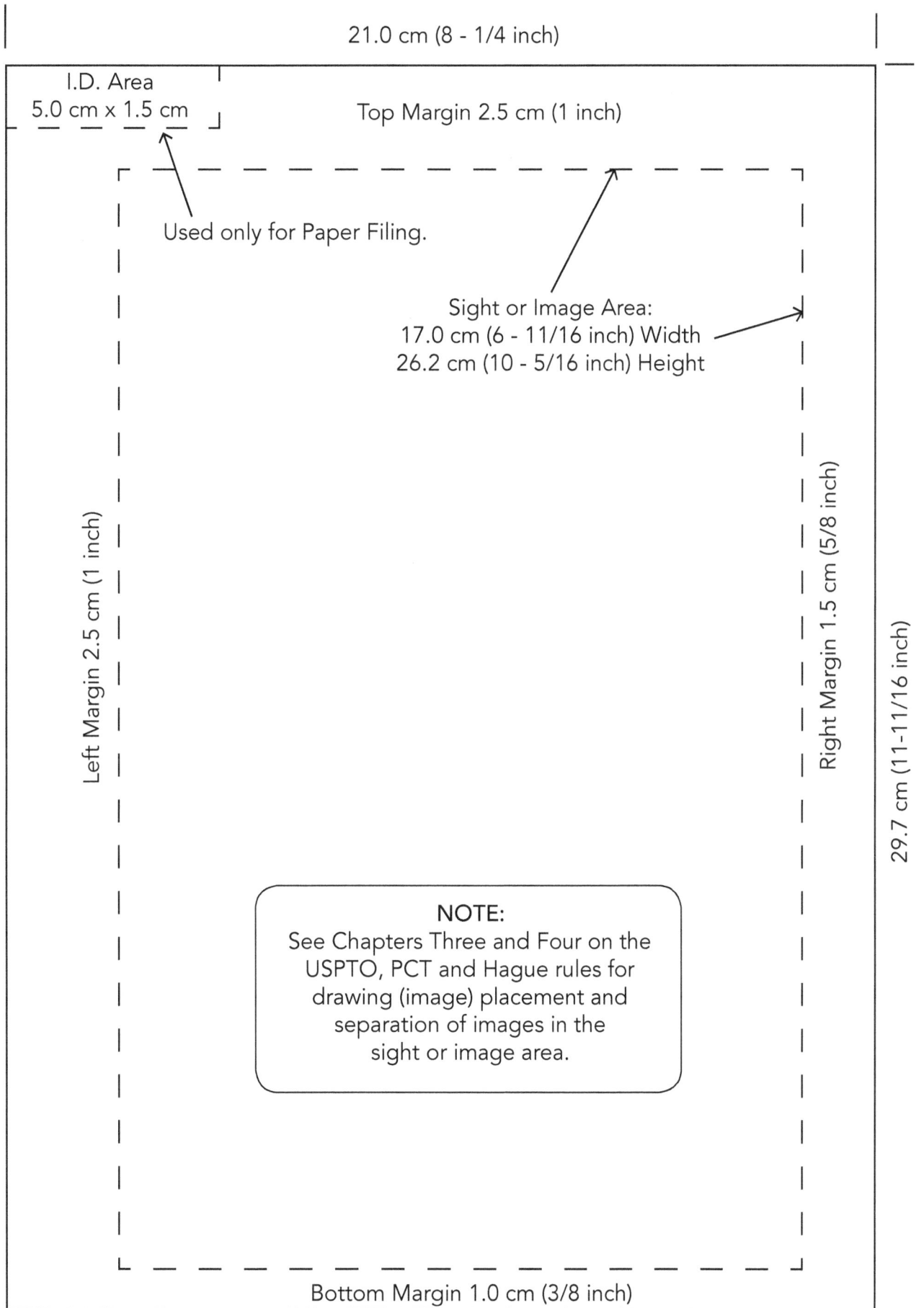

A4 Drawing Sheet Dimensions

U.S. Design Patent Drawing Rules
vs. Hague Agreement Rules

Subject Number:	Subject:	USPTO Design Patent:	USPTO Design Hague Agreement:	WIPO Hague Agreement:
1	Drawing sheet size	Letter/A-4	A-4	A-4
2	Maximum image size	16 x 24 cm	16 x 16 cm	16 x 16 cm
3	Minimum image size	37 CFR 1.84(k)	3 x 3 cm	3 x 3 cm
4	Resolution	300 dpi	300 dpi	300 dpi
5	Max. file size (per file)	5 MB	2 MB	2 MB
6	Black line drawing	Yes	Yes	Yes
7	Grayscale drawing (image)	Yes	Yes	Yes
8	Black & white photograph	Yes	Yes	Yes
9	Color drawing	Yes	Yes	Yes
10	Color Photograph	Yes	Yes	Yes
11	Mix of drawings & photographs	No	Yes	Yes
12	Figures in scale with each other	Yes	No	No
13	Maximum number of 2-D Figures	1	1	1
14	Maximum number of 3-D Figures	6 +	6	6
15	Figure numbering	FIG. 1 . . .	1.1 . . .	1.1 . . .
16	Multiple design protection	No	No	Yes-100
17	Maximum number of reproductions	None Req.	None Req.	None Req.
18	Specimens of design	No	No	Yes
19	Technical application examination	Yes-Chap16	Yes after pub.	No
20	E-Filing requirements	PDF	PDF/JPG	JPG/TIF
21	Prefered E-Filing requirement	PDF	JPG	JPG
22	Design Classification	US/Locarno	Locarno	Locarno
23	Issuance of Patent	Yes	Yes	No
		Sec.1 Chap.16	Section 2	Section 3

The above chart highlights the major differences between the USPTO's drawing rules as apposed to WIPO's Hague Agreement to the registration of industrial design rules.

See Chapter Four - Industrial design drawings and reproductions: (Rules and details)
> Section 1 - USPTO design patent rules (Chap.16)
> Section 2 - USPTO drawing rules under the WIPO Hague Agreement for Industrial Design Registrations (Designating US as a Contracting Party)
> Section 3 - WIPO Hague Agreement for Industrial Design Registration drawing and reproduction rules (International Registration); see pages 198 and 208 for guidance on preparing reproductions for Contracting States: HU, JP, KG, KR, MD, RO, SY and US.

Chapter One
Section 2
How Patent Drawings are Made

How Patent Drawings are Made

Most patent drawings today are done with the aid of a computer and some form of drawing software; if not, the drawings are made by hand using drawing instruments, then scanned either by the patent applicant or, if sent to the USPTO as a paper application, the USPTO will scan the drawings to use in their computer system.
(See illustration of: How patent drawings are made on page 26.)

What's needed to illustrate correct patent drawings?

The patent draftsman needs as much background material as possible to illustrate the various figures required for the patent application. He or she will need materials such as sketches, engineering drawings, photographs, charts, graphs and, on occasion, a prototype, if available.

Successful patent drawings are a collaboration among the inventor, patent attorney or patent agent, and the patent illustrator. Patent drawings must illustrate everything in the claims, thus more drawings may be added as the attorney or agent progresses with the application.

Acceptable patent drawings must satisfy three areas:
1) the drawings must illustrate the invention as described in the written patent application;
2) the patent drawings must illustrate each of the features described in the written patent claims; and
3) the patent drawing must be made in a specific form and uniform style that can be clearly published electronically or on paper.

It is important to have good, clean, understandable patent drawings that reproduce well both on a computer screen and on a printed page, at the same size and at a 50% reduction. One area where I have seen many bad drawings is in the drawing of sectional views where the "cross hatching" is too close together and the lines start to blur as the drawing is reduced in size.

___

The clearer the drawings the sooner the examiner, and everyone else, can understand the patent application.

___

Incorrect drawings can hold up a patent application. Generally, bad drawings are harder to correct and take longer than any other part of the patent application. With the new rules on 18-month publication, sometimes the drawings are examined before the written part of the Patent Application. If there are drawing rejections it may hold up the examination process until the drawings are corrected. (See Chapter Five – Corrections for USPTO/WIPO patent drawings.)

Degree of Accuracy Required in Patent Drawings

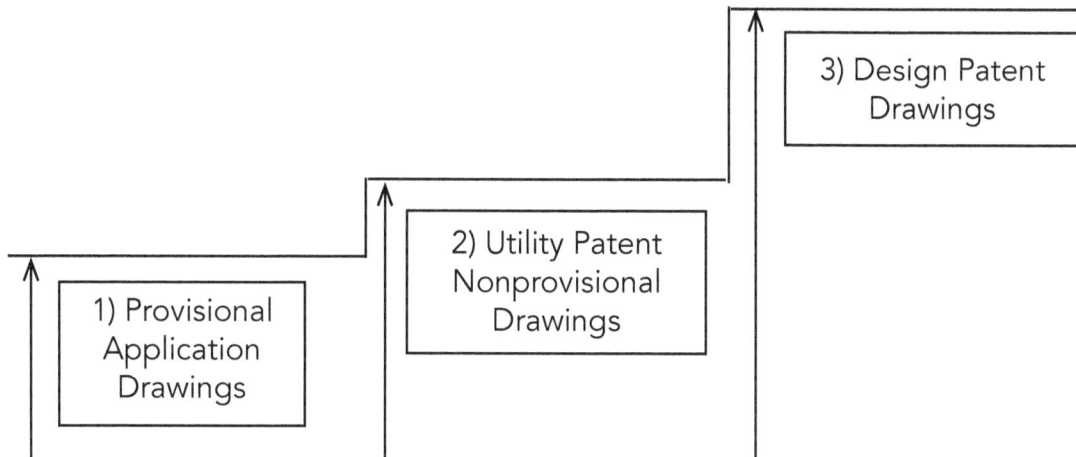

---

1) Provisional Application for Patent:
Graphics for Provisionals can be sketches (informal drawings),
finished formal drawings, photographs and computer-drawn images.

Note: Although generally they are "informal images" they still must represent
what you want to claim in your final Nonprovisional Application.

2) Utility Patent or Nonprovisional Patent:
Graphics for Utility Patents can be formal ink drawings, photographs,
computer-drawn images and analytical instrument images.

Note: Graphics for Utility Patents should be clean, sharp and reproduce well
but they are not required to have the accuracy of Design Patent Drawings.

3) Design Patent:
Graphics required for Design Patent Applications must accurately illustrate
the features of the design.
Note: The choice of media selected to illustrate the features of the design:
- Line drawings
- Photographs (black & white or color)
- Computer Modeling Images (black & white or color)

Patent Drawings are currently made by a preference for one of these three techniques:

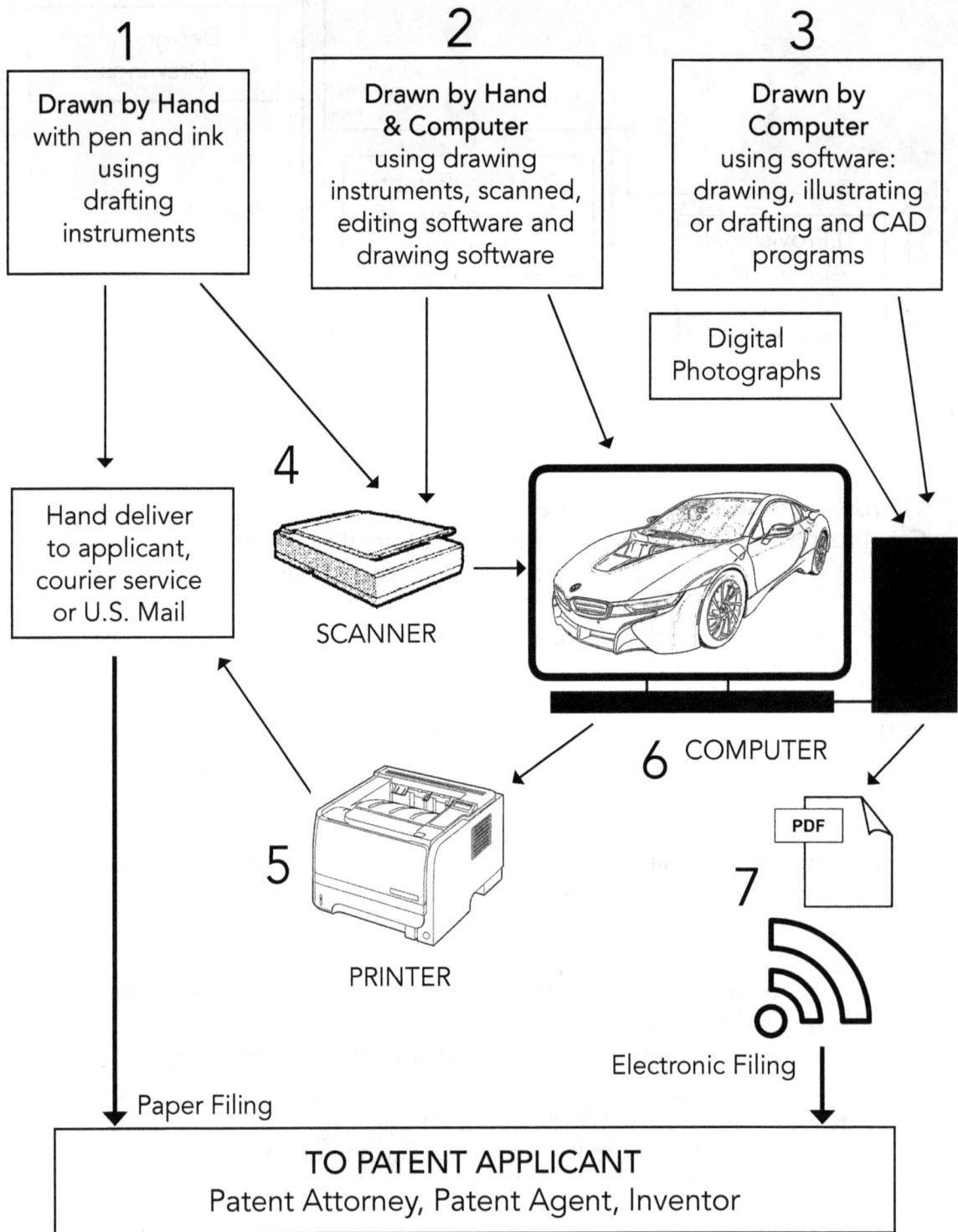

1

Drawn by Hand
with pen and ink
using
drafting
instruments

2

Drawn by Hand
& Computer
using drawing
instruments, scanned,
editing software and
drawing software

3

Drawn by
Computer
using software:
drawing, illustrating
or drafting and CAD
programs

Digital
Photographs

Hand deliver
to applicant,
courier service
or U.S. Mail

4

SCANNER

COMPUTER

6

5

PRINTER

PDF

7

Electronic Filing

Paper Filing

TO PATENT APPLICANT
Patent Attorney, Patent Agent, Inventor

How patent drawings are made; see following page for production details

PATENT DRAWING PRODUCTION DETAILS FOR:

1 – Drawn by Hand. At present, some patent drawings are still drawn by hand using pen and ink on a good quality patent board, or paper. The percentage of drawings produced this way varies with who is doing the drawings; it is estimated that only about 10% of professional patent illustrators are still drawing by hand, while approximately 50% of independent inventors do their own drawings.

2 – Drawn by Hand & Computer. Patent drawings using this method are drawn by hand then scanned as a raster image, edited, cleaned up, sized and finished by adding vector drawing, and lastly, adding the text and numbers to complete the finished drawing sheet.

3 – Drawn by Computer. Patent drawings produced using computer software such as drawing, illustrating, drafting and/or CAD software programs.

Author's Comment: I have produced patent drawings using all three of the above methods and it generally comes down to what you are given to work with and the type of patent application: utility, design or plant patent. If you are given engineering drawings to work with it generally works better with a drafting software program; process patent drawings often work better using drawing or illustrating programs; design patents generally work better drawn by hand or with illustration software; plant patents mostly are done today with good quality color photographs.

4 – Scanner. Patent drawings done by hand and/or drawings supplied by the inventor that can be scanned, edited and cleaned up must be scanned in black & white (1-bit mode). **Note:** Yes, you can scan black ink drawings in color mode and still produce a black-like color, but do not use this method because it will cause viewing problems for the USPTO patent examiners and if it should go through, it will print out poorly.

5 – Printer. Most patent drawings at present are printed out on laser printers instead of ink-drop or ink-jet printers.

Author's Comment: In printing out final patent drawing sheets, I like to use a good-quality 24 or 27 pound white, acid-free paper. If the applicant is submitting the drawings to the USPTO as hard copy then I print out all scanned copies at 600 dpi instead of 300 dpi because the Patent Office, upon receiving the application, will rescan the drawings sheets into 300 dpi. If the drawings are going to be filed by Electronic Submission, then scan black & white, 300 dpi in noncompressed or Group 4 compression. USPTO recommends cropping each graphic image to reduce surrounding white space. Save in a lossless format (e.g., TIFF, PNG, GIF, BMP).Lastly, convert image file to .pdf.

6 – Computer. Fortunately, at the present time, the USPTO's EFS-Web has adopted an electronic application submittal method that allows applicants to submit patents in PDF form over the Internet using the Linux, Macintosh or Windows-based operating systems, whereas some of the Internation electronic filing systems are still setup to only use the Windows OS.

7 – Portable Document Format (PDF). (See complete PDF details further on in this chapter.)

Advantages of CAD/CAM use for Patent Drawings

There are multiple advantages for inventors when they have their patent drawings made on a CAD/CAM based system.
(See schematic on the following page).

The advantages are:

- Input data applied to CAD/CAM has multiple uses.
- Data can be used for patent drawings.
- Data can be used for marketing drawings.
- Data can be used for engineering drawings.
- Data can be revised quickly.
- Data can be used for 3D printing for prototypes.
- Data can be used for machine-tool manufacturing.

AUTHOR'S COMMENT

Do not expect the CAD/CAM service provider to bill you for only one of these services when you ask for more than one.

In other words, just because they have the files of your engineering drawings does not mean they can make your patent drawings, for free, by just a click of their computer mouse.

Advantages of CAD/CAM with 2D & 3D Capabilities
(Computer Aided Design • Computer Aided Manufacturing)

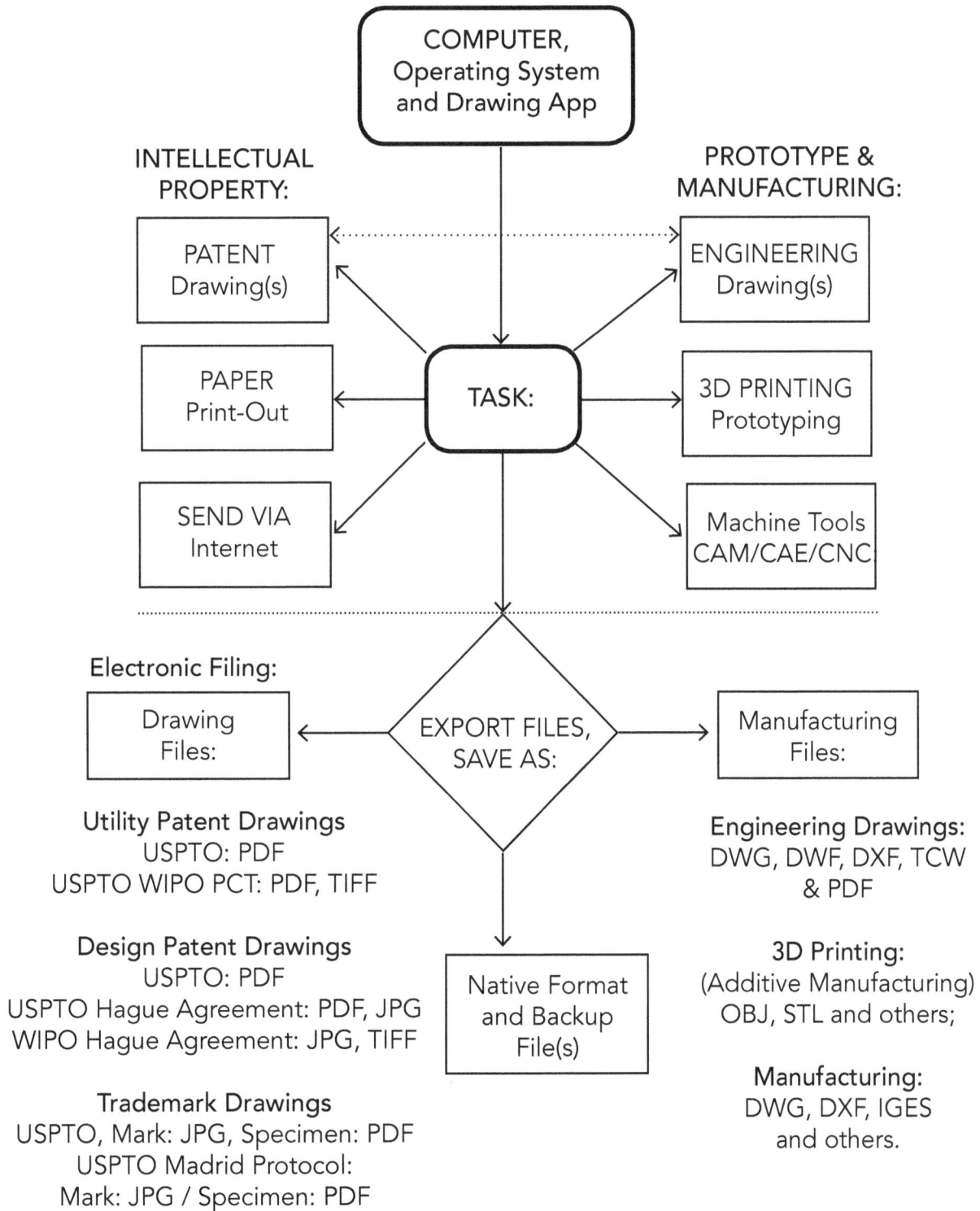

COMPUTER,
Operating System
and Drawing App

INTELLECTUAL PROPERTY:

PROTOTYPE & MANUFACTURING:

PATENT
Drawing(s)

ENGINEERING
Drawing(s)

PAPER
Print-Out

TASK:

3D PRINTING
Prototyping

SEND VIA
Internet

Machine Tools
CAM/CAE/CNC

Electronic Filing:

Drawing
Files:

**EXPORT FILES,
SAVE AS:**

Manufacturing
Files:

Utility Patent Drawings
USPTO: PDF
USPTO WIPO PCT: PDF, TIFF

Engineering Drawings:
DWG, DWF, DXF, TCW
& PDF

Design Patent Drawings
USPTO: PDF
USPTO Hague Agreement: PDF, JPG
WIPO Hague Agreement: JPG, TIFF

Native Format
and Backup
File(s)

3D Printing:
(Additive Manufacturing)
OBJ, STL and others;

Manufacturing:
DWG, DXF, IGES
and others.

Trademark Drawings
USPTO, Mark: JPG, Specimen: PDF
USPTO Madrid Protocol:
Mark: JPG / Specimen: PDF

Raster vs. Vector Use in Producing Patent Drawings

By definition a **raster (bit-map) image** is made up of hundreds/millions of tiny squares of color information, referred to as pixels or dots. (Technically pixels refer to color blocks viewed on an electronic monitor whereas dots refer to the ink dots on a printed piece; often the two terms are used interchangeably.)

A vector graphic uses math to draw shapes using points, lines and curves. A raster image of 1" x 1" square will have 300 dots horizontally and 300 dots vertically, for a total of 90,000 total dots/individual pieces of information per square inch, a vector image will only contain four points, one for each corner; the computer will use math to "connect the dots" and fill in the missing information.

Source: Jen Lombardi of Kiwi Creative, Cleveland, Ohio.

RASTER GRAPHICS:
Photographs & toned images

Raster file format extensions:
jpg/jpeg, psd, png, tiff, bmp and gif

Pros of Raster Images:
• Rich detail
• Precise editing

Cons of Raster Images:
• Blurry when enlarged
• Large file size

VECTOR GRAPHIC:
Line Drawings & Fonts

Vector file format extensions:
eps, ai, dwg, dwf, tcw and pdf

Pros of Vector Images:
• Infinitely scalable
• Smaller file size
• Edibility

Cons of Vector Images:
• Limited details
• Limited effects

AUTHOR'S COMMENTS
Most patent drawings are produced using a combination of raster and vector images that render as they were produced when you do a "save as a PDF file."
(See pages 24 and 36)
A PDF file can contain any combination of text, graphics and images:
Text: fonts used with patent drawings (use vector, do not use raster fonts)
Graphics: such as symbols, arrows, etc. (better to use vector)
Images: photographs and tone drawings (raster), line drawings (vector).

Chapter One
Section 3

(A) Files to be Submitted – Naming PDF Files

(B) Indexing of EFS-Web Submission

(C) EFS-Web PDF Guidelines

(D) USPTO EFS-Web Electronic Filing System for Patent Applications; WIPO PCT and WIPO Hague eFiling

(E) Modernization of Electronic Patent Application Process

(A) Files to be Submitted - Naming PDF Files

Files to be submitted are those relevant to the application in Portable Document Format (PDF), ASCII text file format (.TXT) and if using PCT-SAFE, .ZIP compressed file format.

File naming conventions:
EXAMPLE: Filename.pdf , Filename.txt or Filename.zip

1. Start file name with [A thru Z , a thru z , or 0 thru 9] - do not use brackets or commas; cannot start a file name with an underscore or hyphen.

2. Last 4 characters of the file name must be lowercase .pdf , EXAMPLE: .pdf , .txt or .zip

3. Can consist of any combination* of characters selected from uppercase alphabet, lowercase alphabet and/or digits zero through nine: [A thru Z , a thru z , or 0 thru 9 , _ , -] - do not use brackets, commas or symbols; can use underscore or hyphen within file name

> *any combination except the following reserved device names: CON, PRN, AUX, NUI, COM1, COM2, COM3, COM4, COM6, COM7, COM8, COM9, LPT1, LPT2, LPT3, LPT4, LPT5, LPT6, LPT7, LPT8, LPT9, or CLOCK$. You should also avoid starting a file name with any of these prohibited device names.

4. No spaces are permitted in the actual file name.
5. Spaces are permitted in your local file path.
6. Length of file name is limited to a maximum of 100 characters including the required 4 character .pdf , .txt or .zip file extension.

EXAMPLE: VALID FILE NAMES:
- Up_to_96-Alphabetic_or_Numeric_CharactersPlus.pdf
- RUNonlettersorNUMBERS.txt
- 123-12333_z.zip

EXAMPLE: INVALID FILE NAMES (ERRORS) :
- Over100charactersplusx.pdf (exceeds total 100 character limit)
- Name.PDF (ends in .PDF - must be .pdf)
- Any space.txt (cannot have a space in the file name)
- ~@#$%^&*()+=]}[{"':;?/>.<,.zip (contains invalid characters within file name)

Source: USPTO Data

Sample of Drawing File Identifier
(File Naming)

DRW-1-7-Doc-235-2016.pdf

USPTO Document Description Indexing Code:	APPLICANT Document Identifier:	USPTO / WIPO File Type Ender:
DRW - Drawing SPEC - Written Description CLM - Claims ABST - Abstract IDS - Information Disclosure Statement ADS - Application Data Sheet	(Should be unique to current application) • Docket Number • Case Number • Application Number • Attorney/Agent's Registration Number • Inventor's Name • Invention Title	.pdf: Portable Document Format .txt: Text .zip: Compression File .jpeg / .jpg: Lossy Compressed Image File .tif / .tiff: Tagged Image File .png: Portable Network Graphics

NOTES:

1) - Example **DRW-1-7-Doc-235-2016.pdf** has 24 characters:
    a) - Maximum allowed by USPTO is 100 characters. (Author's Comment: I would not use full amount)
    b) - Maximum allowed by WIPO/PCT is 20 characters
    c) - Maximum allowed by WIPO/Hague is 20 characters

2) - For **"APPLICANT Document Identifier"** I would suggest a unique identifier related to each application, (docket or job number) instead of attorney or inventor's name because of filing multiple applications with the same DRW identification.

3) - DRW Sheet 1 of 7; use "1-7" as can not use 1/7 because the "/" is an invalid character.

4) - Example can be shortened by taking out some of the "dash characters."

AUTHOR'S COMMENT
In regard to Note 1: Maximum number of characters allowed. The number has been getting smaller, generally because of space allowed on "Fillable PDF Forms." Applicants need to check this periodically.

(B) Indexing of EFS-Web Submission

Indexing

- Indexing is applying a document description to a PDF/TXT/ZIP File.
- Page ranges must be specified if multi-document selection is made in a PDF File.
- All files or the documents in a multi-document PDF File must be indexed.
- There are nearly 200 document descriptions offered in EFS-Web.

However, the document description lists are presented based on the filing type chosen.
- The filer still has the ability to choose a category to condense the document description list even more.
- All indexing is checked by the USPTO personnel.
- Indexing has no legal relationship to the patent application; indexing is a function for processing the submission.

Why index?

- Allows for quicker and more accurate downstream processing of your submission:
- Documents are instantly routed to the Image File Wrapper.
- Generates workflow and assigns the submission to the USPTO personnel to be acted upon.

NOTE:
Indexing is used in two areas in filling out electronic patent applications:
1) in appropriate "Application Parts" list, and
2) on the application parts PDF file naming.

Application Parts:
Specification........SPEC
Claims...................CLM
Abstract...............ABST
Drawings..............DRW

(C) EFS-Web PDF Guidelines

PDF Guidelines

The USPTO will be receiving electronic patent application documents in the Adobe PDF (Portable Document Format) format, from which images will be produced for the Image File Wrapper (IFW) system. Because the PDF format is so feature-rich, a standard is required to restrict submitted content to what the USPTO is prepared to receive. The following guidelines set forth here will help to ensure that the created PDF documents meet the requirements for processing at the USPTO.

The following guidelines are based in part on the PDF/A specification; a document conforming to PDF/A will meet the requirements of EFS-Web for submission to the USPTO.

Document Formatting

The page size should be either 21.0 cm by 29.7 cm (DIN size A4) or 21.6 cm by 27.9 cm (8.5 by 11 inches). Pages of a larger size will be reduced to 8.5 by 11 inches, which may affect readability of the document and/or distort any attached image.

PDF Version

The PDF document must conform to any one of versions 1.1 through 1.6 of the Adobe PDF specification. These are the versions supported by the USPTO reference viewer (Adobe Acrobat Reader version 7.0 or higher). This document will be revised to indicate support for any future versions of PDF. A review of the to-be-filed document(s) is strongly recommended before submission.

Fonts

All characters (glyphs) that make up the text of the document must be embedded. Embedding allows the fonts used in the creation of a document to travel with that document, ensuring that a user sees documents exactly as the designer intended them to be seen. Embedded fonts may be limited to a subset containing the glyphs necessary to render the document. All fonts embedded within the document must be licensed and legally embeddable.

Color Text

It is recommended that the text of the document be black. Text of other colors may not convert to image properly, resulting in unreadable or invisible text.

Images

Bi-tonal (black & white), color or grayscale images should be scanned at a minimum resolution of 300 DPI. It is recommended to use images saved in a lossless format (e.g., TIFF, PNG, GIF, BMP). It is strongly recommended that the PDF creation software does not downsample images during the PDF creation process as this could degrade the quality of the image. For color and grayscale images, it is recommended that no compression be used;   (continued on following page)

CCITT Group IV compression is recommended for bi-tonal images. The use of Alternates (a feature within PDF that allows for alternate images to be used for on-screen rendering and printing) is prohibited. Images consisting of multiple layers must be flattened before embedding into the PDF document. The properties of all layers should be marked as "visible" before flattening. This ensures that the complete image is visible to the examiner.

Layers

PDF documents with multiple layers must be flattened prior to submission to ensure that the complete document is available to the examiner. If a document contains layers that are marked as "invisible," the invisible layers will be lost when the received document is processed within the USPTO. Documents submitted with multiple layers will be flattened by the USPTO when converted to an image.

Object Content

Content that cannot render (be viewed) directly or completely to a printed page, including multimedia (e.g., sound, video, animations, slideshows), 3-dimensional models (e.g., CAD drawings), file attachments, multi-page objects (e.g., Microsoft Excel spreadsheets, multi-page TIFF images), and commenting/reviewing features (highlighting, annotations, comments, notes, and the like) are prohibited. There must be no dependencies on external files or resources of any type in order to render the attached image.

Security Features

Password protection and encryption are prohibited. Documents that are protected in this manner will not pass validation, thus will not be submitted. When files are submitted through EFS-Web, the SSL v3 / TLS v1 protocol within the TruePass security application will provide the needed security and protection.

Embedded Code/Viruses

The PDF document must be free of executables, worms, viruses, or any type of potentially malicious content. Any files that found to have potential malicious content will be deleted.

JobOptions File

Most PDF creation tools have the ability to create a customized job option file that configures the print driver to use certain printing settings. This can be used for the user's specification for creating PDF print jobs that are used frequently but are not the standard. It allows users to create PDF files that meet the USPTO guidelines. This job options file may not work with other PDF creation tools.

FONTS and PDF FILES
All PDF readers have 14 fonts built into them

All other fonts must be embedded into your PDF file transmitted to the USPTO through the EFS-Web. If you do not embed the fonts there may be a conflict between the PDF file you send and the PDF file the other party receives.

The conflict can show up in two ways: 1) the USPTO will reject your submitted PDF file; or 2) your PDF will print out one thing and the receiving PDF file will possibly print out something different.

Example of how a font conflict can lead to the wrong information being applied to a patent application:

A patent applicant may have a variety of mathematical formulas in the application and the applicant used a special font that has all the math symbols. The patent application text is typed in Times Roman, with the special mathematical font used as needed on four different pages throughout the application, including the claims.

The application is sent to the USPTO EFS-Web and when received the application text comes up the same but the special font math symbols cannot be read by the computer. The computer first tries to use a substitute and if this takes place it might print out different symbols, therefore changing the intent of the application.

The 14 Fonts built into all PDF Readers:

Courier
Courier Italic
Courier Bold
Courier Bold Italic

Helvetica
Helvetica Italic
Helvetica Bold
Helvetica Bold Italic

Times Roman
Times Roman Italic
Times Roman Bold
Times Roman Bold Italic

Symbol
Dingbat

NOTE: Other fonts used must be embedded in the PDF file.

MERGED and FLATTENED
Black & White Patent Drawings into .pdf File

LAYERS IN SOFTWARE PROGRAMS

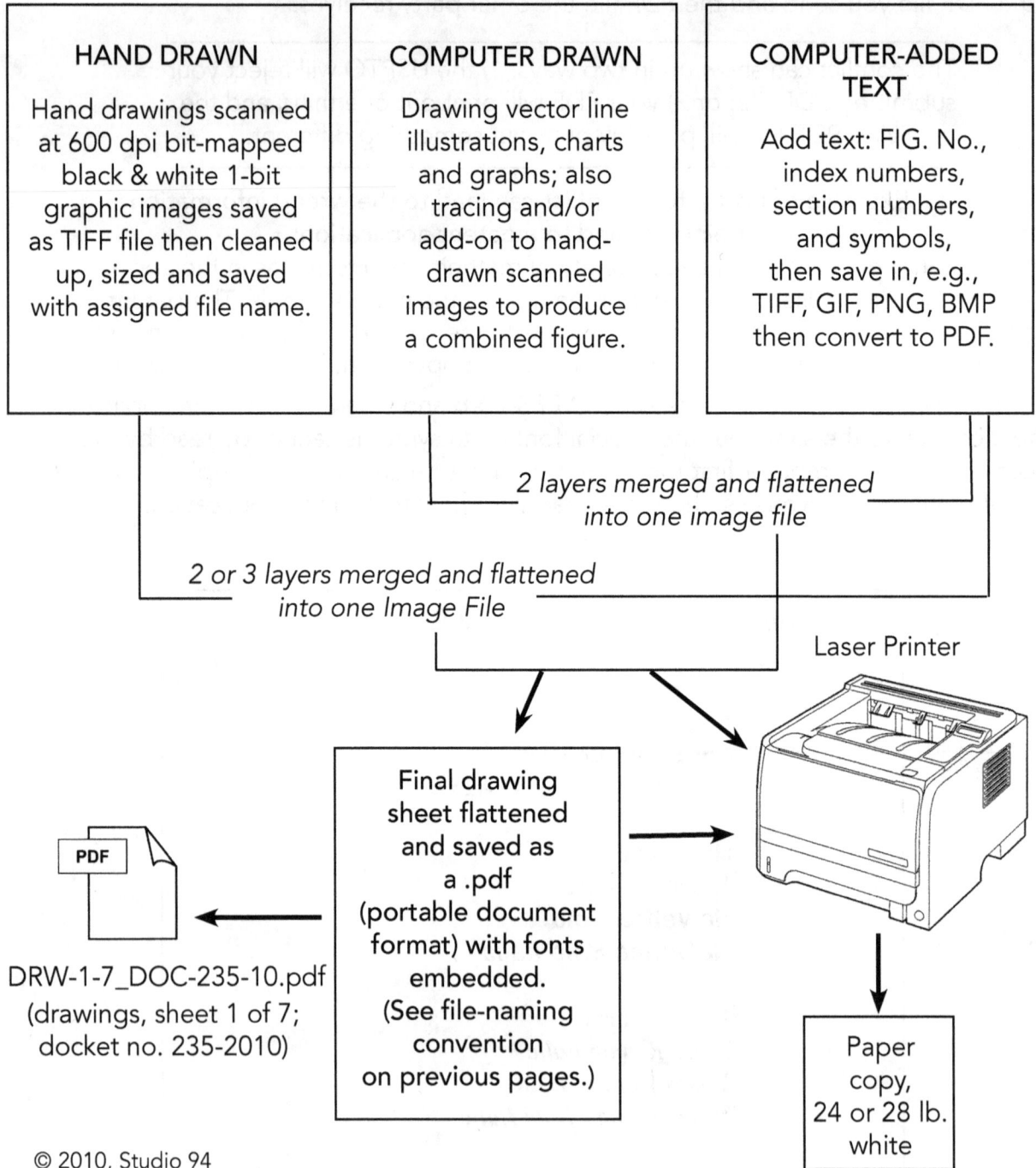

HAND DRAWN

Hand drawings scanned at 600 dpi bit-mapped black & white 1-bit graphic images saved as TIFF file then cleaned up, sized and saved with assigned file name.

COMPUTER DRAWN

Drawing vector line illustrations, charts and graphs; also tracing and/or add-on to hand-drawn scanned images to produce a combined figure.

COMPUTER-ADDED TEXT

Add text: FIG. No., index numbers, section numbers, and symbols, then save in, e.g., TIFF, GIF, PNG, BMP then convert to PDF.

2 layers merged and flattened into one image file

2 or 3 layers merged and flattened into one Image File

Laser Printer

Final drawing sheet flattened and saved as a .pdf (portable document format) with fonts embedded. (See file-naming convention on previous pages.)

PDF

DRW-1-7_DOC-235-10.pdf (drawings, sheet 1 of 7; docket no. 235-2010)

Paper copy, 24 or 28 lb. white

© 2010, Studio 94

Merged & Flattened Patent Drawings into .pdf File.

PDF FORM-FILLABLE BENEFITS AND FEATURES

EFS-Web utilizes standard Web-based screens and prompts to enable you to submit a portable document format (PDF) document directly to the USPTO within minutes. A key component of EFS-Web is the use of PDF Form-Fillable documents, which are interactive forms with various field types and formatting options that auto-load field information directly in USPTO's systems. PDF Form-Fillable files are portable; they may be circulated to various people in your office for completion prior to being submitted to the USPTO.

When used in conjunction with EFS-Web, PDF Form-Fillable documents can help the intellectual property community ease the filing and submission process and accelerate the processing of patent applications and documents in USPTO's technology infrastructure for users.

PDF FORM-FILLABLE BENEFITS
• Form-Fillable PDF's allow USPTO to extract form data directly into the main database used to process forms so that the same information can appear in Patent Application Information Retrieval (PAIR)
• By extracting data directly out of Form-Fillable PDFs, EFS-Web users can minimize rework and improve data accuracy for all types of filings
• Improved data accuracy reduces the need to file additional papers, such as "Correction of Filing" forms
• Form-Fillable PDFs require no PDF creation software; only the latest free version of Acrobat Reader is needed to use the forms. (Author's emphasis.)

IMPORTANT PDF FORM-FILLABLE FEATURES
• Ability to print forms with data entered by the user.
• Ability to save the form electronically with data embedded.
• Capability to re-open the saved form to modify existing data.
• Ability to import data in XML format from document management systems and other databases. **Note:** The "Import Data" feature is not available for the latest ADS form. USPTO is troubleshooting this problem.
• Ability to export data in XML format to document management systems and other databases.

OTHER IMPORTANT INFORMATION
There are many other PDF forms on the USPTO Web site but these do not save data. These legacy PDF forms can be filled out and submitted to USPTO using EFS-Web; however, the field information will not be automatically loaded onto USPTO systems.

Download other USPTO Fillable Forms (all forms are available in Adobe's PDF format for viewing and printing. **To view and use the forms you must install Adobe Acrobat reader on your computer.**) (Author's emphasis.)

If users create their own Form-Fillable PDFs, or modify USPTO Form-Fillable PDFs, the data will be accepted, however data in individual fields will not auto-load into USPTO systems.

Source: USPTO

PORTABLE DOCUMENT FORMAT (PDF) INSTRUCTIONS

PDF Specification

EFS-Web requires the PDF file to conform to any one of versions 1.1 through 1.7 of the PDF specification.

PDF Creation Software Compatibility

The most common versions of PDF Writer software that are compatible with EFS-Web include:

- Adobe Acrobat Professional
- Open Office (Freeware)
- Easy Office (Ad ware)
- CutePDF Writer (Freeware)
- Primo PDF (Freeware)
- FoxIT PDF (Freeware)

PDF creation software products that are not listed above may not be compatible with EFS-Web and their use may result in document image degradation and/or processing delays.

Adobe Reader Compatibility

EFS-Web does not require the use of Adobe Reader, a free software application.

However, to use the EFS-Web eForms, Adobe Reader or Acrobat version 7.0.8 or higher is required. To upgrade to the Adobe Reader or Acrobat software version visit the Adobe website, choose the appropriate operating system and language for downloading the latest version.

NOTE:
The above list of PDF Writers is continually changing due to:
- USPTOs EFS-Web contractors upgrades
- Computer operating system upgrades
- Which OS and browser you are using
- Security caused revisions

Chapter One, Section 3 Part (D)
The United States Patent and Trademark Office
Electronic Filing System for Patent Applications;
WIPO PCT and WIPO Hague eFiling

(D) The USSPTO Electronic Filing System for Patent Applications

EFS-Web Overview
EFS-Web is the United States Patent and Trademark Office's easy-to-use, Web-based patent application and document submission solution. Using EFS-Web, anyone with a Web-enabled computer can file patent applications and documents without downloading special software or changing document preparation tools and processes.

PRODUCT OVERVIEW
EFS-Web utilizes standard Web-based screens and prompts to enable you to submit a portable document format (PDF) document directly to the USPTO within minutes. You choose the tool, process and workflow with which you author your documents; convert them to standard PDF files and then submit them to USPTO's secure servers. EFS-Web is safe, simple and secure and gives you all of the same benefits as paper filings, including an electronic receipt that acknowledges your submission date.

Quick Start Guides Available at USPTO
- **Quick Start Guide for EFS-Web [PDF 981KB]**
- Quick Start Guide for EFS-Web Contingency [PDF 516KB]
- Quick Start Guide for EFS-Web ePetitions [PDF 997KB]
- Quick Start Guide for Quick Path Information Disclosure Statement (QPIDS) [PDF 573KB]
- Quick Start Guide for eTerminal Disclaimer [PDF 2108KB]
- **Quick Start Guide for PCT [PDF 47KB]**
- Quick Start Guide for Petition to Accept Unintentionally Delayed Payment of Maintenance Fee in an Expired Patent (37 CFR 1.378(c)) [PDF 190KB]
- Quick Start Guide for Petition to Make Special Based on Age [PDF 669KB]
- Quick Start Guide for Pre-Grant Publications [PDF 199KB]
- Quick Start Guide for Supplemental Examination [PDF 2511KB]
- Quick Start Guide for Third-Party Preissuance Submissions under 37 CFR 1.290 [PDF 1918KB]
- **Quick Start Guide for EFS-Web International Design Application (Hague) Submissions [PDF 2680KB]**
- Quick Start Guide for EFS-Web Issue Fee Transmittal (Web 85b) [PDF 3360KB]
- Quick Start Guide for Web-based Application Data Sheet (Web ADS) [PDF 3121KB]
- Quick Start Guide for Corrected Web-based Application Data Sheet (Corrected Web ADS) [PDF 2.95 MB]

USPTO Supported Operating Systems, Browser, and JRE/JVM version combinations

Operating Systems	Web browsers	Java Runtime Version
• Microsoft Windows Vista Home Edition SP 2 (32-bit / 64-bit) • Microsoft Windows 7 (32-bit / 64-bit) • Microsoft Windows 8 • Microsoft Windows 10 *	• Microsoft Internet Explorer 11 • Mozilla Firefox 44 and above	• Latest version of Java JRE
• Mac OS X 10.7.3 (Lion) - 10.8 (Mountain Lion)	• Apple Safari 6 • Mozilla Firefox 44 and above	• Latest version of Java JRE
• Mac OS X 10.9 (Mavericks)	• Apple Safari 7*** • Mozilla Firefox 44 and above	• Latest version of Java JRE
• Mac OS X 10.10 (Yosemite) - 10.11 (El Capitan)	• Apple Safari 8 • Mozilla Firefox 44 and above	• Latest version of Java JRE

*** For Safari 7 users, additional configurations may be required. Please contact the **Electronic Business Center** (PEBC) for assistance.

Please note that each browser version (major and minor releases) may have specific issues that USPTO cannot always address. If you install a later browser version, please be sure to maintain one of the supported browsers in order to ensure access to EFS-Web. Additional browsers and Java versions are not supported. However, a workaround may be available. Please contact the Patent EBC for general support.

Please check the vendor website for additional information relating to vulnerabilities and end of life support.

Source: USPTO

NOTES:
1) - Example of USPTO EFS-Web Supported Operating Systems is for reference only and will change periodically.
2) - See page on WIPO E-filing for similar information.
3) - The USPTO uses a larger variety of operating systems and Web browsers than the WIPO-E-filing at the time of publication.

Filing Patent Applications with the USPTO EFS-Web

What Can Be Filed

New Applications:
- Utility: Accelerated Exam, Provisional, Reexam, Nonprovisional under 111(a), Reissue and 371 National Stage
- Design: Accelerated Exam, Reexam, Nonprovisional under 171 with Color Drawings and Reissue
- International applications for filing in the U.S. Receiving Office

Existing Applications:
- Follow-on papers.
- Pre-Grant publications under 37 CFR 1.211 - 1.221
- Petition to Accept Unintentionally Delayed Payment of Maintenance Fees in an Expired Patent (37 CFR 1.378(c))
- Petition to Make Special Based on Age
- Request for Continued Examination (RCE)

What Cannot be Filed

- Credit Card Authorization Form - PTO-2038
- Assignments
- Maintenance Fees
- New Plant Applications or Color Plant Drawings
- Documents related to Registration Practice & Disciplinary Proceedings
- Certified Copies (Ribbon Copies)
- Secrecy Order Applications and/or Documents
- Contested Cases at the Board of Appeals and Interferences
- Third-party papers under 37 CFR 1.99
- Protests under 37 CFR 1.291
- Public use hearing papers under 37 CFR 1.292

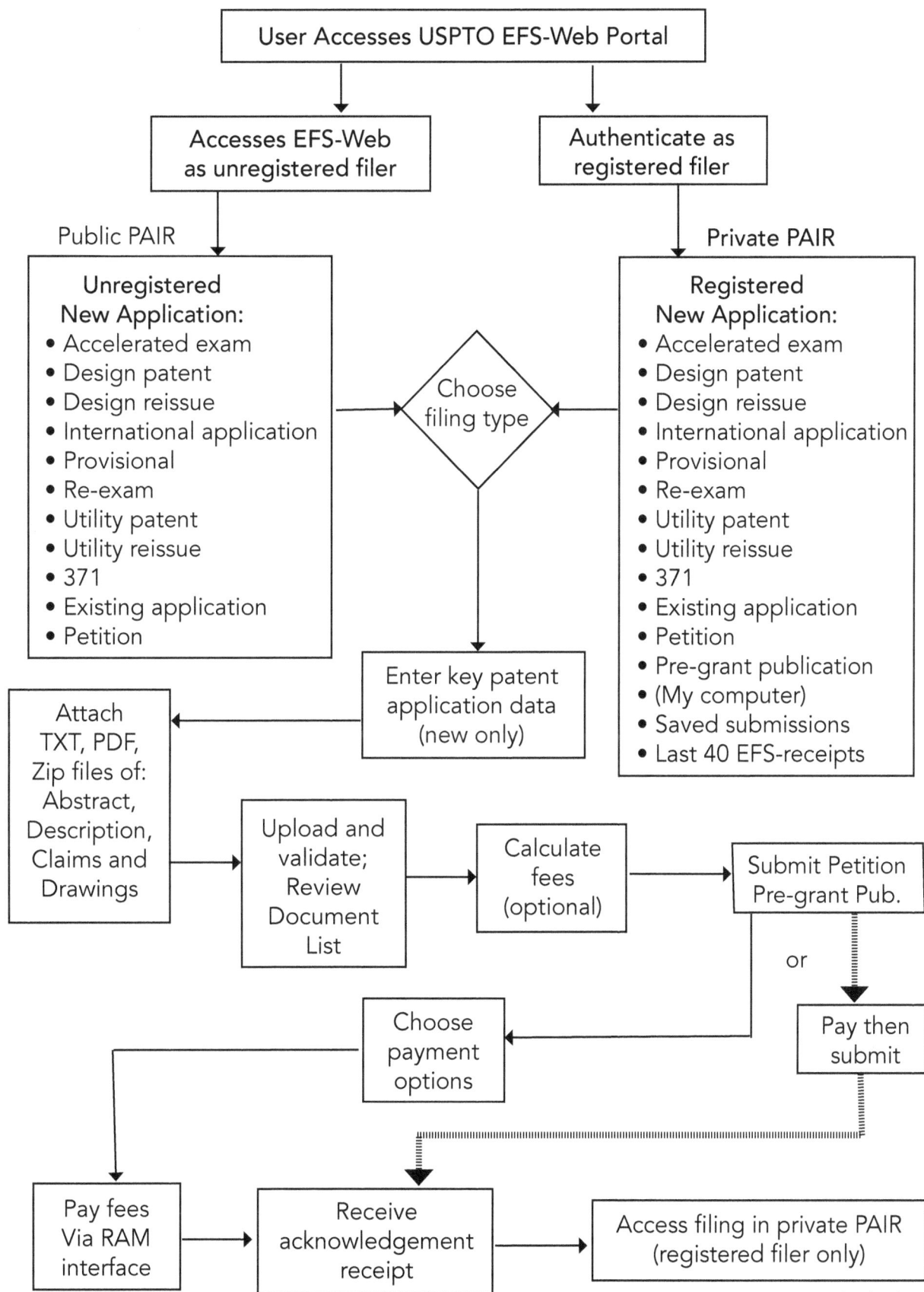

```
                  ┌─────────────────────────────────────┐
                  │  User Accesses USPTO EFS-Web Portal  │
                  └─────────────────────────────────────┘
                          │                    │
                          ▼                    ▼
          ┌──────────────────────┐   ┌──────────────────────┐
          │   Accesses EFS-Web   │   │    Authenticate as   │
          │ as unregistered filer│   │   registered filer   │
          └──────────────────────┘   └──────────────────────┘
                     │                          │
Public PAIR          ▼                          ▼         Private PAIR
┌─────────────────────────────┐         ┌─────────────────────────────┐
│        Unregistered         │         │         Registered          │
│      New Application:       │         │       New Application:       │
│  • Accelerated exam         │         │  • Accelerated exam         │
│  • Design patent            │  ┌────┐ │  • Design patent            │
│  • Design reissue           │◄─│Choose│◄│  • Design reissue           │
│  • International application │  │filing│ │  • International application │
│  • Provisional              │  │ type │ │  • Provisional              │
│  • Re-exam                  │  └────┘ │  • Re-exam                  │
│  • Utility patent           │     │    │  • Utility patent           │
│  • Utility reissue          │     │    │  • Utility reissue          │
│  • 371                      │     ▼    │  • 371                      │
│  • Existing application     │  ┌──────┐│  • Existing application     │
│  • Petition                 │  │Enter key│ • Petition                 │
└─────────────────────────────┘  │patent  ││  • Pre-grant publication    │
                                 │application│ • (My computer)            │
                                 │data     ││  • Saved submissions        │
                                 │(new only)│ • Last 40 EFS-receipts      │
                                 └──────┘ └─────────────────────────────┘
```

Choose filing type

Enter key patent application data (new only)

Attach TXT, PDF, Zip files of: Abstract, Description, Claims and Drawings

Upload and validate; Review Document List → **Calculate fees (optional)** → **Submit Petition Pre-grant Pub.**

or

Pay then submit

Choose payment options

Pay fees Via RAM interface → **Receive acknowledgement receipt** → **Access filing in private PAIR (registered filer only)**

Studio 94

Filing a Patent Application with USPTO EFS-Web.

WEB-ENABLED U.S. PATENT FILING
Subject to change with Patent-End-To-End upgrade

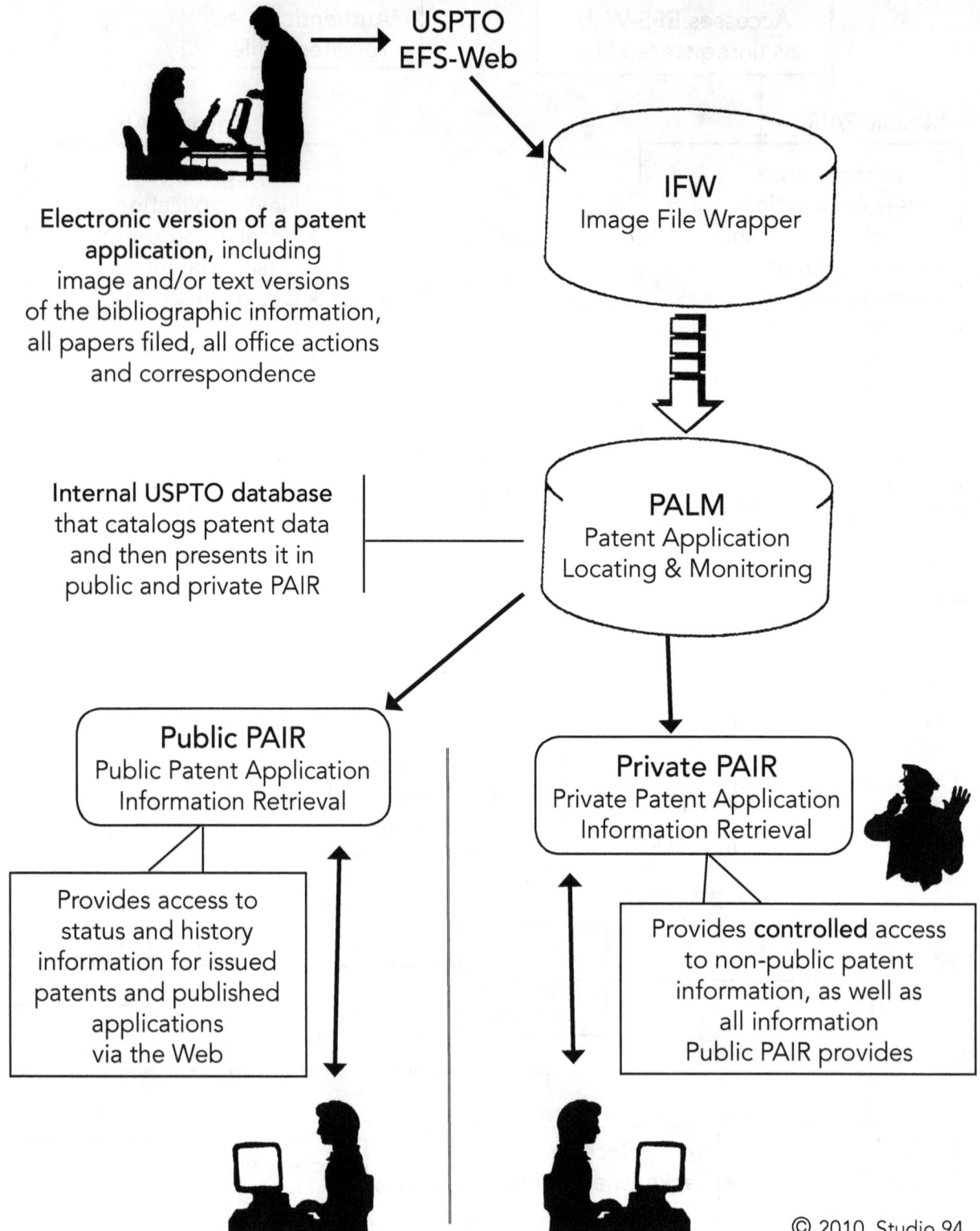

USPTO EFS-Web

IFW
Image File Wrapper

Electronic version of a patent application, including image and/or text versions of the bibliographic information, all papers filed, all office actions and correspondence

PALM
Patent Application
Locating & Monitoring

Internal USPTO database that catalogs patent data and then presents it in public and private PAIR

Public PAIR
Public Patent Application
Information Retrieval

Provides access to status and history information for issued patents and published applications via the Web

Private PAIR
Private Patent Application
Information Retrieval

Provides **controlled** access to non-public patent information, as well as all information Public PAIR provides

© 2010, Studio 94

Web-Enabled U.S. Patent Filing.

44

Electronic Filing with WIPO PCT & Hague

NOTE:
Filing PCT patent drawings using USPTO EFS-Web:
- File sheet size A4 as a PDF
- PCT patent drawings in black line mode
- File drawing sheet in portrait position
- Black & white photographs only with exceptions
- Color drawings and photographs not accepted
- Index drawings as DRW

WIPO ePCT FAQ
Frequently Asked Questions
September 1, 2015 ePCT Version 3.1
Software and operating system requirements

Which browsers are supported?
Mozilla Firefox (recommended) from version 3.6 and above
Internet Explorer versions 7.0 and above

Note: If you use Internet Explorer 11, the following setting may need to be configured to be able to access the system: Go to "Tools" > "Internet options" > select the "Advanced" tab > scroll down to the end and uncheck the box "Use TLS 1.2".

Note on WIPO digital certificates: Firefox or Internet Explorer MUST be used to enroll and pick up certificates. However, other browsers e.g., Google Chrome or Safari may be used subsequently for accessing the ePCT.

Useful tip: If you have obtained a WIPO digital certificate with Internet Explorer, and you also have Google Chrome installed on your PC, the certificate is automatically also available in Google Chrome. If you encounter login problems to private services with Internet Explorer, you should be able to log into ePCT using Chrome.

Can I use the ePCT service on a Macintosh platform?
Yes, it is possible; both the ePCT private and public services work on a Mac; we strongly recommend that you use Mozilla Firefox.

For private-services access, if you require a WIPO digital certificate, Mozilla Firefox must be used to request and pick up the certificate on a Mac.

Source: WIPO PCT System (look for upgrades)

This section shows how to file an industrial design application through the Hague System.

- **Entitlement:** Who can help you determine if you have the right to file an international application through the Hague System.
- **Fees and payment:** Helps you estimate the final cost and describes the payment options.
- **Preparing reproductions:** Gives practical advice and helps you prepare your reproductions before filing.
- **Create user account:** Walks you through the creation of a user account, which is mandatory to use the E-Filing.
- **File:** Walks you through the filing of your application.
- **After filing:** Describes what happens to your application once the International Bureau of WIPO receives it.

http://www.wipo.int/hague/en/how_to/file/file.html

What is the resolution (or dpi) of my image?

The resolution corresponds to the density of information of your image. 300x300 dpi means that there are 300 pixels (or points) in a surface of one inch (2.54 cm).
For optimal quality, your images should be between 250x250 dpi and 300x300 dpi. Less or more than that, the system will automatically resize your images to a resolution of 266x266 dpi.

The E-filing interface has the following advantages:

- personalized workbench environment (Portfolio Manager);
- uploading of multiple reproductions simultaneously;
- real-time checking of certain formalities;
- saving of applications in progress;
- a fully integrated fee calculator;
- online payment by credit card;
- faster delivery of the application;
- lower fees when the application contains many reproductions of the industrial designs to be registered, since reproductions submitted on paper are subject to a fee for each page beyond the first (refer to "Fees due" in "Payment of fees"); and
- instant acknowledgement of receipt with all the details of the submitted application.

However, please note that the E-filing interface may not be used if the applicant wishes to include specimens of the industrial design(s) instead of reproductions.

Summary of technical requirements for image files used in the Hague System E-Filing Portfolio Manager

Image format	JPEG or TIFF
Resolution	300 x 300 dpi
Minimum size	3 cm x 3 cm (at 300 dpi)
Maximum size	16 cm x 16 cm (at 300 dpi)
Maximum file size (per file)	2 Megabytes
Color	RGB or Grayscale
Borders	Between 1 and 20 pixels

NOTES:
1) - Image format JPEG or TIFF:
    a) - WIPO prefers you use JPEG
    b) - USPTO format JPEG or PDF, WIPO prefers JPEG

2) - Using USPTO RO for Hague Industrial Design Registrations, if you submit
    drawings in a PDF file WIPO will reformat the figures to JPEG for publishing;
    you may lose some detail. I would advise submitting in JPEG. (JPEG also has
    the advantage of you knowing where the border on the image is opposed
    to where it is in a PDF file.)

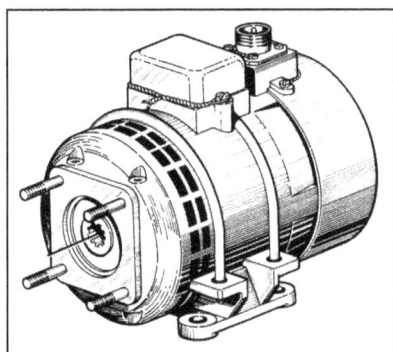

JPEG with close cropping

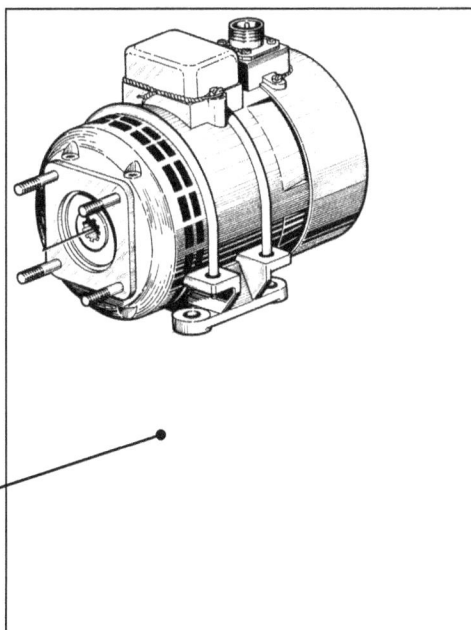

PDF drawing file with lots of white space can be a problem with applicant using a PDF writer that is not made to the ISO 32,000-1 standards.

(E) Modernization of Electronic Patent Application Process

Guest Blog by Deputy Under Secretary of Commerce for Intellectual Property and Deputy Director of the USPTO Russ Slifer

I'm excited to let you know about one of our newest initiatives, eCommerce Modernization (eMod), which will improve the electronic patent application process by modernizing the filing and viewing systems. Development with the initial pilot program anticipated to start in the summer or autmn of 2016. The new system will be implemented in phases over the next few years, and once completed, will replace our current EFS-Web, Public PAIR, and Private PAIR.

For patent applicants, eMod will help provide a simpler authentication process, improved functionality, and a more user friendly interface and documents. For patent examiners, the updated systems will streamline patent submission, review, and management processes, and increase accuracy of application processing and publication. Overall, a more easy-to-use electronic patent application process will improve efficiency, communication, and patent quality.

Posted at 11:51AM Aug 06, 2015

AUTHOR'S COMMENTS

In the USPTO's adoption of the "Modernization of Electronic Patent Application Process" there will be a two components: 1) the conversion of existing "big data," and 2) the adoption of new application specifications to incorporate XML (Extensible Markup Language) into both text and graphics used in new patent applications.

Looking forward to the USPTO and WIPO accepting color drawings and color photographs, without petitions, in nonprovisional (utility) patent drawings when they are best utilized, since most granted patents are in an electronic file format and viewed on color hardware screens of all sizes. Print copies of granted patents can be printed on Print On Demand (POD) systems.

In the up-and-coming use of XML I'm expecting there to be conversion software that converts text and graphics automatically to XML, because patent draftsmen, attorneys and agents are not computer programmers. Most newer versions of drawing software will save drawing files to the Scalable Vector Graphics (SVG) which is XML-based. XML and SVG are currently built into Internet browsers and search engines, which will make the job of patent examiners and searchers more efficient. XML supports multilingual documents and Unicode.

Move Toward XML (Extensible Markup Language)

The XMLs are coming! The XMLs are coming!

Image: Public Domain

Patents End-to-End (PE2E) will be the United States Patent & Trademark Office's next-generation IT infrastructure, supporting Patents business operations. The PE2E system will replace the nearly four dozen aging legacy systems used today with a single system that unifies electronic processing over the entire patent application lifecycle (hence "end-to-end").

Certain documents will contain figures or drawings.
DRW: *This doc code represents patent drawings filed by the applicant. Patent drawings should be captured as cropped images, with no more than one figure per image. Where there are drawing pages that contain multiple figures, each figure shall be captured in a separate image file. Text components of a figure, such as a caption, figure number, and any reference numbers or letters, shall be captured as text and tagged as link targets within the image file. References to figures or drawings in the text of the specification shall be tagged as XML resource links to their corresponding targets in the image files.*

Drawing and Drawing Software Tips

You get what you pay for: Using cheap or "freebie" drawing software and fonts will generally cost you more in time and money in Office Action-ordered corrections. With the advent of digital copy machines, scanners and cameras along with computers, everyone thinks they are an illustrator, then complain about the drawing rejections or blame the USPTO.

(Slide show presentation programs do not replace good quality drawing software.)

DRAWING TIP

Patent Drawings – While making your drawings either by pen and ink by hand or with the use of a computer, stop and make file copies before you add the shading 37 CFR 1.84(m) then add the shading if required; then save the drawings as a second set. This allows you, if required, to make corrections easier and also some Contracting States do not require shading.

You will notice that some of my patent illustrations used in this book have more shading than is required at the present time; this is because my drawings are from 1953 to 2003 and that was the rule at that time.

SCANNING TIPS

Scanner or Copy Machine – If you need to copy or scan an image that is on paper that has show-through printing from the reverse-side, place a sheet of black paper behind the print side; this will cancel out the show-through when copying or scanning.

Multi-page rapid scanners – While scanning patent applications of TXT and DRW files into PDF files, occasionally the rapid-scanner will position a page or two in the "landscape" orientation; if this happens and the applicant is in a rush to file, the USPTO EFS-Web will reject the application. It pays to inspect the multi-page PDF before submittal and fix the page rotation.

The rotation fix is easy with either Adobe Acrobat® or Apple Preview®. (But it can be hard with some freebie software.)

Both the USPTO and WIPO require all filed pages to be submitted in the "portrait" orientation.

MATCHING DIGITAL TOOLS
How to play nice together and work with printed and electronic video images

PAPER:

Properties of printed images:

Image size measured in inches.

Image size does **NOT vary** with scanned resolution.

Image size is modified on paper **by scaling.**

Image pixels are spaced on paper using specified scaled resolution.

Monochrome (black & white) laser printer generally 600 to 1200 dpi.

ELECTRONIC:

Properties of video images:

Image size measured in pixels.

Image size **varies** with scanned resolution.
Ah ha! This is why, when you scan at a higher resolution, the image is so large on your computer's monitor screen.

Image size is modified on screen **by resampling.**

Image pixels are located at each screen pixel location, one for one.

One screen pixel location contains one image pixel, and can be of any RGB value.
A line art value of 0 (black) is shown as RGB 0, 0, 0.
A line art value of 1 (white) is shown as RGB 255, 255, 255.

NOTE: Chart relates to black & white line drawings and text only, no color.

Information used with permission from:
Wayne Fulton © 1997 - 2010
www.scantips.com

AUTHOR'S COMMENTS
In submitting patent drawings on printed paper, I used 24- or 28-pound acid free brite-white paper, and generally gave the applicant three to five sets of the patent drawing sheets. On occasion, patent attorneys would ask for drawings on heavier paper and I would then print them out on a 65-pound paper.

What happens to a patent application once the examiner allows it for issuance as a patent?

Listed below are the stages through which an allowed patent application goes within the PTO:

When the examiner allows an application, a message concerning the application number is sent to the Office of Data Management. The application is then electronically exported to Initial Data Capture for electronic capture of the patent file. It takes approximately six weeks from the date that the allowed file is exported for the completion of the Initial Data Capture of the application.

[6 weeks]

Upon IDC completion, a message is then sent to the File Maintenance Facility (FMF) to ensure that all post allowance correspondence, fees and drawings have been updated. The application may stay in the FMF for approximately one - two weeks. However, if all requirements are not yet fulfilled the application will remain at the FMF until the requirements are met.

[1-2 weeks]

Once the fee and any correspondence and/or drawings are matched with the application and all requirements have been met for issuance as a patent, the application is then electronically exported to the Final Data Capture (FDC) stage of the process. The FDC makes any updates necessary to the electronic file and places the allowed patent application in an issue. The average time that an allowed application is in the FDC process is five weeks (two weeks of processing time for assignment of issue date). The "Issue Notification" is mailed approximately three weeks prior to the issue date of the patent.

[5 weeks]

The patent grant is mailed on the issue date of the patent. It includes any references to prior patents, the names of the inventors, specification, and claims (to name a few). It is bound in an attractive cover and includes a gold seal and red ribbon on the cover.

[Total approximately; 12 - 13 weeks]

The Reed Tech PDCap System

Initial Filing of the U.S. Patent Application

↓

The Reed Tech PDCap system is designed to perform data capture and conversion of patent applications to produce the final published patent.

The PDCap system helps manage the entire lifecycle of the patent application in collaboration with USPTO processing, from the initial filing of the application to the final published document.

Applications are submitted either electronically or on paper to the United States Patent and Trademark Office.

Reed Tech then processes the applications through several stages and ultimately produces the finished patent document.

↓

Final Published Patent Document ◄••••►

Reed Tech and the USPTO have entered into an agreement to make the following USPTO products available to the public at no charge:
Patents (grants, published applications, assignments, classification information, and maintenance fee events).

Trademarks (registrations, applications, assignments, and TTAB proceedings).

All data originated from the USPTO. Reed Tech is hosting this data unchanged, except for repackaging some of the data into zip files.

http://patents.reedtech.com

Published Application Alert Service (PAAS)
Allows the public to create queries against current patent applications published and generate alerts in the form of emails for notification of matches to their queries.

Source:
Chart by: Studio 94 Publishing 2015
Data by: United States Department of Commerce
  Reed Technology and Information Services, Inc.
  Patent Data Capture (PDCap) DOC50PAPT0905000
  September 11, 2015

USPTO DATA CONVERSION SYSTEM

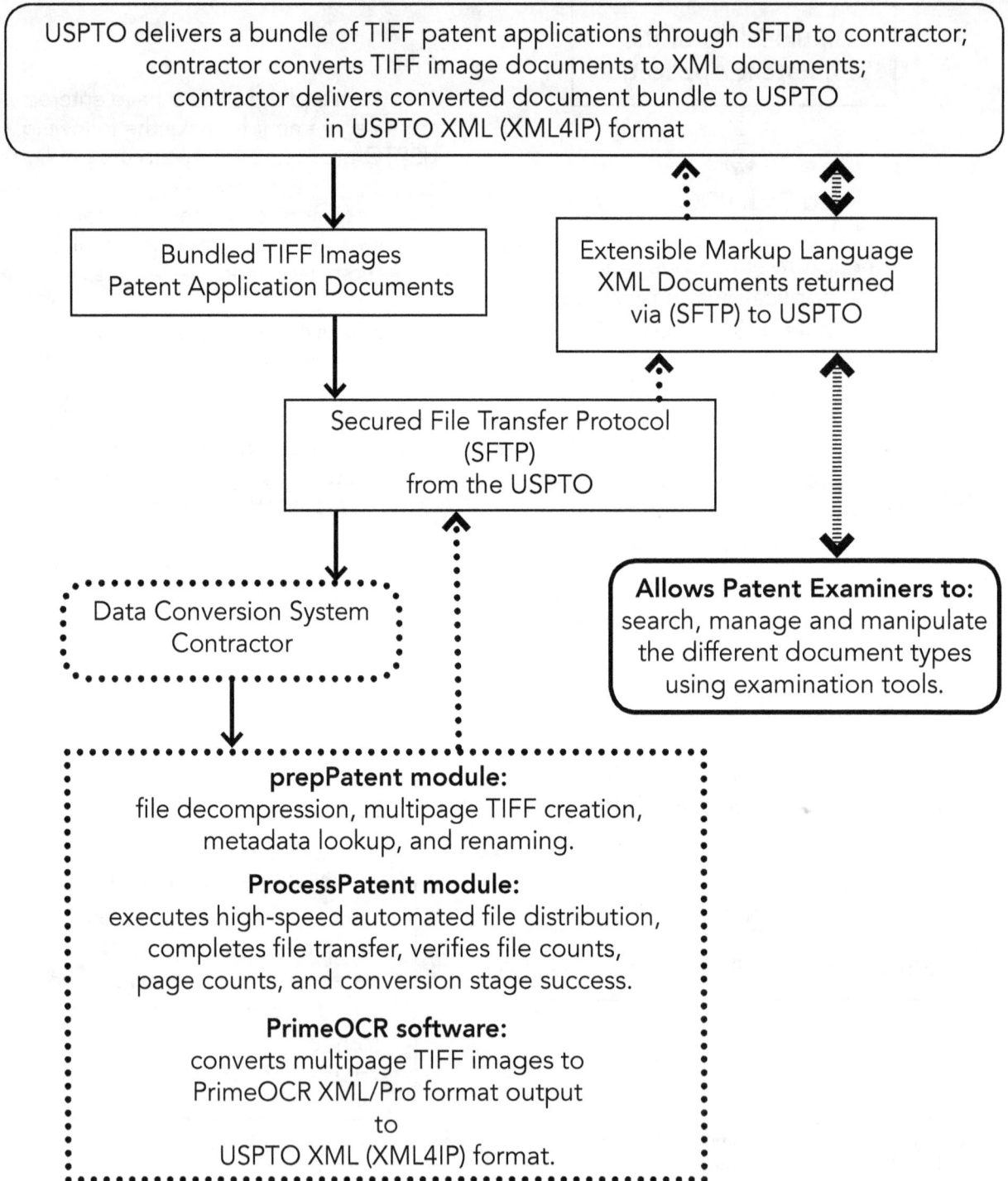

USPTO delivers a bundle of TIFF patent applications through SFTP to contractor; contractor converts TIFF image documents to XML documents; contractor delivers converted document bundle to USPTO in USPTO XML (XML4IP) format

Bundled TIFF Images
Patent Application Documents

Extensible Markup Language
XML Documents returned
via (SFTP) to USPTO

Secured File Transfer Protocol
(SFTP)
from the USPTO

Data Conversion System
Contractor

Allows Patent Examiners to:
search, manage and manipulate
the different document types
using examination tools.

prepPatent module:
file decompression, multipage TIFF creation,
metadata lookup, and renaming.

ProcessPatent module:
executes high-speed automated file distribution,
completes file transfer, verifies file counts,
page counts, and conversion stage success.

PrimeOCR software:
converts multipage TIFF images to
PrimeOCR XML/Pro format output
to
USPTO XML (XML4IP) format.

Source Material: Department of Commerce PTOC-004-00
Data Conversion Laboratory Patent Support (DCLPS) 01/07/2015
Chart by Studio 94 Publishing.

Chapter Two

Preparing Drawings and Photographs for U.S. Provisional Applications

Preparing Drawings for Provisional Applications

Generally drawings submitted along with a Provisional Application consist of: sketches, line drawings, engineering drawings, charts, graphs, inventors' journal sketches and photographs. If any of the above listed drawings are in color, you may want to put in a statement in the "Brief Description of the Drawings" of why the drawings are in color, or that they will not be in color, in the later filed nonprovisional application.

If your provisional application will be used later for a nonprovisionnal PCT application, PCT drawing rules do not allow the use of color at this time.

Parts of an Application

- Title
- Abstract
- Drawings
- Background of the Invention
- Summary of the Disclosure
- Brief Description of the Drawings
- Detailed Description of the Invention [35 USC § 112(a)]
- Claims [35 USC § 112(b)] some attorneys recommend, a least, one claim

---

35 U.S.C. 112 Specification.
[MPEP Editor Note: Applicable to any patent application filed on or after September 16, 2012. See 35 U.S.C. 112 (pre-AIA) for the law otherwise applicable.]

(a) IN GENERAL.—The specification shall contain a written description of the invention, and of the manner and process of making and using it, in such full, clear, concise, and exact terms as to enable any person skilled in the art to which it pertains, or with which it is most nearly connected, to make and use the same, and shall set forth the best mode contemplated by the inventor or joint inventor of carrying out the invention.

(b) CONCLUSION.—The specification shall conclude with one or more claims particularly pointing out and distinctly claiming the subject matter which the inventor or a joint inventor regards as the invention.

Provisional Application for Patent

A provisional patent application allows you to file without a formal patent claim, oath or declaration, or any information disclosure (prior art) statement.

Since June 8, 1995, the United States Patent and Trademark Office has offered inventors the option of filing a provisional application for patent, which was designed to provide a lower-cost first patent filing in the United States and to give U.S. applicants parity with foreign applicants under the GATT Uruguay Round Agreements.

A provisional application for patent (provisional application) is a U.S. national application filed in the USPTO under 35 U.S.C. §111(b). A provisional application is not required to have a formal patent claim or an oath or declaration. Provisional applications also should not include any information disclosure (prior art) statement since provisional applications are not examined. A provisional application provides the means to establish an early effective filing date in a later filed nonprovisional patent application filed under 35 U.S.C. §111(a). It also allows the term "Patent Pending" to be applied in connection with the description of the invention.

NOTE:
Before U.S. Provisional Applications were established
many independent inventors could not afford the cost of a utility patent so
they would then file a design patent, so they could say "Patent Pending."

AUTHOR'S COMMENTS
I was the president of a nonprofit independent inventor's organization
in 1995 when U.S. Provisional Applications first were established and
we had a rush of independent inventors ask,
"How can I get a $75 patent?"

We, as volunteer advocates for independent inventors
have attempted to, on every occasion, use the title
"Provisional Application for Patent"
not a . . .
"Provisional Patent Application."
I know it seems like a matter of semantics, but it helps new inventors.

The USPTO references the title both ways in their various documents.

A provisional application for patent has a pendency lasting 12 months from the date the provisional application is filed. The 12-month pendency period cannot be extended. Therefore, an applicant who files a provisional application must file a corresponding nonprovisional application for patent (nonprovisional application) during the 12-month pendency period of the provisional application in order to benefit from the earlier filing of the provisional application. However, a nonprovisional application that was filed more than 12 months after the filing date of the provisional application, but within 14 months after the filing date of the provisional application, may have the benefit of the provisional application restored by filing a grantable petition (including a statement that the delay in filing the nonprovisional application was unintentional and the required petition fee) to restore the benefit under 37 CFR 1.78.

In accordance with 35 U.S.C. §119(e), the corresponding nonprovisional application must contain or be amended to contain a specific reference to the provisional application. For nonprovisional applications filed on or after September 16, 2012, the specific reference must be included in an application data sheet. Further, a claim under 35 U.S.C. §119(e) for the benefit of a prior provisional application must be filed during the pendency of the nonprovisional application, and within four months of the nonprovisional application filing date or within 16 months of the provisional application filing date (whichever is later). See 37 CFR 1.78.

Once a provisional application is filed, an alternative to filing a corresponding nonprovisional application is to convert the provisional application to a nonprovisional application by filing a grantable petition under 37 C.F.R. 1.53(c)(3) requesting such a conversion within 12 months of the provisional application filing date.

Converting a provisional application into a nonprovisional application (versus filing a nonprovisional application claiming the benefit of the provisional application) will have a negative impact on patent term. The term of a patent issuing from a nonprovisional application resulting from the conversion of a provisional application will be measured from the original filing date of the provisional application.
By filing a provisional application first, and then filing a corresponding nonprovisional application that references the provisional application within the 12-month provisional application pendency period, a patent term endpoint may be extended by as much as 12 months.

The provisional application must name all of the inventor(s). In view of the one-year grace period provided by 35 U.S.C. 102(b)(1) in conjunction with 35 U.S.C. 102(a)(1), a provisional application can be filed up to 12 months following an inventor's public disclosure of the invention. (Such a pre-filing disclosure, although protected in the United States, may preclude patenting in foreign countries.) A public disclosure (e.g., publication, public use, offer for sale) more than one year before the provisional application filing date would preclude patenting in the United States. Keep in mind that a publication, use, sale, or other activity only has to be made available to the public to qualify as a public disclosure.

A filing date will be accorded to a provisional application only when it contains a written description of the invention, complying with all requirements of 35 U.S.C. §112(a).

---

35 U.S.C. 112
Specification.

[Note: Applicable to any patent application filed on or after September 16, 2012. See 35 U.S.C. 112 (pre-AIA) for the law otherwise applicable.]

(a) In general —The specification shall contain a written description of the invention, and of the manner and process of making and using it, in such full, clear, concise, and exact terms as to enable any person skilled in the art to which it pertains, or with which it is most nearly connected, to make and use the same, and shall set forth the best mode contemplated by the inventor or joint inventor for carrying out the invention.

Although the application will be accorded a filing date regardless of whether any drawings are submitted, applicants are advised to file with the application any drawings necessary for the understanding of the invention, complying with 35 U.S.C. 113.

35 U.S.C. 113 Drawings.

The applicant shall furnish a drawing where necessary for the understanding of the subject matter sought to be patented. When the nature of such subject matter admits of illustration by a drawing and the applicant has not furnished such a drawing, the director may require its submission within a time period of not less than two months from the sending of a notice thereof. Drawings submitted after the filing date of the application may not be used (i) to overcome any insufficiency of the specification due to lack of an enabling disclosure or otherwise inadequate disclosure therein, or (ii) to supplement the original disclosure thereof for the purpose of interpretation of the scope of any claim.

---

37 CFR 1.53(c)

(c) Application filing requirements — Provisional application. The filing date of a provisional application is the date on which a specification as prescribed by 35 U.S.C. 112(a), and any drawing required by § 1.81(a) are filed in the Patent and Trademark Office. No amendment, other than to make the provisional application comply with the patent statute and all applicable regulations, may be made to the provisional application after the filing date of the provisional application.

> A drawing necessary to understand the invention cannot be introduced into an application after the filing date because of the prohibition against new matter. Further, 37 CFR 1.53(c) prohibits amendments from being filed in provisional applications that are not required to comply with the patent statute and all applicable regulations.

To be complete, a provisional application must also include the filing fee as set forth in 37 CFR 1.16(d) and a cover sheet* identifying:
- the application as a provisional application for patent;
- the name(s) of all inventors;
- inventor residence(s);
- title of the invention;
- name and registration number of attorney or agent and docket number (if applicable);
- correspondence address; and
- any U.S. Government agency that has a property interest in the application.

* A cover sheet, form PTO/SB/16, pages 1 and 2, is available at www.uspto.gov/forms/index.jsp.

> The information in this PTO brochure is general in nature and is not meant to substitute for advice provided by a patent practitioner. Applicants unfamiliar with the requirements of U.S. patent law and procedures should consult an attorney or agent registered to practice before the USPTO.
> A list of attorneys and agents can be searched at the USPTO Website at www.uspto.gov.

Source: USPTO brochure

CAUTIONS

- The benefits of the provisional application cannot be claimed if the 12-month deadline for filing a nonprovisional application has expired (unless the benefit of the provisional application has been restored under 37 CFR 1.78).

- A provisional application cannot result in a U.S. patent unless one of the following two events occur within 12 months of the provisional application filing date:

1 - a corresponding nonprovisional application for patent entitled to a filing date is filed that claims the benefit of the earlier filed provisional application (unless the benefit of the provisional application was restored under 37 CFR 1.78, in which case the nonprovisional application may be filed within 14 months from provisional application filing date); or

2 - a grantable petition under 37 CFR 1.53(c)(3) to convert the provisional application into a nonprovisional application is filed.

- Provisional applications for patent may not be filed for design inventions.
- Provisional applications are not examined on their merits.

- Provisional applications for patent cannot claim the benefit of a previously filed application, either foreign or domestic.

- It is recommended that the disclosure of the invention in the provisional application be as complete as possible.

- In order to obtain the benefit of the filing date of a provisional application, the claimed subject matter in the later filed nonprovisional application must have support in the provisional application.

- If there are multiple inventors, each inventor must be named in the application.

- All inventor(s) named in the provisional application must have made a contribution, either jointly or individually, to the invention disclosed in the application.

- The nonprovisional application must have at least one inventor in common with the inventor(s) named in the provisional application to claim benefit of the provisional application filing date.

- A provisional application must be entitled to a filing date and include the basic filing fee in order for a nonprovisional application to claim benefit of that provisional application.

- There is a surcharge for filing the basic filing fee or the cover sheet on a date later than filing the provisional application.

- Amendments are not permitted in provisional applications after filing, other than those to make the provisional application comply with applicable regulations.

- No information disclosure statement may be filed in a provisional application.

FEE

Fees are subject to change annually. See current fees (37 CFR 1.16(d)) at www.uspto. gov. Call the USPTO Contact Center (UCC) Monday through Friday (except federal holidays) at 800-786-9199 for fee information. Payment by check or money order must be made payable to "Director of the U.S. Patent and Trademark Office."

HOW TO FILE

The provisional application papers (written description and drawings), filing fee and cover sheet can be filed electronically using EFS-Web or filed by mail.

Electronically Using EFS-Web: The provisional application can be filed electronically only if EFS-Web is used. EFS-Web allows patent applications, including provisional applications, to be filed securely via the Internet. Applicants prepare documents in **Portable Document Format (PDF)**, attach the documents, validate that the PDF documents will be compatible with USPTO internal automated information systems, submit the documents, and pay fees with real-time payment processing. When fillable EFS-Web forms are used, the data entered into the forms is automatically loaded into USPTO information systems. Further information on EFS-Web is available at http://www.uspto.gov/patents/process/file/efs/guidance.

By Mail: The provisional application and filing fee can be mailed to:

Commissioner for Patents
P.O. Box 1450
Alexandria, VA 22313-1450

FEATURES

- Provides simplified filing with a lower initial investment with 12 months to assess the invention's commercial potential before committing to higher cost of filing a prosecuting a nonprovisional application for patent.
- Establishes official United States patent application filing date for the invention.
- Permits authorized use of "Patent Pending" notice for 12 months in connection with the description of the invention.
- Begins the Paris Convention priority year.
- Enables immediate commercial promotion of invention with greater security agaist having the invention stolen.
- Permits applicant(s) to obtain USPTO certified copies.

WARNINGS

A provisional application automatically becomes abandoned when its pendency period expires 12 months after the provisional application filing date by operation of law. Applicants must file a nonprovisional application claiming benefit of the earlier provisional application filing date in the USPTO before the provisional application pendency period expires in order to preserve any benefit from the provisional application filing (unless the benefit of the provisional application has been restored under 37 CFR 1.78).

Beware that an applicant who publicly discloses his or her invention (e.g., publishes, uses, sells, or otherwise makes available to the public) during the 12-month provisional application pendency period may lose more than the benefit of the provisional application filing date if the 12-month provisional application pendency period expires before a corresponding nonprovisional application is filed. Such an applicant may also lose the right to ever patent the invention.
See 35 U.S.C. §§102(a)(1) and (b)(1).

> Independent inventors should fully understand that a provisional application will not mature into a granted patent without further submissions by the inventor. **Some invention promotion firms misuse the provisional application process leaving the inventor with no patent.**

CONTACTS

Direct questions regarding regulations or procedures to the Office of the Deputy Commissioner for Patent Examination Policy.
Telephone: 571-272-8800 Fax: 571-273-0125
Direct questions regarding legislative changes to the Office of Policy and External Affairs.
Telephone: 571-272-9300 Fax: 571-273-0085

The Inventors Assistance Center (IAC) provides patent information and services to the public. The IAC is staffed by former Supervisory Patent Examiners and experienced Primary Examiners who answer general questions concerning patent examining policy and procedure. Send e-mail to: IndependentInventor@uspto.gov (link sends e-mail).
See also http://www.uspto.gov/inventors/iac/index.jsp.
For additional copies of this brochure, or for further information, contact the USPTO Contact Center.
Telephone: 800-786-9199
Send e-mail to: usptoinfo@uspto.gov.
Access USPTO's Website at www.uspto.gov.
Provisional application mailing address:
COMMISSIONER FOR PATENTS
P.O. BOX 1450
ALEXANDRIA, VA 22313-1450

Source: USPTO except where author boxed in items to highlight them.

PROVISIONAL APPLICATION FOR PATENT

There is no requirement that the written description and any drawings filed in a provisional application and a later-filed nonprovisional application be identical; however, the later-filed nonprovisional application is only entitled to the benefit of the common subject matter disclosed in the corresponding nonprovisional application filed not later than 12 months after the provisional application filing date. **Additionally, the specification shall disclose the manner and process of making and using the invention in such full, clear, concise, and exact terms as to enable any person skilled in the art to which the invention pertains to make and use the invention and set forth the best mode contemplated for carrying out the invention.**
See 35 U.S.C. § 112, 1st paragraph.

It is recommended that the disclosure of the invention in the provisional application **be as complete as possible.** In order to obtain the benefit of the filing date of a provisional application the claimed subject matter in the later filed nonprovisional application **must have support in the provisional application.**

A filing date will be accorded to a provisional application only when it contains: a written description of the invention, complying with all requirements of 35 U.S.C. §112 1st paragraph and any **drawings necessary to understand the invention,** complying with 35 U.S.C. §113. If either of these items are missing or incomplete, no filing date will be accorded to the provisional application.

AUTHOR'S COMMENTS

In preparing drawings to be submitted with a provisional application, you can submit: marked-up photographs, formal and informal drawings, clips of engineering drawings, charts and graphs. The graphics you submit should be on 8-1/2 x 11 paper, or the same on a PDF file for EFS-Web submittal (see Section 6). Remember, whatever you submit should represent what you determine will be submitted as formal drawings in your final nonprovisional patent application. The trick is to send in just enough, but not too much. Most patent attorneys have different ways of filing provisional applications and it generally has to do to the inventor's particular situation.

With all the tools available at the present it is easy to put together informal graphics for your application. Tools include such things as copy machines, digital cameras, compuers, scanners, sketches and engineering drawings. *Never forget that even though these graphics may be informal, they should be done correctly.*

Photographs can be loaded into a computer and with photo-editing software you can clean up or remove background, size, and then add FIG. and part numbers.

Most large engineering drawings can be cut into sections where the image of the invention is, and if you can cut the image area into 8-1/2 x 11 inch sheets they can be FIG. and part numbered. If the image area is larger than 8-1/2 x 11 inches it can be reduced on a copy machine. (See examples on following pages.)

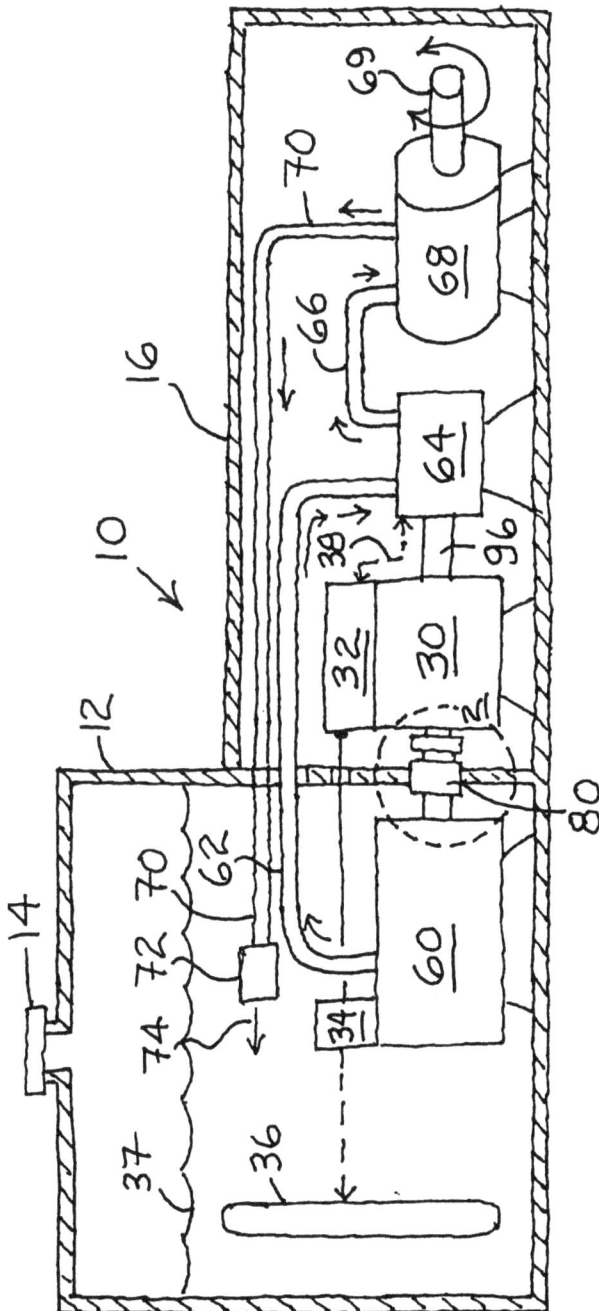

FIG. 1

EXAMPLE ONLY
NOT AN ACTUAL PATENT APPLICATION

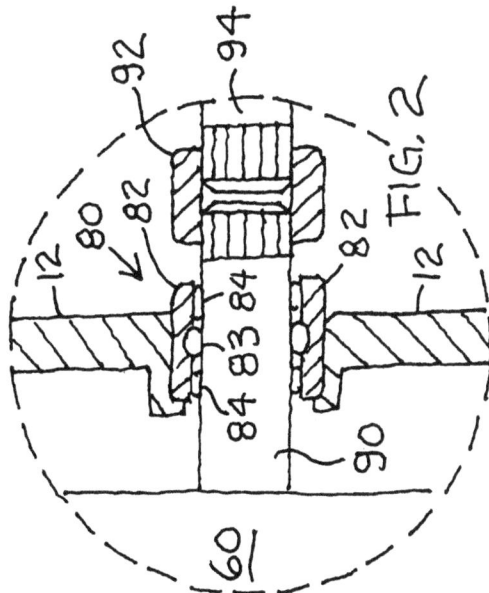

FIG. 2

Example of how to use informal drawings in a provisional application for patent.

Photographs Submitted with a Provisional Application for Patent

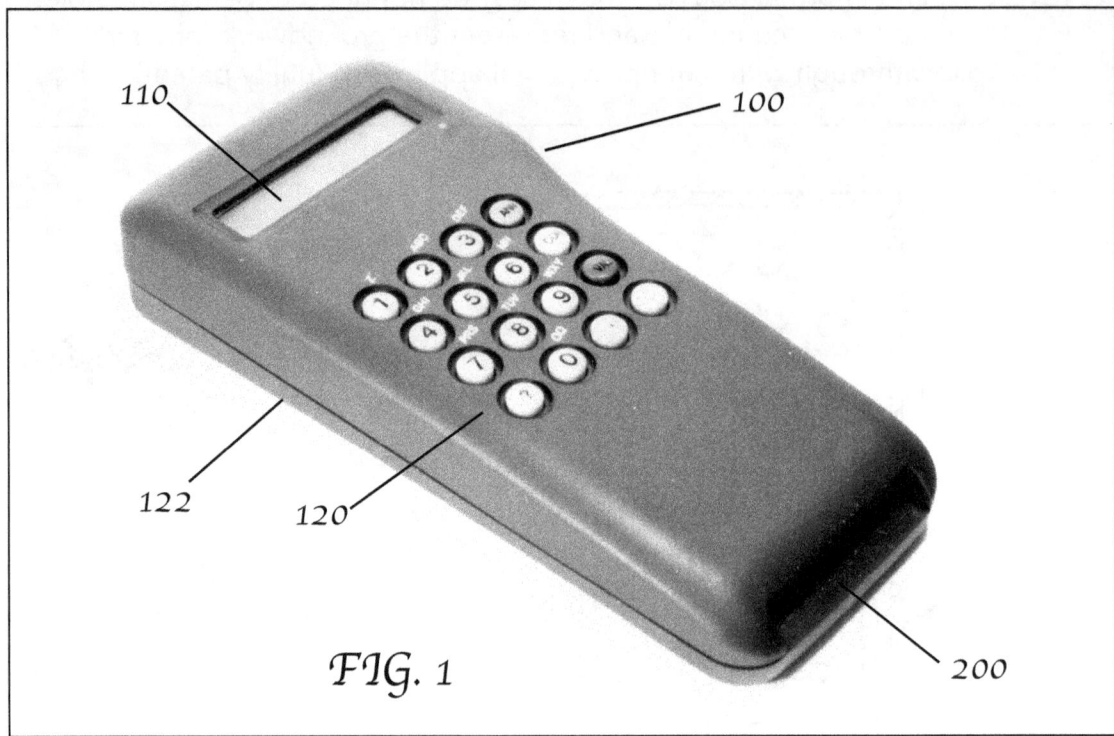

FIG. 1

Example of how photographs can be used in a provisional application for patent.
Parts can be hand-marked, computer-marked, or can even be formal photographs
to be used in the later nonprovisional application.
Remember to keep photo sheet no larger than 8-1/2 x 11 inches.

EXAMPLE ONLY
NOT USED IN A PATENT APPLICATION

Photograph by Studio 94, 1991 before
provisional applications were available.

Example of how to use photographs in a provisional application for patent.

EXAMPLE ONLY
Not part of an actual
patent application

300 B

BSH-300-01 ASSY.

FIG. 6A

FIG. 6

1 — 301-02 SHAFT
2 1654 DCTN BEARING (
3 302 INSULATOR TUBE
4 303 INSULATOR END
5 304 COIL (SEE DRW for DATA)
6 304 LEAD WIRES
7 305 COMUTATOR
8 306 KEY
9 307 TIMING DEVICE
10 11 UPRIGHT

UPRIGHT REF. ONLY

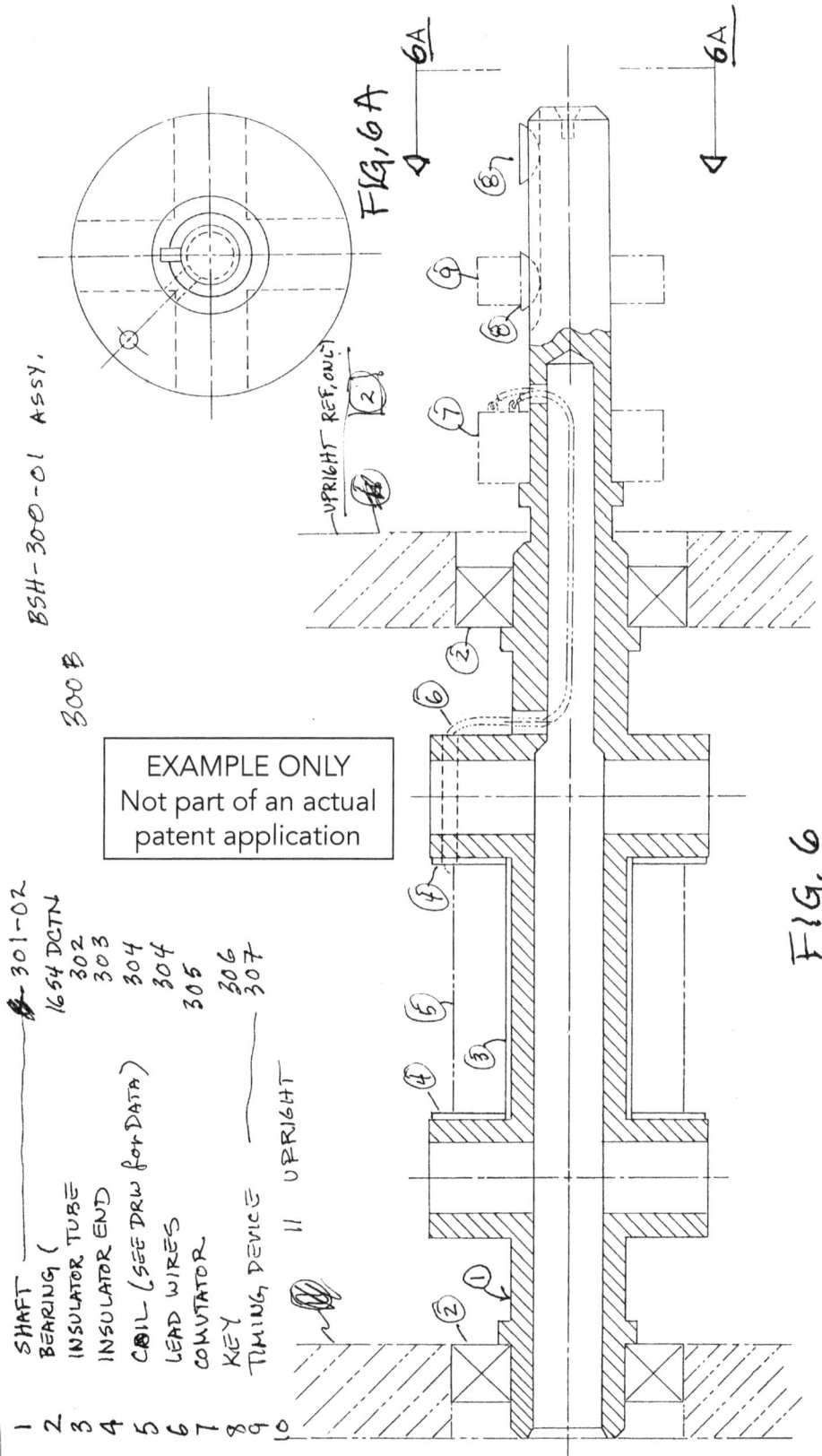

Example of how to use an engineering drawing in a provisional application for patent.

67

Example of graphic image submitted in a Provisional Application

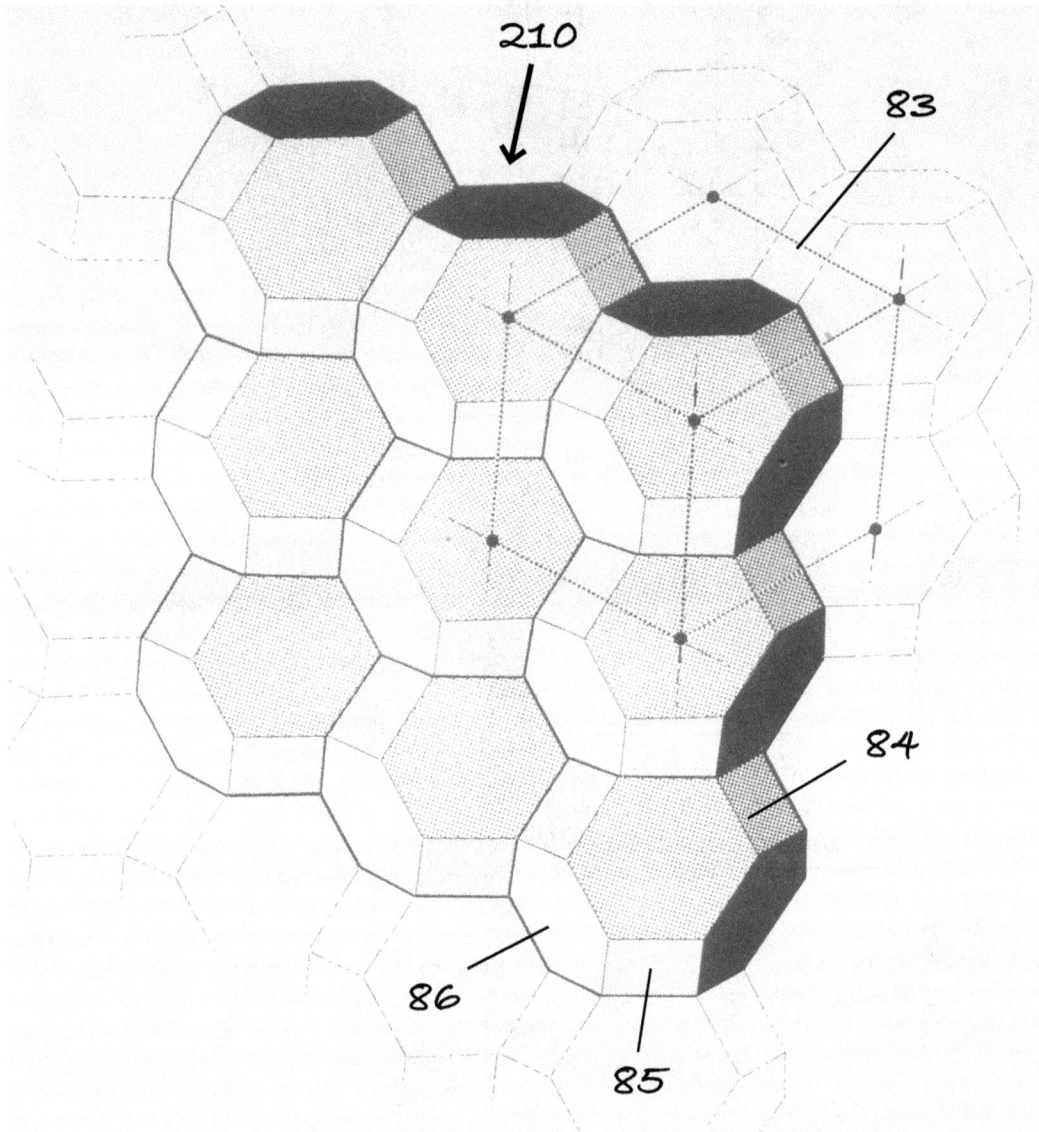

FIG. 3

Example Only:
Marked up copy of geometric dampening
device used in a seaship's fuel tank.

AUTHOR'S COMMENTS

Patent drawings for provisional applications can be anything from formal patent drawings to informal drawings, sketches, engineering data and photographs. What you put into your application generally depends on what the patent attorney recommends. Each case is different and the attorney will generally have a reason to select how much drawing information to put in or leave out.

On occasion I have completed formal patent drawings for a nonprovisional patent application and for reasons of time constraints attorneys used these drawings to apply for a provisional application so that the inventor was able to exhibit the invention and say "patent pending," while the attorney a few months later filed the nonprovisional application.

USPTO COMMENT

It is recommended that the disclosure of the invention in the provisional application **be as complete as possible.** In order to obtain the benefit of the filing date of a provisional application the claimed subject matter in the later filed nonprovisional application **must have support in the provisional application.**

IMPROVEMENTS
(Sometimes inventors need to freeze the design)

Working with prolific inventors, I have observed many times, where they never stop fine-tuning their inventions and between the time they file for a provisional application and then the nonprovisional, there is too much "new matter" introduced to be able to claim the provisional's filing date.

"I can give you a six-word formula for success:
Think things through – then follow through."
Sir Walter Scott

Chapter Three

Section 1 - Drawing & Reproduction Rules For USPTO Nonprovisional (Utility) Patents

Location:
MPEP 9th Edition November 2015
Laws, Rules & Index
Appendix R - Patent Rules 37 CFR 1.84(a) through (w)

Section 2 - Drawing & Reproduction Rules For WIPO PCT Nonprovisional (Utility) Patents

Location:
MPEP 9th Edition November 2015
Laws, Rules & Index
Appendix T - Patent Cooperation Treaty
Article 7 - The Drawings, Rule 11 through 11.14

Chapter Three
Section 1

**Drawing & Reproduction Rules For
USPTO Nonprovisional (Utility) Patents**
Location:
MPEP 9th Edition November 2015
Laws, Rules & Index
Appendix R - Patent Rules 37 CFR 1.84(a) through (w)

35 U.S.C. 113 Drawings

The applicant shall furnish a drawing where necessary for the understanding of the subject matter sought to be patented. When the nature of such subject matter admits of illustration by a drawing and the applicant has not furnished such a drawing, the director may require its submission within a time period of not less than two months from the sending of a notice thereof. Drawings submitted after the filing date of the application may not be used (i) to overcome any insufficiency of the specification due to lack of an enabling disclosure or otherwise inadequate disclosure therein, or (ii) to supplement the original disclosure thereof for the purpose of interpretation of the scope of any claim.

37 CFR 1.58 Chemical and mathematical formulae and tables.

(a) The specification, including the claims, may contain chemical and mathematcal formulae, but shall not contain drawings or flow diagrams. The description portion of the specification may contain tables, but the same tables should not be included in both the drawings and description portion of the specification. Claims may contain tables either if necessary to conform to **35 U.S.C. 112** or if otherwise found to be desirable.

(b) Tables that are submitted in electronic form **(§§ 1.96(c) and 1.821(c))** must maintain the spatial relationships (e.g., alignment of columns and rows) of the table elements when displayed so as to visually preserve the relational information they convey. Chemical and mathematical formulae must be encoded to maintain the proper positioning of their characters when displayed in order to preserve their intended meaning.

(c) Chemical and mathematical formulae and tables must be presented in compliance with **§ 1.52(a) and (b)**, except that chemical and mathematical formulae or tables may be placed in a landscape orientation if they cannot be presented satisfactorily in a portrait orientation. Typewritten characters used in such formulae and tables must be chosen from a block (nonscript) type font or lettering style having capital letters which should be at least 0.422 cm (0.166 inch) high (e.g., preferably Arial, Times Roman, or Courier, with a font size of 12), but may be no smaller than 0.21 cm (0.08 inch) high (e.g., a font size of 6). A space at least 0.64 cm (1/4 inch) high should be provided between complex formulae and tables and the text. Tables should have the lines and columns of data closely spaced to conserve space, consistent with a high degree of legibility.

37 CFR 1.81 Drawings required in patent application

(a) The applicant for a patent is required to furnish a drawing of his or her invention where necessary for the understanding of the subject matter sought to be patented; this drawing, or a high-quality copy thereof, must be filed with the application. Since corrections are the responsibility of the applicant, the original drawing(s) should be retained by the applicant for any necessary future correction.

(b) Drawings may include illustrations, which facilitate an understanding of the invention (for example, flowsheets in cases of processes, and diagrammatic views).

(c) Whenever the nature of the subject matter sought to be patented admits of illustration by a drawing without its being necessary for the understanding of the subject matter and the applicant has not furnished such a drawing, the examiner will require its submission within a time period of not less than two months from the date of the sending of a notice thereof.

(d) Drawings submitted after the filing date of the application may not be used to overcome any insufficiency of the specification due to lack of an enabling disclosure or otherwise inadequate disclosure therein, or to supplement the original disclosure thereof for the purpose of interpretation of the scope of any claim.

---

37 CFR 1.83 Content of drawing

(a) The drawing in a nonprovisional application must show every feature of the invention specified in the claims. However, conventional features disclosed in the description and claims, where their detailed illustration is not essential for a proper understanding of the invention, should be illustrated in the drawing in the form of a graphical drawing symbol or a labeled representation (e.g., a labeled rectangular box). In addition, tables that are included in the specification and sequences that are included in sequence listings should not be duplicated in the drawings.

(b) When the invention consists of an improvement on an old machine the drawing must, when possible, exhibit, in one or more views, the improved portion itself, disconnected from the old structure, and also in another view, only as much of the old structure as will suffice to show the connection of the invention therewith.

(c) Where the drawings in a nonprovisional application do not comply with the requirements of paragraphs (a) and (b) of this section, the examiner shall require such additional illustration within a time period of not less than two months from the date of the sending of a notice thereof. Such corrections are subject to the requirements of § 1.81(d).

CONTENTS
37 CFR 1.84 Drawing Standards

Contents of 37 CFR 1.84 Drawing Standards used in non-provisional (utility) patent applications.

37 CFR 1.84(a) Drawings.

(a) Drawings. There are two acceptable categories for presenting drawings in utility and design patent applications.

(1) Black ink. Black & white drawings are normally required. India ink, or its equivalent that secures solid black lines, must be used for drawings; or

(2) Color. Color drawings are permitted in design applications. Where a design application contains color drawings, the application must include the number of sets of color drawings required by paragraph (a)(2)(ii) of this section and the specification must contain the reference required by paragraph (a)(2)(iii) of this section. On rare occasions, color drawings may be necessary as the only practical medium by which to disclose the subject matter sought to be patented in a utility patent application. The color drawings must be of sufficient quality such that all details in the drawings are reproducible in black and white in the printed patent. Color drawings are not permitted in international applications **(see PCT Rule 11.13).** The Office will accept color drawings in utility patent applications only after granting a petition filed under this paragraph explaining why the color drawings are necessary. Any such petition must include the following:

(i) The fee set forth in **§ 1.17(h);**

(ii) One (1) set of color drawings if submitted via the Office electronic filing system or three (3) sets of color drawings if not submitted via the Office electronic filing system; and

(iii) An amendment to the specification to insert (unless the specification contains or has been previously amended to contain) the following language as the first paragraph of the brief description of the drawings:

The patent or application file contains at least one drawing executed in color.

Copies of this patent or patent application publication with color drawing(s) will be provided by the Office upon request and payment of the necessary fee.

37 CFR 1.84(a) USPTO COMMENTS

See the notice titled Interim Waiver of Parts of 37 CFR 1.84 and 1.165, and Delay in the Enforcement of the Change in 37 CFR 1.84(e) to No Longer Permit Mounting of Photographs, as published in the Official Gazette on May 22, 2001 (1246 OG 106):

• WAIVER: The Office has waived the requirement set forth in 37 CFR 1.84(a)(2)(iii) and 1.165(b) by which the applicant was to file a black & white photocopy of a color drawing or color photograph. The black & white photocopy of the color drawing or color photograph is not required.

In general, "black ink" drawings must be prepared with the aid of drafting instruments.

The Office will also accept computer-generated "black ink" drawings provided that the drawings are substantially equivalent in quality to drawings made with drafting instruments. The jagged and wavy lines characteristic of some computer-generated drawing systems must be kept to an absolute minimum. **The artwork in drawings submitted to the Office should be of a professional quality.**

The "black ink" drawing may be a computer screen image when such an image is necessary for the understanding of the invention.

When color drawings are accepted after the granting of a petition, the three sets are distributed as follows:

• One set remains in the patent application file wrapper.

• One set is included within the official grant of the Letters Patent for routing to the applicant.

• One set is maintained in the Office of Public Records, Document Services Division, and is to be used for color-copying purposes when the Office of Public Records sells color copies of the patent for the fee set forth in 37 CFR 1.19(a)(2) or (3).

In patent application publications, the drawings are published in black & white, even when the applicant has filed color drawings. In utility and design patents and statutory invention registrations, the drawings are published in black & white, even when the applicant has filed color drawings, except (as described above) any color drawings will be included in the official grant of the Letters Patent and in color copies of the patent sold by the Office of Public Records. Only the paper copies of plant patents are published in color.

37 CFR 1.84(b) Photographs

(b) Photographs.

(1) Black & white. Photographs, including photocopies of photographs, are not ordinarily permitted in utility and design patent applications. The Office will accept photographs in utility and design patent applications, however, if photographs are the only practicable medium for illustrating the claimed invention. For example, photographs or photomicrographs of: electrophoresis gels, blots (e.g., immunological, western, Southern, and northern), autoradiographs, cell cultures (stained and unstained), histological tissue cross sections (stained and unstained), animals, plants, in vivo imaging, thin layer chromatography plates, crystalline structures, and, in a design patent application, ornamental effects, are acceptable. If the subject matter of the application admits of illustration by a drawing, the examiner may require a drawing in place of the photograph. The photographs must be of sufficient quality so that all details in the photographs are reproducible in the printed patent.

(2) Color photographs. Color photographs will be accepted in utility and design patent applications if the conditions for accepting color drawings and black & white photographs have been satisfied. See paragraphs (a)(2) and (b)(1) of this section.

---

37 CFR 1.84(b) USPTO COMMENTS

Patent practitioners are cautioned that photographs cannot be removed from applications pending in the Office. Therefore, practitioners should make sure they retain an original set of photographs.

The Office is willing to accept black & white photographs or photomicrographs (not photolithographs or other reproductions of photographs made by using screens) developed on photographic paper in lieu of ink drawings to illustrate inventions which are incapable of being accurately or adequately depicted by ink drawings. The photographs or photomicrographs must show the invention more clearly than it can be shown by ink drawings and otherwise comply with the rules concerning such drawings. Examples of acceptable categories of photographs are listed in the rule.

There are instances when photographs are produced through use of equipment such as tunneling electron microscopy (TEM). For example, in areas such as solid state electronics, wherein single atoms or single atomic layers can form part of the invention, only TEM or comparable equipment images can resolve single atoms or radicals. In such instances, the Office will not necessarily object to the images for not being completely sharp as long as the content of such TEMs adds to the understanding of the invention and as long as the TEMs can be adequately reproduced in the printed patent.

Continuation of 37 CFR 1.84(b) USPTO COMMENTS

Photographs taken with such specialized equipment must meet the same standards as photographs that do not require such specialized equipment. Images produced through use of specialized equipment may not always appear with secure black solid lines. However, the drawing review will consider such limitations and accept full-tone photographs that meet the specified requirements.

Although photographs are not mentioned in PCT Rule 11, it is possible for black & white photographs to appear as drawings in an international application. In part, MPEP 1825 states the following:

The PCT makes no provision for photographs. Nevertheless, they are allowed by the International Bureau where it is impossible to present in a drawing what is to be shown (for instance, crystalline structures). Where, exceptionally, photographs are submitted, they must be on sheets of A4 size, they must be black & white, and they must respect the minimum margins and admit of direct reproduction. Color photographs are not accepted.

In the U.S. national stage, the Office will accept the photographs that have been approved in the international application. Since MPEP 1893.03(f) prohibits the Office from imposing requirements beyond those in PCT Rule 11, it is not necessary for national stage cases to meet the petition requirement or three-set requirement set forth in 37 CFR 1.84(b). (See Section 5).

The Office will object to mounted photographs. See Page 1-13.

The Office will not object if photographs are submitted on shiny or glossy paper. See Page 1-13.

The Office has waived the requirement that the applicant submit a black & white photocopy of a color photograph.

AUTHOR'S COMMENTS

My experience with using black & white photographs as figures was in the various Government Research Centers, and these photographs were captured by filming through various scientific instruments that illustrated the invention's findings, or the results of the research. On a few occasions the patent examiner requested a traced-in-ink, over the photo, a "fingerprint" drawing with numbered call-outs that described what was shown on the scientific photograph. This was done in the 1960s. I believe that, today, these photographs would be digital and in color.

---

37 CFR 1.84(c)

(c) Identification of drawings. Identifying indicia should be provided, and if provided, should include the title of the invention, inventor's name, and application number, or docket number (if any) if an application number has not been assigned to the application. If this information is provided, it must be placed on the front of each sheet within the top margin. Each drawing sheet submitted after the filing date of an application must be identified as either **"Replacement Sheet" or "New Sheet"** pursuant to **§ 1.121(d).** If a marked-up copy of any amended drawing figure including annotations indicating the changes made is filed, such marked-up copy must be clearly labeled as **"Annotated Sheet" pursuant to § 1.121(d)(1).**

USPTO COMMENTS

Identifying indicia, if provided, should include the title of the invention, the inventor's name, the application number (if known), and docket number (if any). This information must be placed within the top margin of each sheet of drawings. *The name and telephone number of a person to call if the USPTO is unable to match the drawings to the proper application may also be provided in the event the drawings are filed in paper, rather than via EFS-Web.*

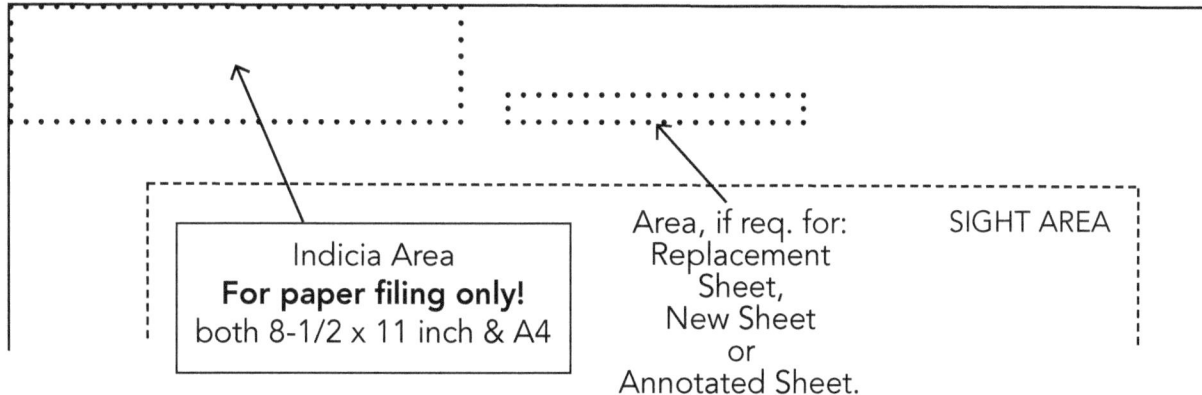

Indicia Area
For paper filing only!
both 8-1/2 x 11 inch & A4

Area, if req. for:
Replacement
Sheet,
New Sheet
or
Annotated Sheet.

SIGHT AREA

AUTHOR'S COMMENTS
Because of the limited space it is better to include just the application number, amendment date, reply to Office action date and Replacement, New or Annotated Sheet notification. Generally, attorneys, large corporations and government agencies have their own way of doing this, and in the past a lot of them also put in their telephone number.

Note: Also see Chapter 5 Corrections for USPTO patent drawings

37 CFR 1.84(c) Identification of drawings.

37 CFR 1.84(d) Graphic Forms in Drawings

(d) Graphic forms in drawings. Chemical or mathematical formulae, tables, and waveforms may be submitted as drawings and are subject to the same requirements as drawings. Each chemical or mathematical formula must be labeled as a separate figure, using brackets when necessary, to show that information is properly integrated. Each group of waveforms must be presented as a single figure, using a common vertical axis with time extending along the horizontal axis. Each individual waveform discussed in the specification must be identified with a separate letter designation adjacent to the vertical axis.

---

37 CFR 1.84(d) USPTO COMMENTS

Under 37 CFR 1.58 chemical formulas, mathematical equations, and tables may be included in the specification. However, the specification may not contain flow diagrams, waveforms, graphs, etc., which must be submitted as drawings.

If a computer program listing is 300 or fewer lines and each line is 72 or fewer characters, the listing may be submitted as drawings. See 37 CFR 1.96.

Nucleotide and/or amino acid sequence data may be submitted as drawings, but the application is nevertheless subject to the Sequence Listing rules set forth in **37 CFR 1.821 through 1.825;** that is, the applicant must submit a computer-readable form, etc. if the application (including the drawings) contains "an unbranched sequence of four or more amino acids or an unbranched sequence of 10 or more nucleotides."

AUTHOR'S COMMENTS

There are professional software programs for both chemical and mathematical formulae that can be used to insert into the "specification" and/or "claims," under **37 CFR 1.58**, or can be used to create drawing figures.

Caution:

If you are submitting text or figures electronically using the above mentioned software, remember to "embed" your drawings into the submittal PDF to the USPTO EFS-Web.

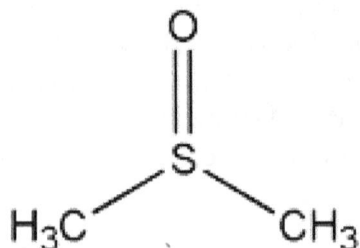

Sample of:
Chemical structure of
dimethyl sulfoxide
from the ChemDrawPro (R)
Used with permission.

---

37 CFR 1.84(d) Graphic Forms in Drawings.

Graphic Forms used in Figures

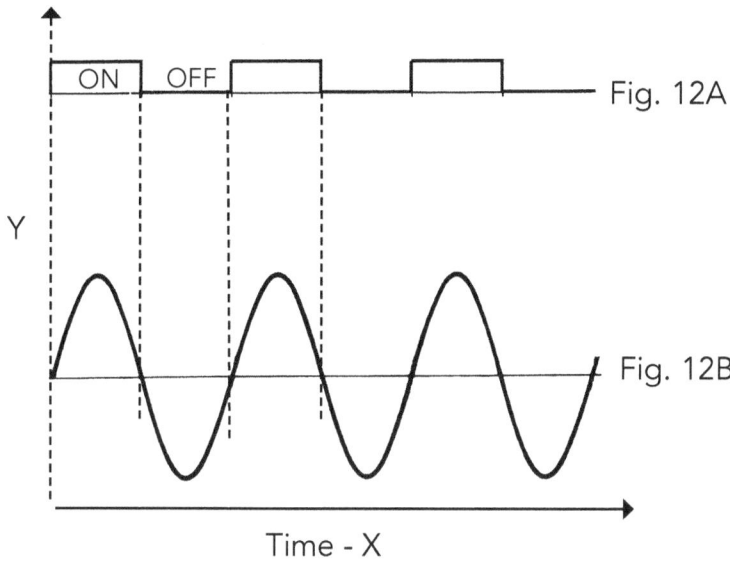

Fig. 12A

Fig. 12B

Y

Time - X

(a) Waveform figure using common vertical axis with time extending along horizontal axis and each individual waveform described as an individual figure but grouped with A, B, C, etc.

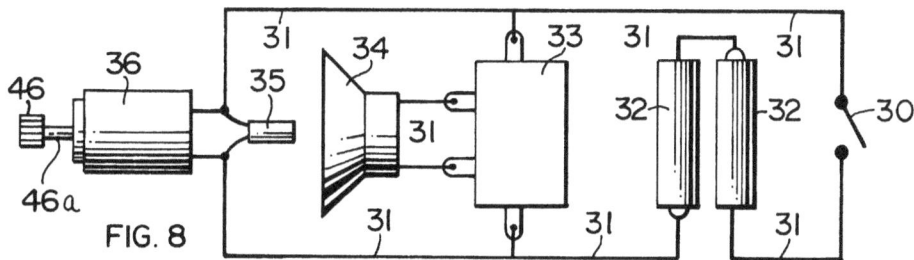

(b) Pictorial of a simple electrical diagram.

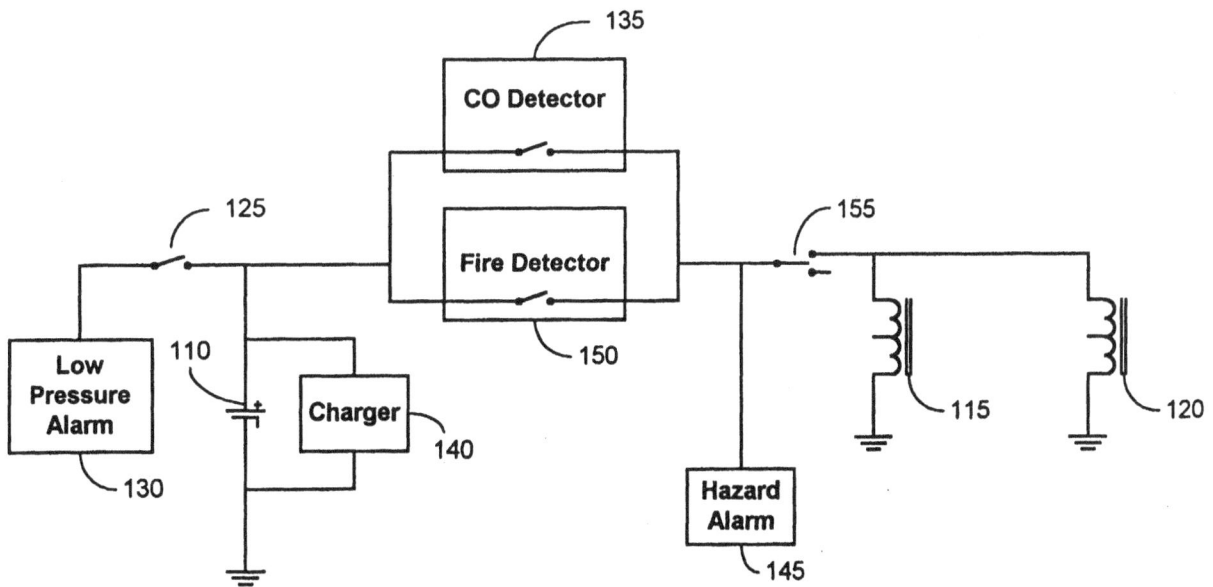

(c) Sample of another simple electrical diagram with call-out numbers and legends.

37 CFR 1.84(d) Graphic Forms, examples of Waveforms, and two simple electrical diagrams.

37 CFR 1.84(e) Type of paper

(e) Type of paper. Drawings submitted to the Office must be made on paper which is flexible, strong, white, smooth, non-shiny, and durable. All sheets must be reasonably free from cracks, creases, and folds. Only one side of the sheet may be used for the drawing. Each sheet must be reasonably free from erasures and must be free from alterations, overwritings, and interlineations. Photographs must be developed on paper meeting the sheet-size requirements of paragraph (f) of this section and the margin requirements of paragraph (g) of this section. See paragraph (b) of this section for other requirements for photographs.

AUTHOR'S COMMENTS

Approximately 95% of all patent applications presently
are filed electronically, both U.S. and PCT International.
You will note that most of the patent drawing rules were
written for paper filing and little by little the various rules
are being converted to accept electronic filing.

(f) Size of paper, most filing at the present time is directed
toward international markets and it generally is better
to plan on using the A4 size requirements.

It is almost impossible to keep products off the World Wide Web!

See page 86 for universal "image area" dimensions
so that your patent drawings will fit either paper size.
If you use an image area that is the width of an A4 sheet (16 cm - 6-3/8 inch)
and the height of a 8-1/2 x 11 inch sheet (24 cm - 9-1/2 inch)
it will work for either drawing sheet size.

(f) Size of paper. All drawing sheets in an application must be the same size. One of the shorter sides of the sheet is regarded as its top. The size of the sheets on which drawings are made must be:

    (1) 21.0 cm. by 29.7 cm. (DIN size A4), or

    (2) 21.6 cm. by 27.9 cm. (8 1/2 by 11 inches).

37 CFR 1.84(g) Margins

(g) Margins. The sheets must not contain frames around the sight (i.e., the usable surface), but should have scan target points (i.e., cross-hairs) printed on two cater-corner margin corners. Each sheet must include a top margin of at least 2.5 cm. (1 inch), a left side margin of at least 2.5 cm. (1 inch), a right side margin of at least 1.5 cm. (5/8 inch), and a bottom margin of at least 1.0 cm. (3/8 inch), thereby leaving a sight no greater than 17.0 cm. by 26.2 cm. on 21.0 cm. by 29.7 cm. (DIN size A4) drawing sheets, and a sight no greater than 17.6 cm. by 24.4 cm. (6 15/16 by 9 5/8 inches) on 21.6 cm. by 27.9 cm. (8½ by 11 inch) drawing sheets.

---

37 CFR 1.84(g) USPTO COMMENTS
(in reference to Scan Target Points)

See PCT Rule 11.6(e) in Section 5. This rule states that "the margins of the international application ... must be completely blank." It has been suggested that scan target points are in conflict with this rule. As indicated above, ***the applicant may elect not to place scan target points on the drawing sheets.*** Otherwise, an applicant filing drawings that were previously filed in an international application may add the scan target points only to the copies of the drawing sheets being filed in the Office. Similarly, an applicant filing drawings that will later be filed as part of an international application may place scan target points only on the copies of the drawings being filed in the Office.

AUTHOR'S COMMENTS

Scan target points are only used on drawing sheets where the patent application is submitted as a printed paper copy; you do not need the scan target points on patent drawing sheets that are submitted electronically through the USPTO EFS-Web, or on PCT submittal (either paper or electronic submittal).

I never submitted drawings with "scan target points" on them and was never asked to put them on.

**See following pages for page size and margin templates.
Also see Chapter 4.**

37 CFR 1.84(g) Margins

Top & Left side alignment

Letter Sheet 8.5 inch (21.6 cm) wide

A4 Sheet 8.25 inch (21 cm) to scale

Image area

Preferred drawing sheet number area

Alternate

Notes on drawing (reproduction) image areas:

1 - For Nonprovisional (Utility) PCT Drawings common image areas can be: (A4)
16 cm (6 - 3/8 inch) wide x 24 cm (9.5 inch) high.

2 - For U.S. Design Patent image area can be: (Letter)
16 cm (6 - 3/8 inch) wide x 24 cm (9.5 inch) high.

3 - For WIPO Hague Industrial Design Registrations (A4) image area can be: 16 cm wide x 16 cm high.

4 - See individual A4 and Letter drawings sheets for complete dimensional information in this chapter.

Letter Sheet 11 inch (27.9 cm) high

A4 Sheet 11-11/16 inch (21 cm)

Image Area

(A4 - Sheet)

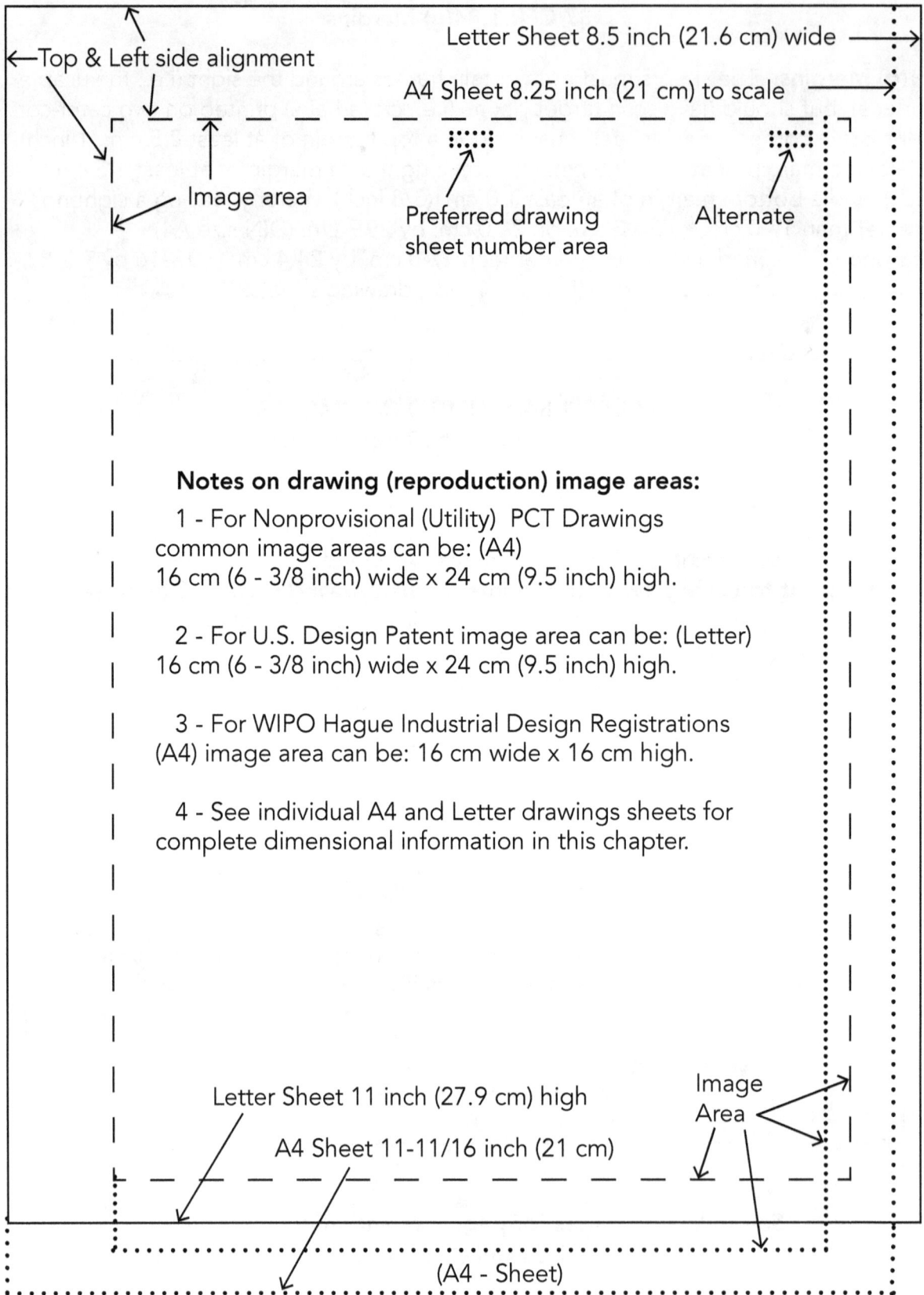

Letter/A4 Drawing Sheet image (sight) area differences.

1 inch Top Margin (2.5 cm)

37 CFR 1.84(c)
Identification
of drawings
Indicia Area,
**paper filing
only.**

5/8 inch Right Margin (1.5 CM)

1 inch Left Margin (2.5 cm)

Sight or Image Area:
6 - 7/8 inch wide (17.6 cm)
9 - 5/8 inch high (24.4 cm)
NOTE:
When positioning drawing figures within the "sight area,"
leave at least a 1/8 inch space between the outside edge
of the figures and the invisible sight line.

11 inch Drawing Sheet Height (27.9 cm)

3/8 inch Bottom Margin (1 cm)

8.5 inch Drawing Sheet Width (21.6 cm)

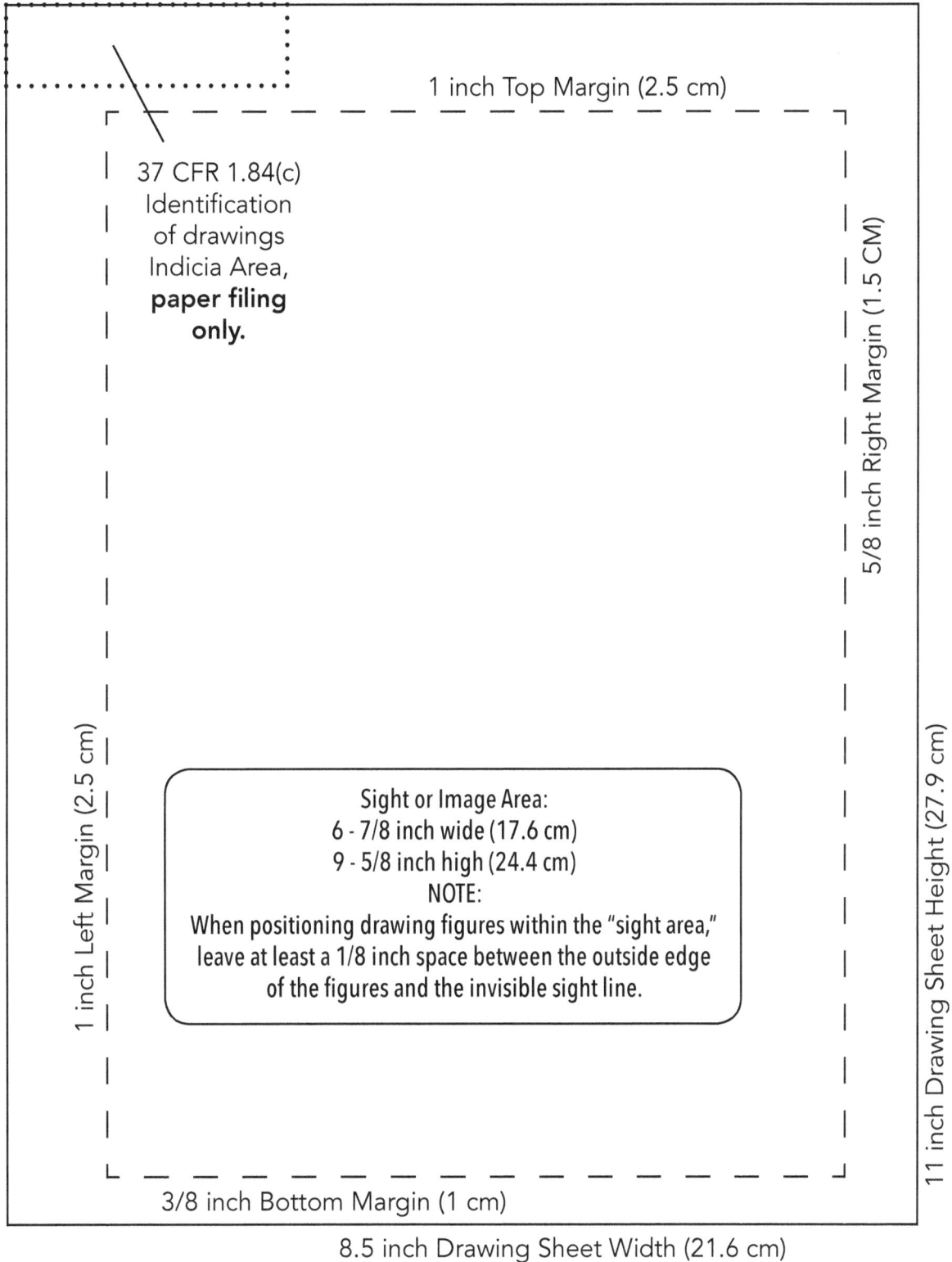

37 CFR 1.84(g) Margins (2) U.S. 8-1/2 x 11 inch drawing sheet
and location of items allowed in the "margin" area.

37 CFR 1.84(h) Views

(h) Views. The drawing must contain as many views as necessary to show the invention. **The views may be plan, elevation, section, or perspective views. Detail views of portions of elements,** on a larger scale if necessary, may also be used. All views of the drawing must be grouped together and arranged on the sheet(s) without wasting space, preferably in an upright position, clearly separated from one another, and must not be included in the sheets containing the specifications, claims, or abstract. Views must not be connected by projection lines and must not contain center lines. **Waveforms of electrical signals may be connected by dashed lines to show the relative timing of the waveforms (see page 83).**

AUTHOR'S COMMENTS

(h) Views. Generally, you can break views down into two categories:
1) for an introduction or description of the invention; and
2) the more detailed drawings to illustrate the features of the claims.

**The second category is too often overlooked.
Therefore, I am repeating the USPTO description below:**

"The drawing must show every feature of the invention specified in the claims, and is required by the Office rules to be in a particular form ... ."

The first category, "description" of the invention, is generally done with plan (top bottom); elevation (side, front, rear), and perspective views.

The second category, "illustrating the features of the claims," is generally done with section, detailed or enlarged, alternate, and exploded views, and the use of PRIOR ART views; charts, graphs, symbols, steps and lists of procedures; and photographs both black & white and color (when allowed by petition), especially when they are used to record test results from various devices and instruments.

CAUTION:

When illustrating PRIOR ART views for your application, do not alter or put your own interpretation on the look of the Pre-Grant, or Granted patent drawing. Your drawing must illustrate the original published application.

---

37 CFR 1.84(h) Views, see examples on following pages.

37 CFR 1.84(h) Views

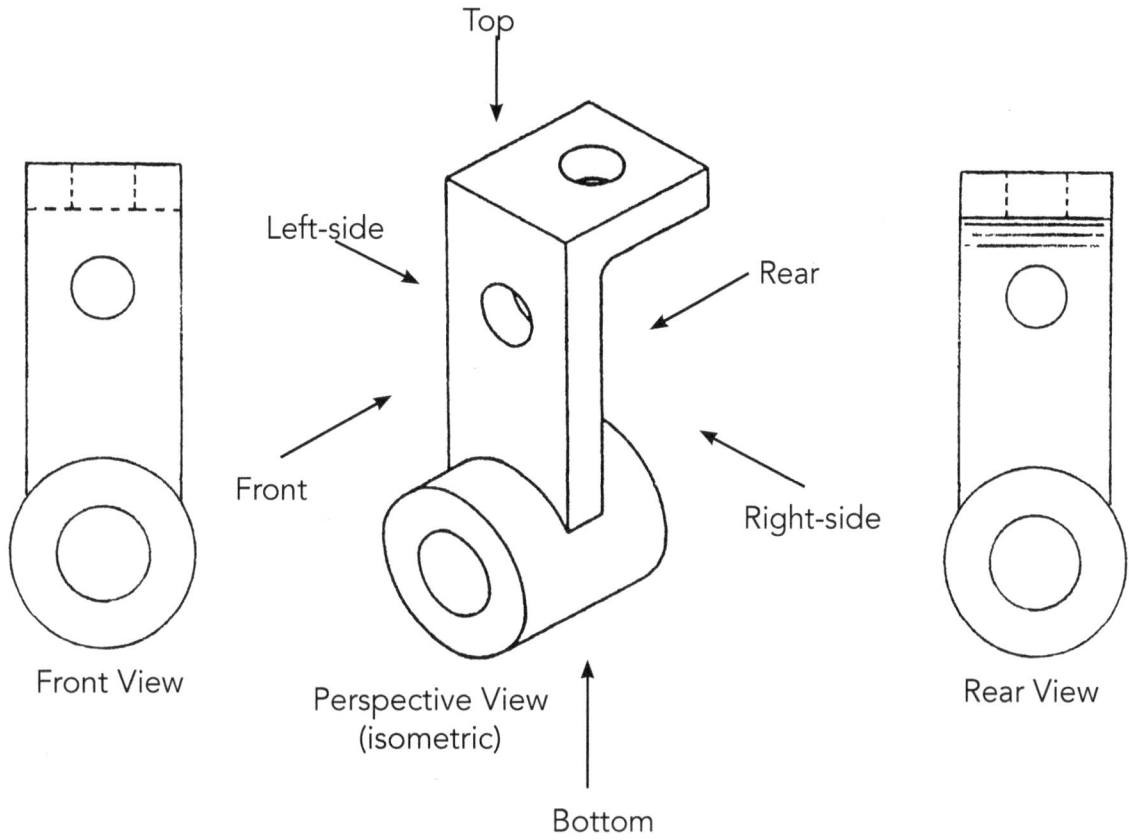

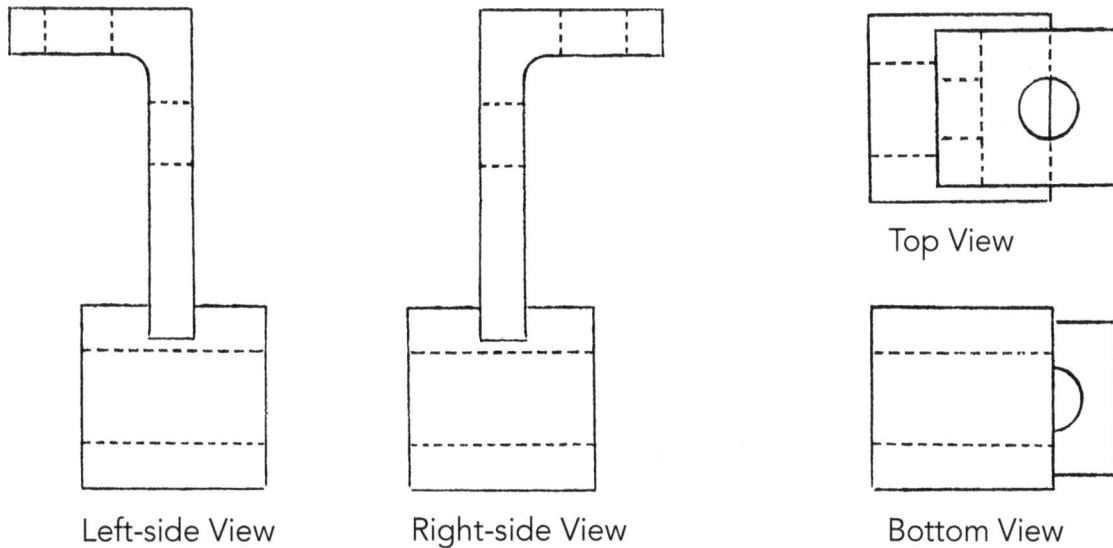

37 CFR 1.84(h) Views, example illustrating the six views in reference to perspective view.

37 CFR 1.84(h) Views

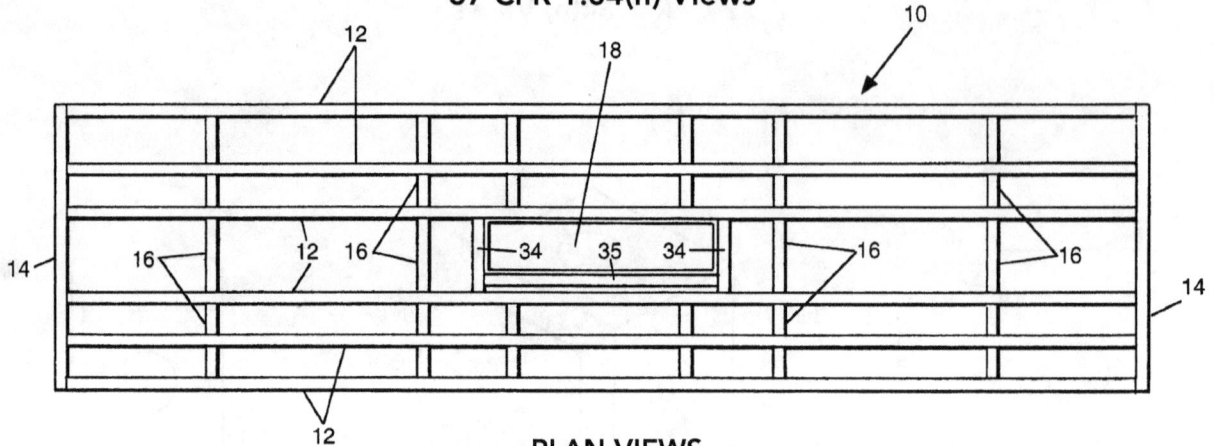

PLAN VIEWS

A plan view of a 3-dimensional object is from the position of a horizontal plane through the object. In other words, a plan is a section viewed from the top. In such views, the portion of the object above the plane is omitted to reveal what lies beyond. In the case of a floor plan, the roof and upper portion of the walls may be omitted. (Ref. Wikipedia)

AUTHOR'S COMMENTS
The description of plan and elevational views are mostly associated with architectural drawings and over time these descriptions were used and added to a lot of patent drawing descriptions in areas, in my opinion, that are not needed. They only add to the unnecessary length of the drawing descriptions. Example: FIG. 3 is a right-side elevational view of my electric motor; or FIG. 3 is a right-side view of my electric motor.

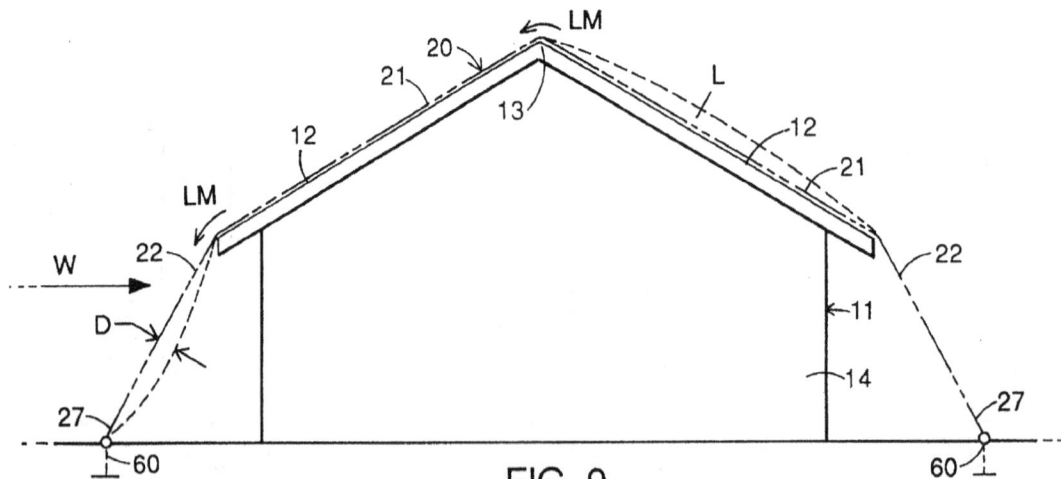

FIG. 9

ELEVATIONAL VIEWS

An elevation is a view of a 3-dimensional object from the position of a horizontal plane beside an object. In other words, an elevation is a side-view as viewed from the front, back, left or right. An elevation is a common method of depicting the external configuration and detailing of a 3-dimensional object in two dimensions. Building façades are shown as elevations in architectural drawings and technical drawings. (Ref. Wikipedia)

37 CFR 1.84(h) Views, Plan and Elevational Views.

37 CFR 1.84(h) Views

Perspective Views: Most perspective views in patent drawings are actually isomeric drawings that are a form of graphical projection; more specifically, a form of axonometric projection. It is a method of visually representing three-dimensional objects in two dimensions in which the three coordinate axes appear equally foreshortened and the angles between any two of them are 120 degrees.

The advantage of this type of drawing is there is no foreshortening as in a true "perspective drawing," whereas in an isometric drawing like objects look the same size, in the foreground or the background.

There are three main types of axonometric projection: isometric, dimetric and trimetric projection. Most of the time isometric is used, but sometimes the other two are used because they may show a better angle illustrating the invention.

If you are drawing an isometric figure by hand you may need a 35° ellipse guide, and remember to match the **"minor axis" on the guide with the center line of your drawing**. Keep in mind that if you are drawing with a computer, most drafting software offers by default only isometric and perspective projections. For dimtric or trimetric you may need to purchase an additional "plug-in" to work with your software.

Oblique drawing is another widely used method for patent figures (see following page).

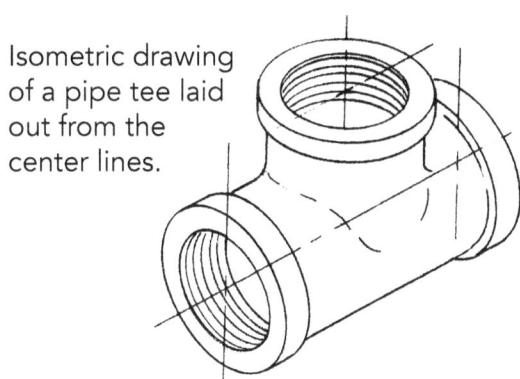

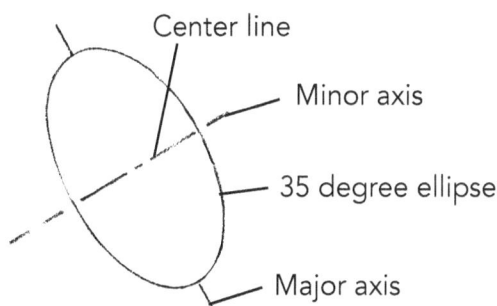

Isometric drawing of a pipe tee laid out from the center lines.

Center line
Minor axis
35 degree ellipse
Major axis

At times inventors and/or draftsmen will trace a photograph of the invention; this type of drawing is closer to a true perspective view.

Regardless of the drawing technique that is used in patent drawings, it is generally worded as a "perspective view" in the title of the figures.

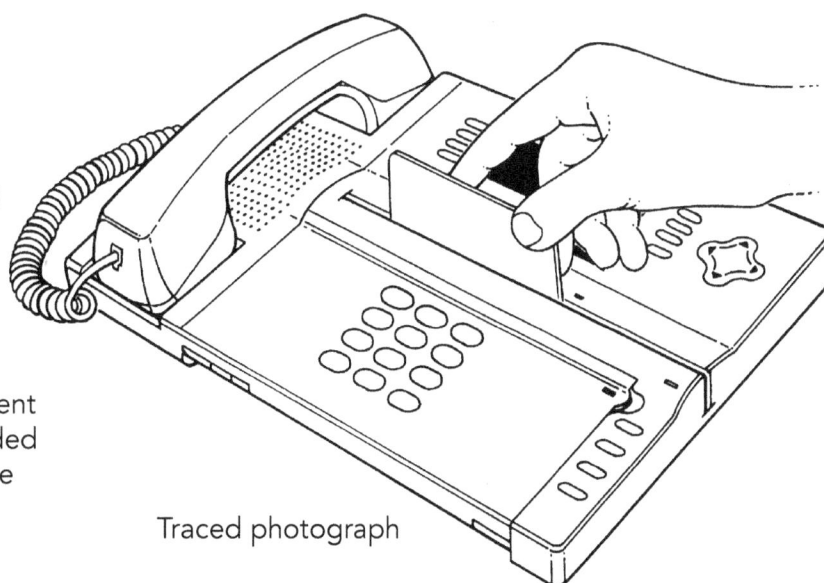

Traced photograph

37 CFR 1.84(h) Views, See following page for forms of axonometric views.

Forms of Axonometric Projection as views of a cube

OBLIQUE

Circle

X
Y
Z
A

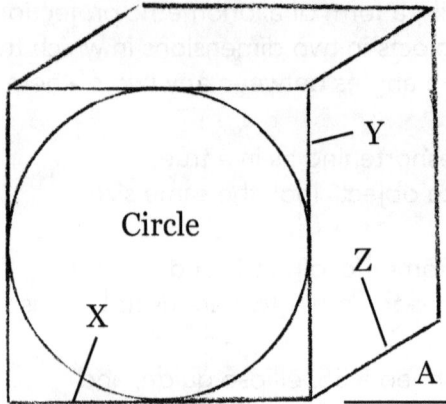

Oblique projection with the three
axes of projection as
horizontal (X), vertical (Y),
and receding (Z).
Angle (A) can generally be 30, 45
or 60 degrees, and can be right,
left, up or down.

ISOMETRIC

35°
35°
35°
Y
Z
X
30°
30°

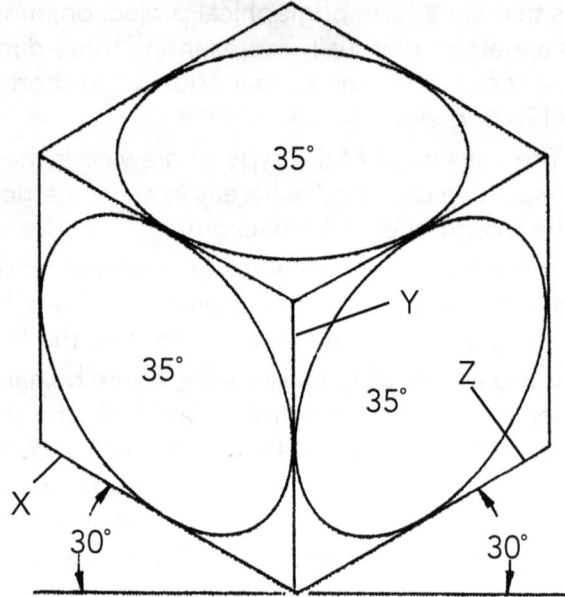

Isometric projection in which the three axes
appear equally foreshortened and the
angles between any two of them
are 120 degrees.

DIMETRIC

20°
40°
40°
X
Z
20°
20°

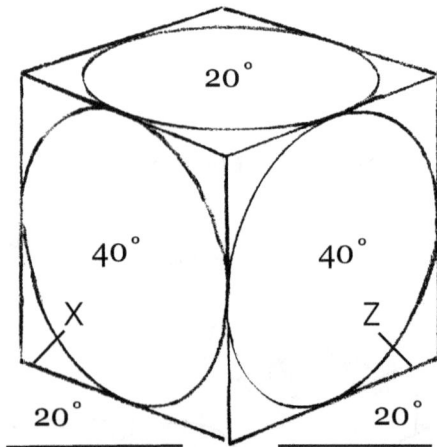

Dimetric projection in which the
view is shown with two of its three
axes (X/Z) tilted equally from the
plane of viewing.

This is a popular form
for exploded views
used in military manuals.

© 2010 Studio 94

TRIMETRIC

35°
Y
15°
60°
Z
X

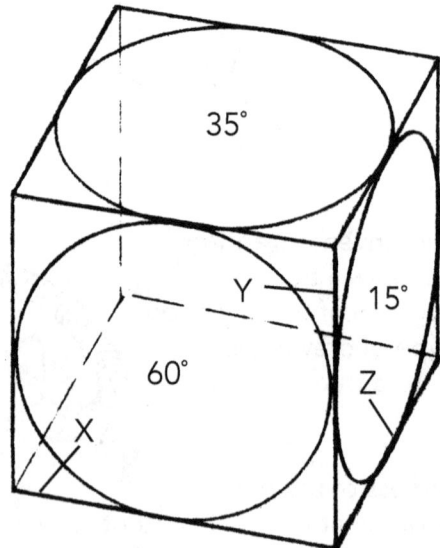

Trimetric projection in which the
view is shown with all three of its
principal axes tilted unequally from
the plane of viewing.

37 CFR 1.84(h) Views, using axonometric projections as perspective.

(1) Exploded views. Exploded views, with the separated parts embraced by a bracket, to show the relationship or order of assembly of various parts are permissible. When an exploded view is shown in a figure that is on the same sheet as another figure, the exploded view should be placed in brackets.

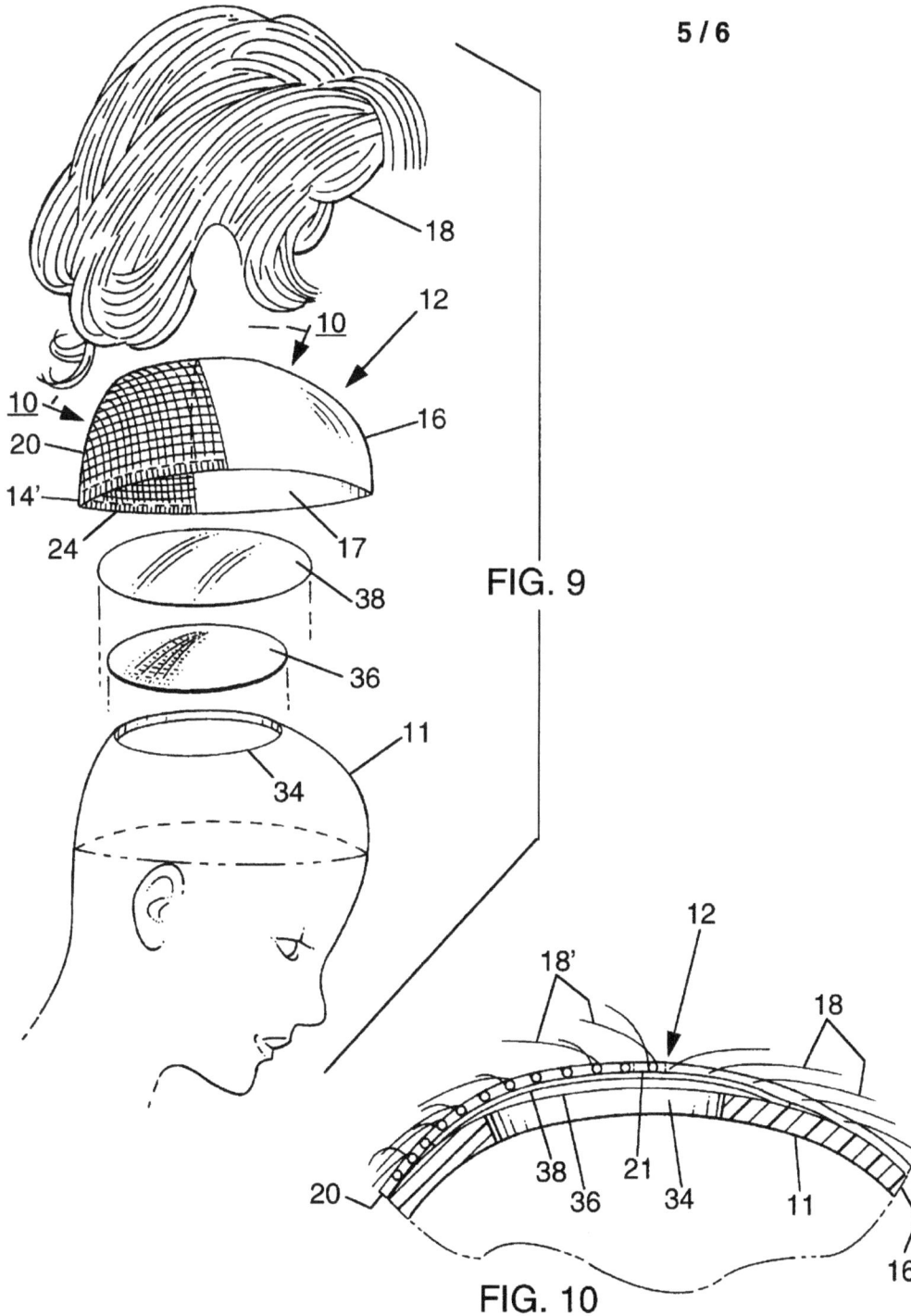

FIG. 9

FIG. 10

Ref: 37 CFR 1.84(h) Views, (1) Exploded Views.

(2) Partial views. When necessary, a view of a large machine or device in its entirety may be broken into **partial views on a single sheet,** or **extended over several sheets** if there is no loss in facility of understanding the view. Partial views drawn on separate sheets must always be capable of being linked edge to edge so that no partial view contains parts of another partial view. **A smaller scale view should be included** showing the whole formed by the partial views and indicating the positions of the parts shown. When a portion of a view is enlarged for magnification purposes, the view and the enlarged view must each be labeled as separate views.

(i) Where views on two or more sheets form, in effect, a single complete view, the views on the several sheets must be so arranged that the complete figure can be assembled without concealing any part of any of the views appearing on the various sheets.

(ii) A very long view **may be divided into several parts** placed one above the other on a single sheet. However, the relationship between the different parts must be clear and unambiguous.

AUTHOR'S COMMENTS
See following pages for additional examples.

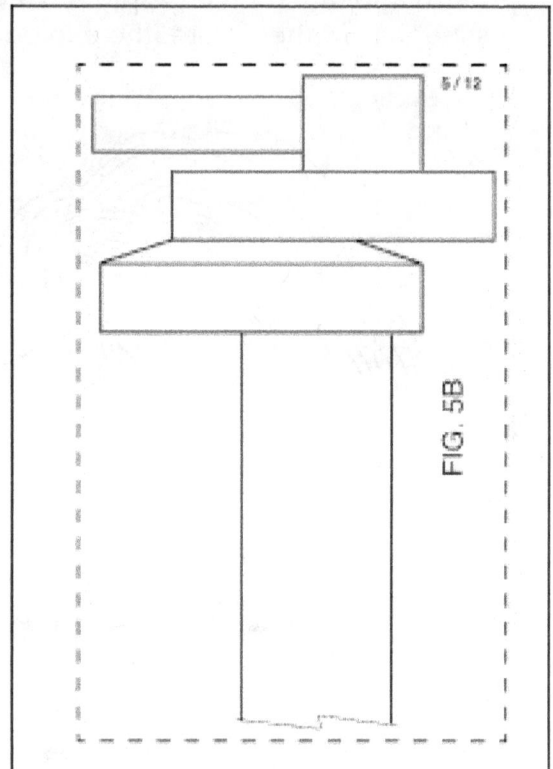

FIG. 5B

5 / 12

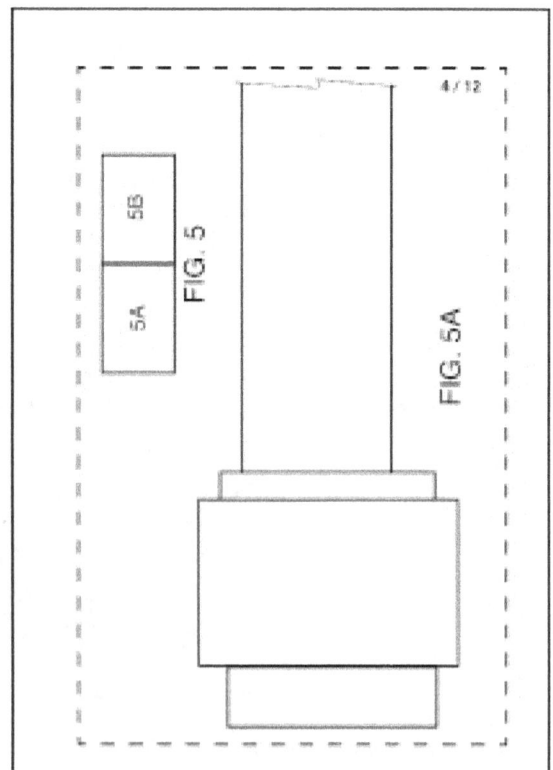

FIG. 5

5B

5A

FIG. 5A

4 / 12

37 CFR 1.84(h)(2) Partial views.

37 CFR 1.84(h)(2) Partial Views

(2) Partial views. When necessary, a view of a large machine or device in its entirety may be broken into **partial views on a single sheet.**

(ii) A very long view **may be divided into several parts** placed one above the other on a single sheet. However, the relationship between the different parts must be clear and unambiguous.

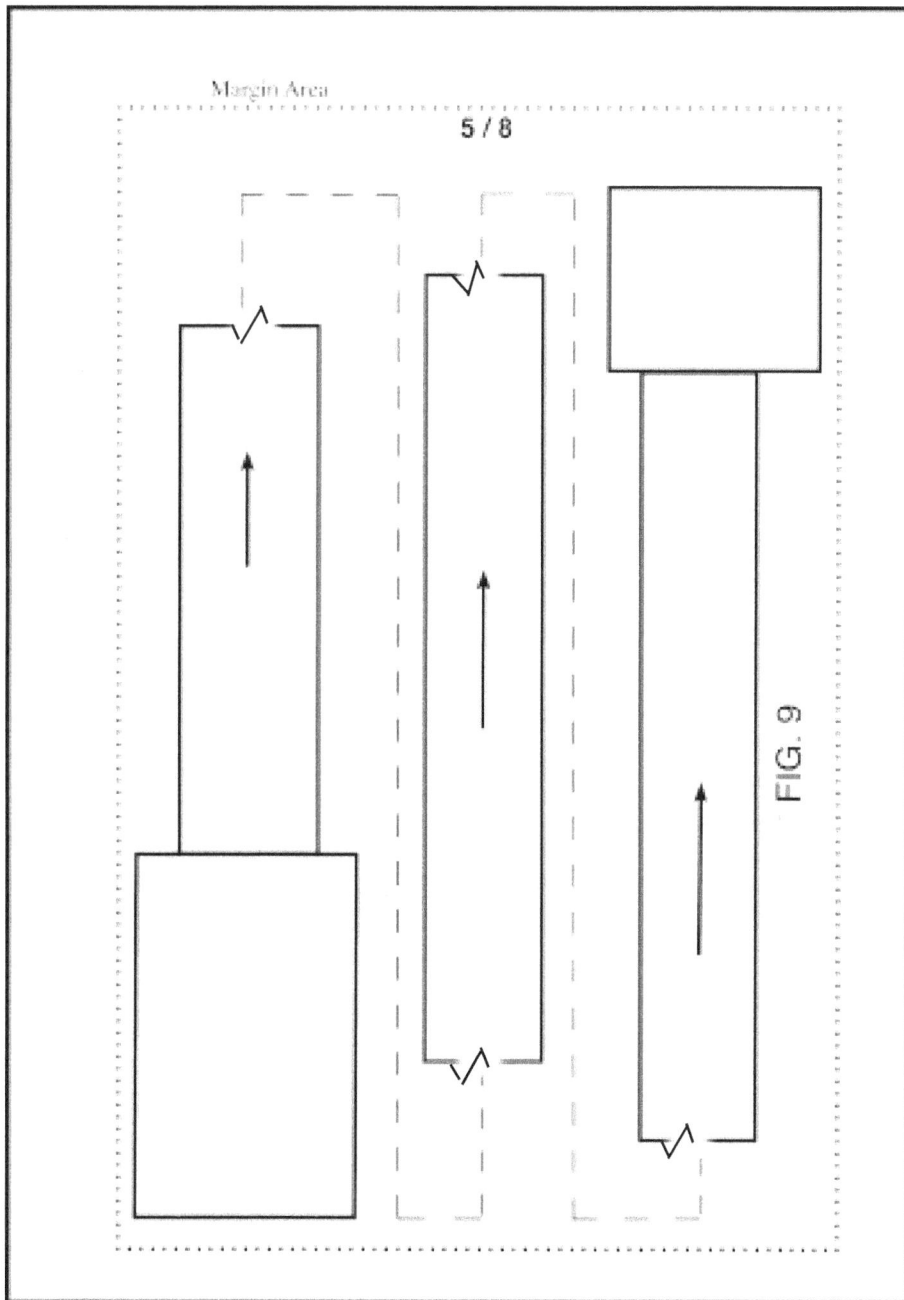

Margin Area

5 / 8

FIG. 9

37 CFR 1.84(h)(2) Partial views, example of long view divided on one sheet.

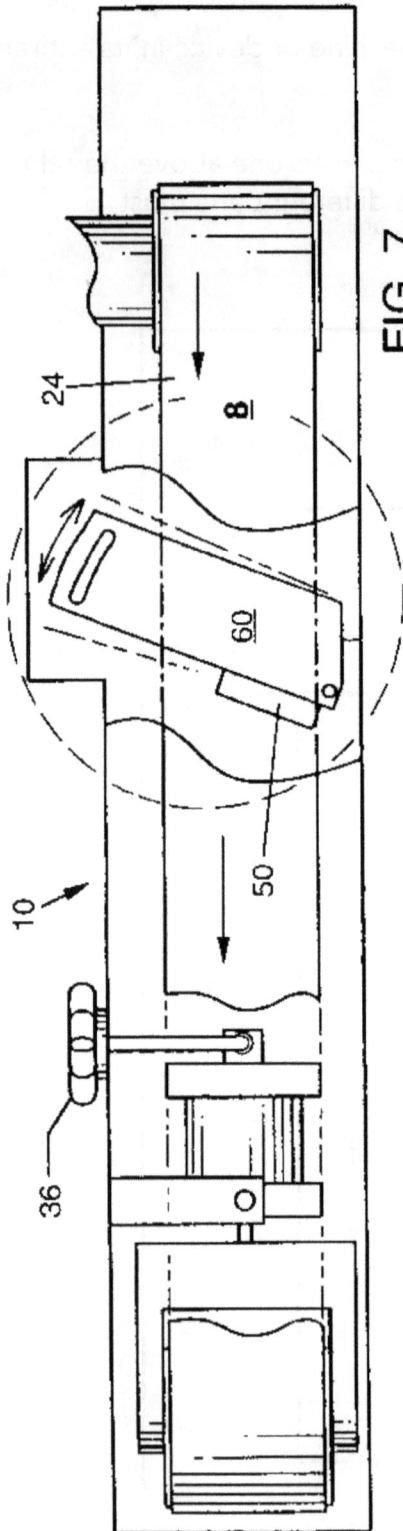

NOTE:
Partial enlarged view FIG. 8
is taken from area 8 indicated
with the dashed line in circle.

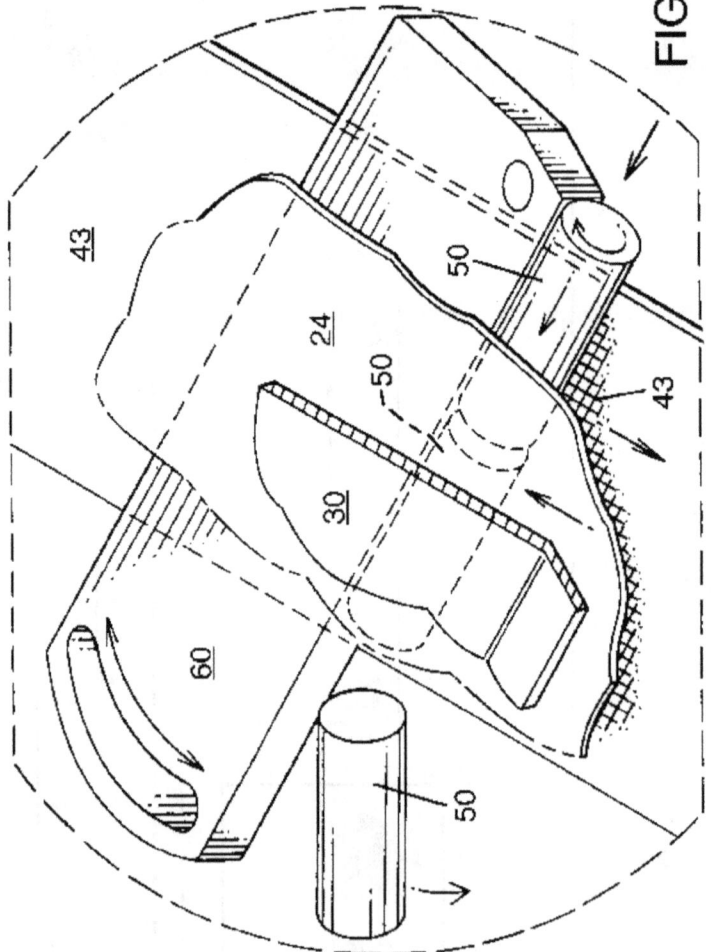

FIG. 7

FIG. 8

NOTE:
If space permitted
FIG. 8 would be in full circle.

37 CFR 1.84(h) (2) Example of partial view (enlarged view).

(3) Sectional views. The plane upon which a sectional view is taken should be indicated on the view from which the section is cut by a broken line. The ends of the broken line should be designated by **Arabic** or Roman numerals **corresponding to the view number of the sectional view,** and should have arrows to indicate the direction of sight. Hatching must be used to indicate section portions of an object, and must be made by regularly spaced oblique parallel lines spaced sufficiently apart to enable the lines to be distinguished without difficulty. Hatching should not impede the clear reading of the reference characters and lead lines. If it is not possible to place reference characters outside the hatched area, the hatching may be broken off wherever reference characters are inserted. Hatching must be at a substantial angle to the surrounding axes or principal lines, preferably 45°. A cross section must be set out and drawn to show all of the materials as they are shown in the view from which the cross section was taken. The parts in cross section must show proper material(s) by hatching with regularly spaced parallel oblique strokes, the space between strokes being chosen on the basis of the total area to be hatched. The various parts of a cross section of the same item should be hatched in the same manner and should accurately and graphically indicate the nature of the material(s) that is illustrated in cross section. The hatching of juxtaposed different elements must be angled in a different way. In the case of large areas, hatching may be confined to an edging drawn around the entire inside of the outline of the area to be hatched. Different types of hatching should have different conventional meanings as regards the nature of a material seen in cross section. (See examples on the following pages).

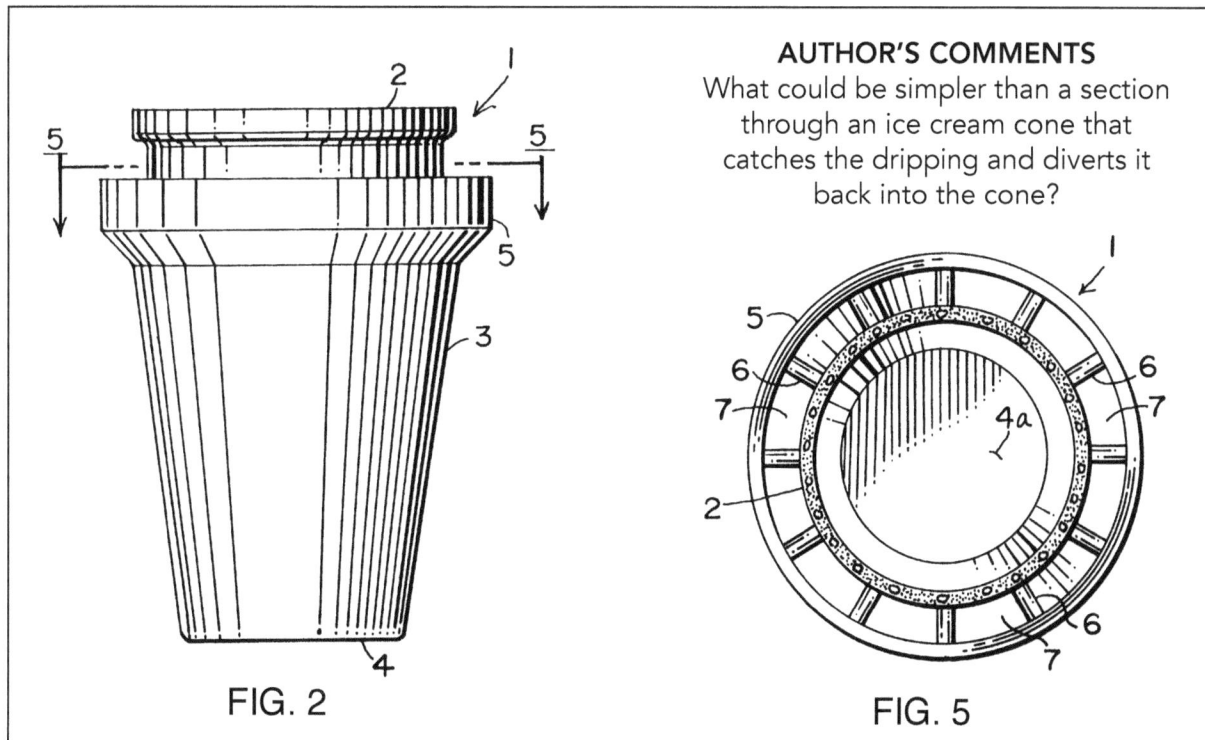

AUTHOR'S COMMENTS
What could be simpler than a section through an ice cream cone that catches the dripping and diverts it back into the cone?

FIG. 2

FIG. 5

37 CFR 1.84(h)(3) Sectional views.

AUTHOR'S COMMENTS
A good practice in illustrating
cross section hatching is to
set the spacing between the lines
wide enough so that the lines
do not close-up
when the figure is reduced 50%.
This is a good rule to follow whether the
hatching is done by hand or computer.

Be cautious when purchasing drawing
software: a lot of low-priced software
will not allow you to set the line spacing,
and the software default spacing
is generally too close together.

NOTE:
See Appendix for examples of
USPTO Surface & Sectional Coding.

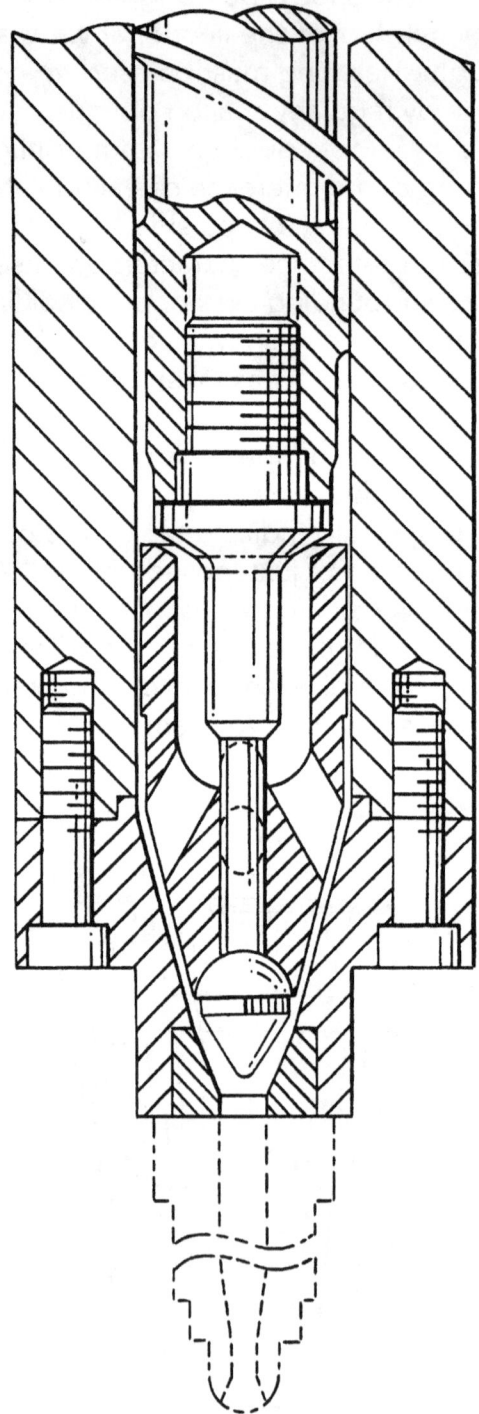

37 CFR 1.84(h) (3) Sectional views.

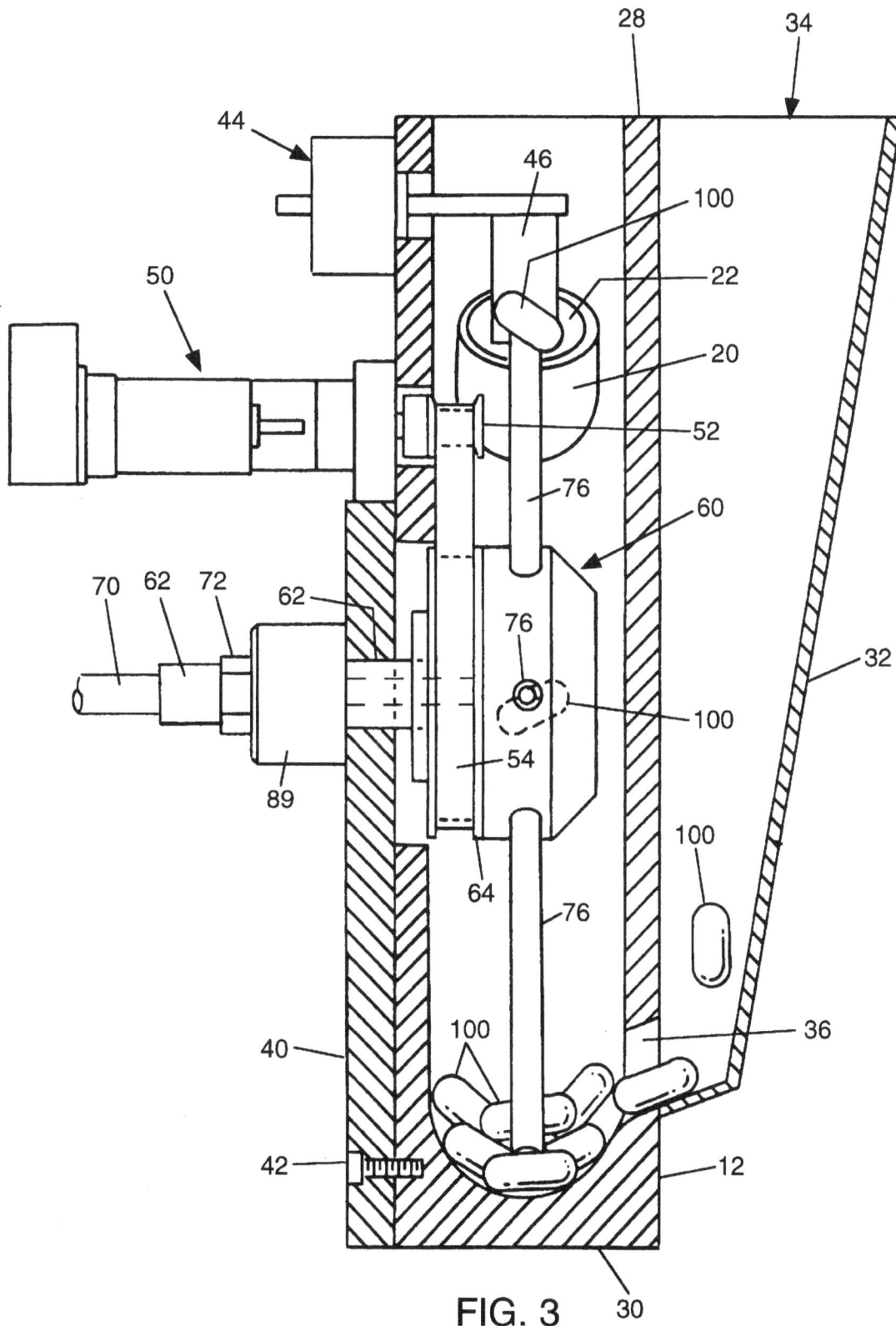

FIG. 3

37 CFR 1.84(h) (3) Sectional views.

99

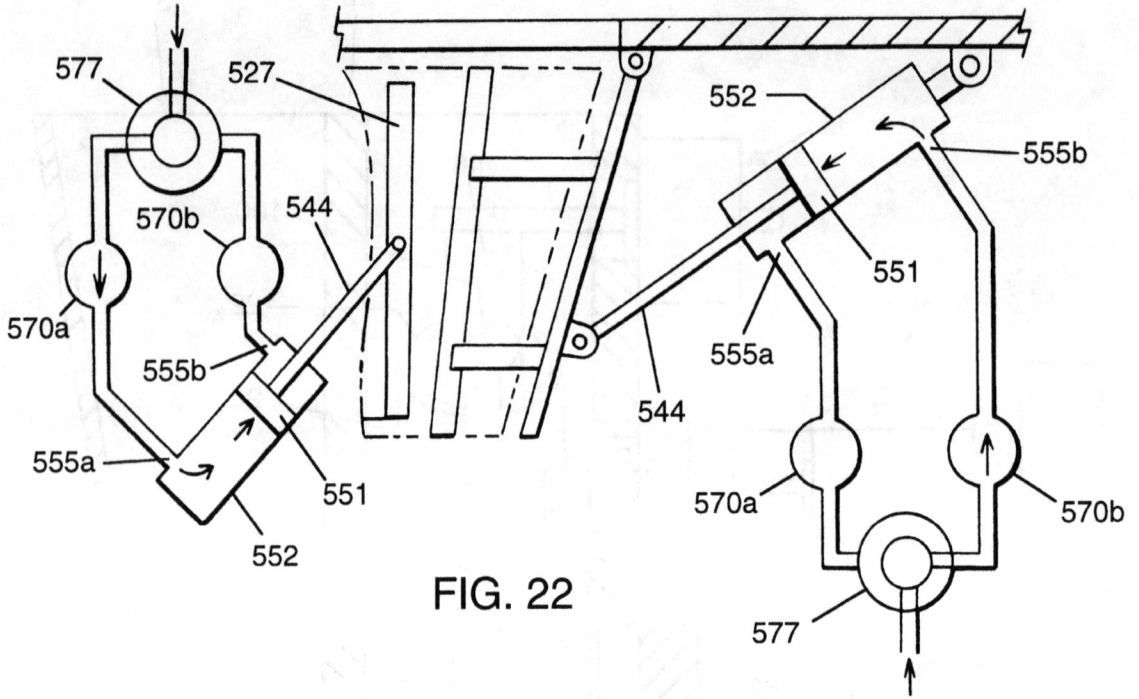

FIG. 22

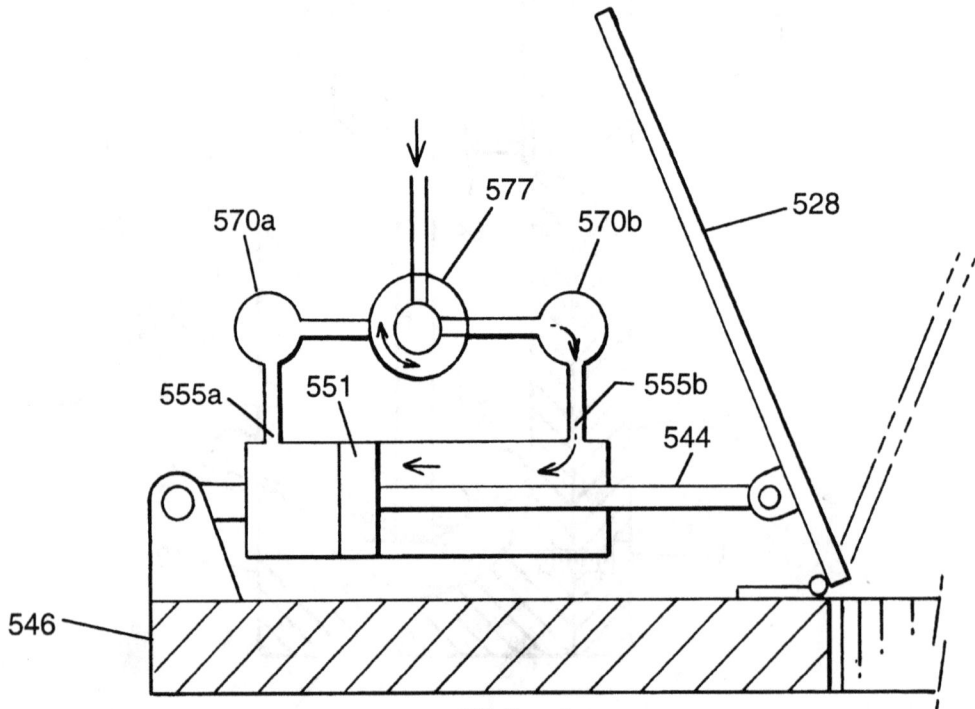

FIG. 23

37 CFR 1.84(h) (3) Sectional views illustrating minor section cut.

100

(4) Alternate position. A moved position may be shown by a broken line superimposed upon a suitable view if this can be done without crowding; otherwise, a separate view must be used for this purpose.

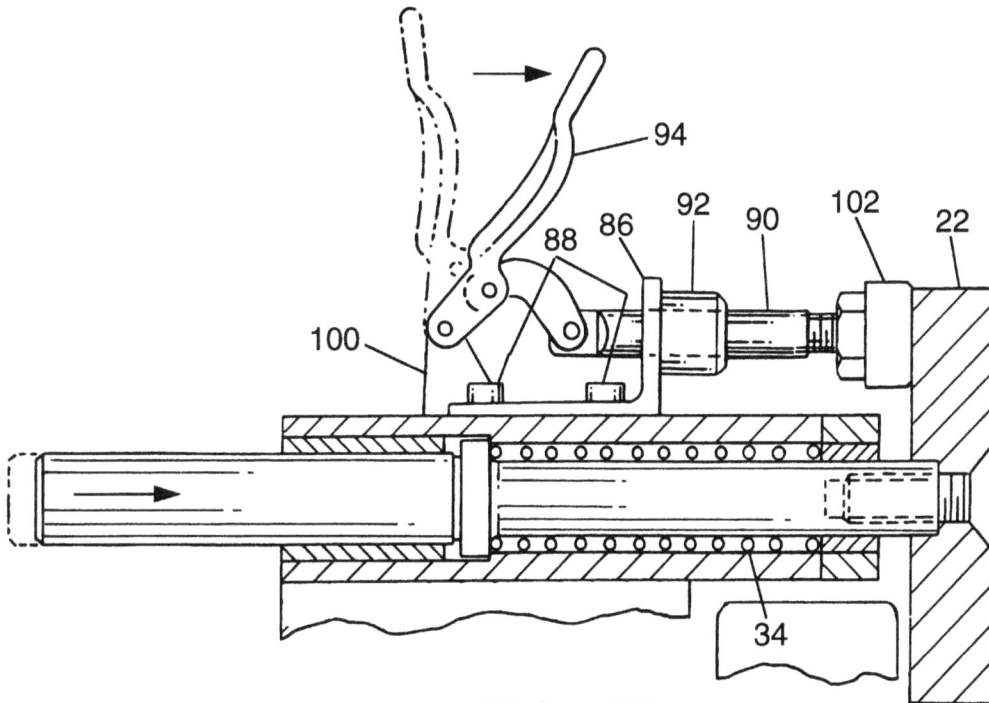

FIG. 5B

37 CFR 1.84(h) (5) Modified Forms

(5) Modified forms. Modified forms of construction must be shown in separate views.

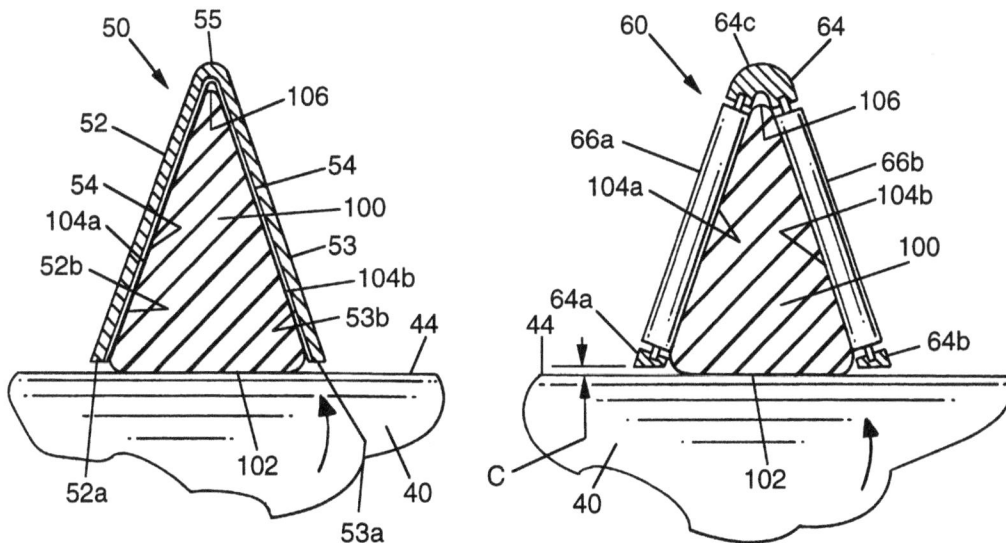

37 CFR 1.84(h)(4) Alternate position and 37 CFR 1.84(h)(5) Modified forms.

37 CFR 1.84(i) Arrangement of views

(i) Arrangement of views. One view must not be placed upon another or within the outline of another. All views on the same sheet should stand in the same direction and, if possible, stand so that they can be read with the sheet held in an upright position. If views wider than the width of the sheet are necessary for the clearest illustration of the invention, the sheet may be turned on its side so that the top of the sheet, with the appropriate top margin to be used as the heading space, is on the right-hand side. Words must appear in a horizontal, left-to-right fashion when the page is either upright or turned so that the top becomes the right side, **except for graphs utilizing standard scientific convention to denote the axis of abscissas (of X) and the axis of ordinates (of Y).**

---

37 CFR 1.84(i) USPTO COMMENTS

One view is not to be superimposed within the outline of another. The requirement that "Words ... appear in a horizontal, left-to-right fashion when the page is either upright or turned so that the top becomes the right side ..." expands the possibilities for presenting graphs to conform to standard scientific conventions, while using a format compatible with automated patent searching displays, such that drawings can be viewed on a monitor in such a manner that words/numbers appear either in the upright position or rotated 90° to the right.

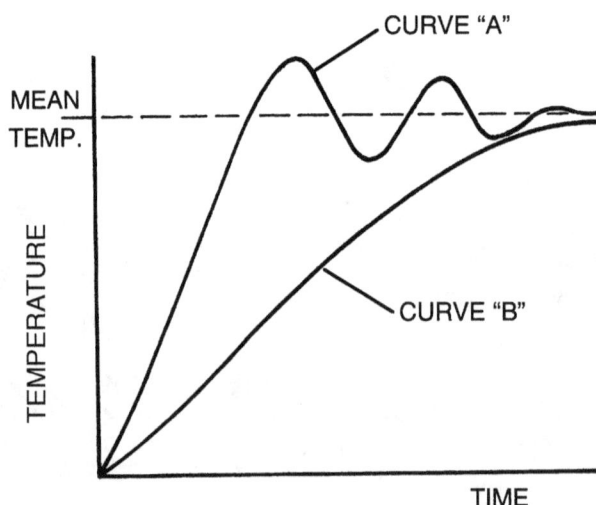

FIG. 10

37 CFR 1.84(i) Arrangement of views, see following pages.

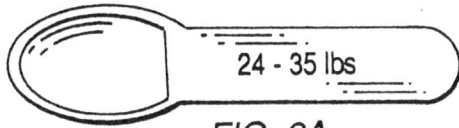

FIG. 6A

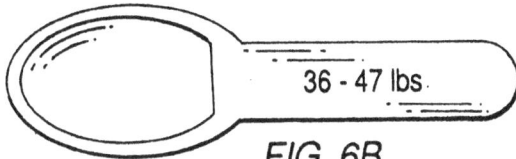

FIG. 6B

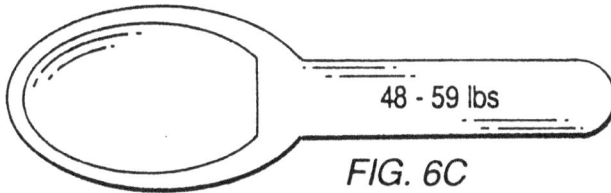

FIG. 6C

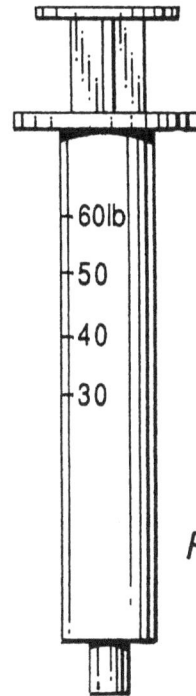

FIG. 7

DOSAGE TABLE

Weight (lb)	Dispense (ml)
15	1.00
14	.93
13	.87
12	.80
11	.73
10	.67
9	.60
8	.53
7	.47

F @ .055 mg / kg = ml / lb

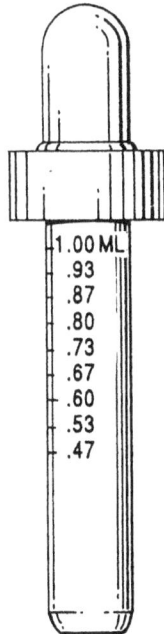

FIG. 8

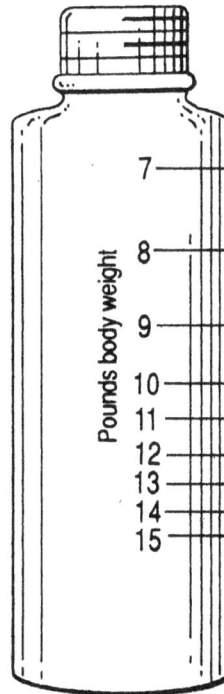

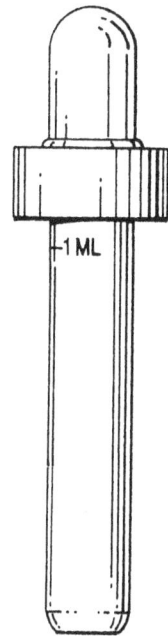

FIG. 9

37 CFR 1.84(i) Arrangement of views.

FIG. 1

FIG. 2

37 CFR 1.84(i) Arrangement of views showing long machine with center areas cut out.

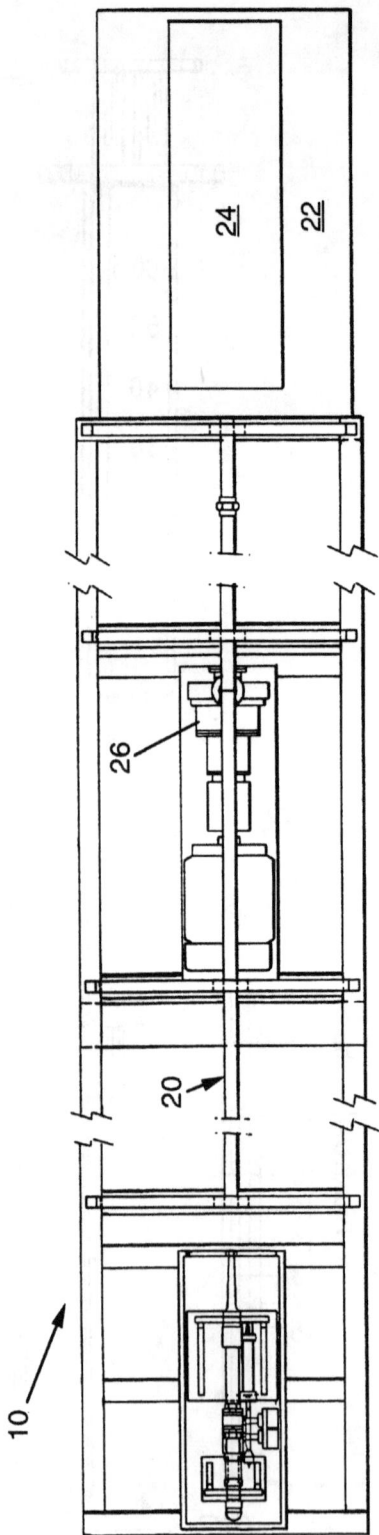

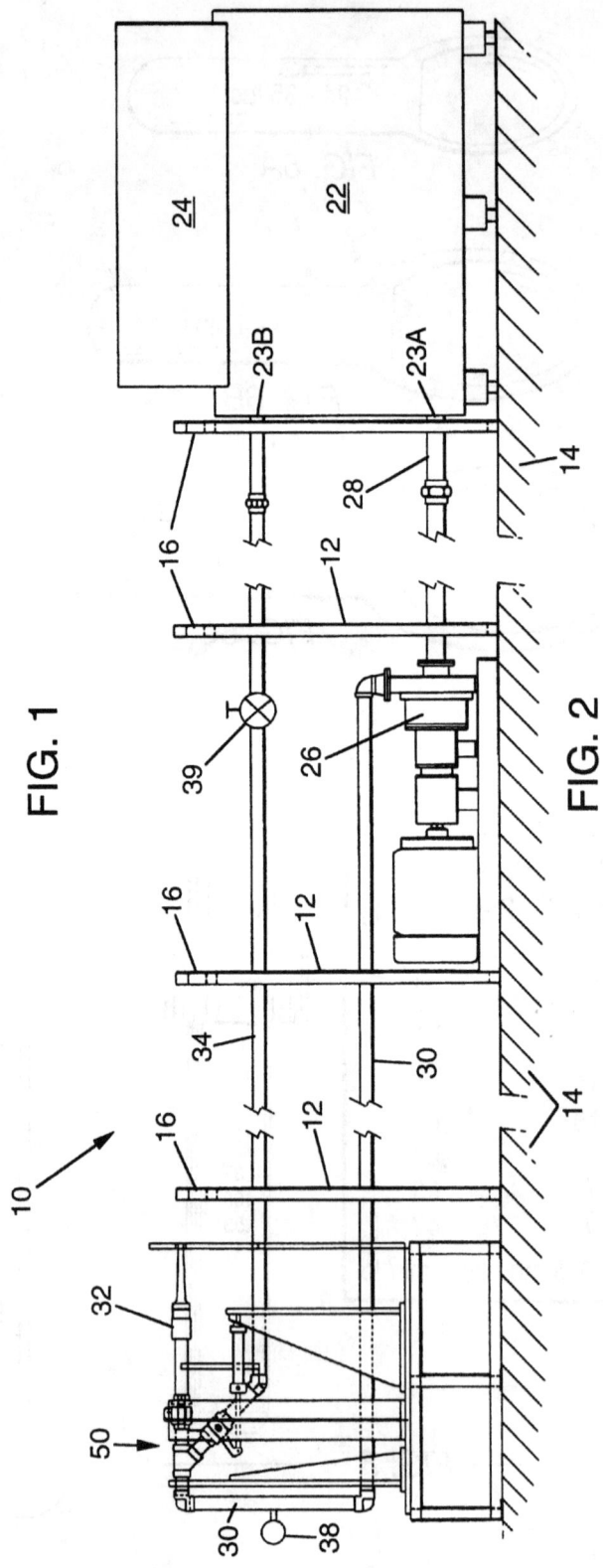

37 CFR 1.84(j) Front page view

(j) Front page view. The drawing must contain as many views as necessary to show the invention. One of the views should be suitable for inclusion on the front page of the patent application publication and patent as the illustration of the invention. Views must not be connected by projection lines and must not contain center lines. Applicant may suggest a single view (by figure number) for inclusion on the front page of the patent application publication and patent.

USPTO COMMENTS

Although the applicant may suggest a "front page" figure, the Office may decide that another figure will better illustrate the invention on the patent application publication's front page or on the patent's front page. As stated in the preamble to the final rulemaking titled Changes to Implement Eighteen-Month Publication of Patent Applications, 1239 Off. Gaz. Pat. Office 6396 (October 10, 2000):

. . . **Section 1.84(j)** is . . . amended to provide that: (1) one of the views should be suitable for inclusion on the front page of the patent application publication and patent as illustration of the invention; and (2) applicant may suggest a single view (by figure number) for inclusion on the front page of the patent application publication and patent. Applicants should indicate in the application transmittal letter the figure number of the view suggested for inclusion on the front page of the patent application publication and patent. The Office, however, is not bound by the applicant's suggestion. . . .

The view that is shown on the front page of the patent will also be shown in the Official Gazette for patents. (There is no Official Gazette for patent application publications.)

The selected view should be at a scale that will clearly illustrate details after being subjected to as much as two-thirds reduction. **See 37 CFR 1.84(k) Scale.**

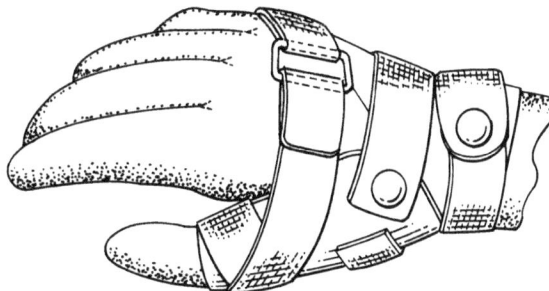

Example of patent figure after a two-thirds reduction.
Drawing may be with or without numbers.

37 CFR 1.84(j) Front page view.

37 CFR 1.84(k) Scale

(k) Scale. The scale to which a drawing is made must be large enough to show the mechanism without crowding when the drawing is reduced in size to two-thirds in reproduction. Indications such as "actual size" or "scale ½" on the drawings are not permitted since these lose their meaning with reproduction in a different format.

---

37 CFR 1.84(k) USPTO COMMENTS

Although indications such as "actual size" or "scale ½" are not allowed, measurement indications such as " *1 inch* " or " *45°* " are acceptable.

AUTHOR'S COMMENTS

There are occasions where it is necessary to put a scale indicator on a drawing and there are many "clip art" graphic scales that can be attached to the patent drawing either by hand or computer. Also, some of the drawing software programs have graphic scales built into them.

If it is necessary to use a graphic scale it is best to choose one that is simple, clear and holds up well when reduced in size.

Do not use a graphic scale that is "decorative" in design.

There are other occasions when it is necessary to put dimensions, angles and mathematical ratios on a patent drawing. These "identifiers" are generally used only when they are necessary to the claims of the patent application.

37 CFR 1.84(l) Character of lines, numbers and letters

(l) Character of lines, numbers and letters. All drawings must be made by a process, which will give them **satisfactory reproduction characteristics.** Every line, number, and letter must be durable, clean, black (except for color drawings), sufficiently dense and dark, and uniformly thick and well-defined. The weight of all lines and letters must be heavy enough to permit adequate reproduction. This requirement applies to all lines however fine, to shading, and to lines representing cut surfaces in sectional views. Lines and strokes of different thicknesses may be used in the same drawing where different thicknesses have a different meaning.

---

37 CFR 1.84(l) USPTO COMMENTS

Use a **continuous thick line** for edging and outlining views and cross sections.

Use a **continuous thin line** for leading lines, hatching, outlining parts of adjoining elements, fictitious lines of intersection of surfaces connected by curved or rounded edges.

Use a **continuous thin line drawn freehand** for delimiting views, part sections, or interrupted views.

Use a **thin broken line made up of short dashes** for hidden edges and contours.

Use a **dot-dash thin line** for axes and planes of symmetry, extreme positions of moveable elements, in front of a cross section.

Use a **thin line terminating in one heavy line** for outlines of cross sections.

AUTHOR'S COMMENTS

All drawings must be made by a process that will give them satisfactory reproduction characteristics.
There are a variety of tools and instruments that may cause patent drawings not to publish in a clean reproduction.
They are: ink pens that are not permanent and smudge; hatching that is too close together; ink lines that are too thin; computer-drawn lines that have a "saw tooth" look; low-quality printers; worn-out copy machines; printer paper that has a rough surface; and cracks, creases and smudges.
Most people new to drawing have a tendency to see their drawing from closer up, about 12 inches away and, not how others will generally view it at a greater distance.

---

37 CFR 1.84(l) Character of lines, numbers and letters.

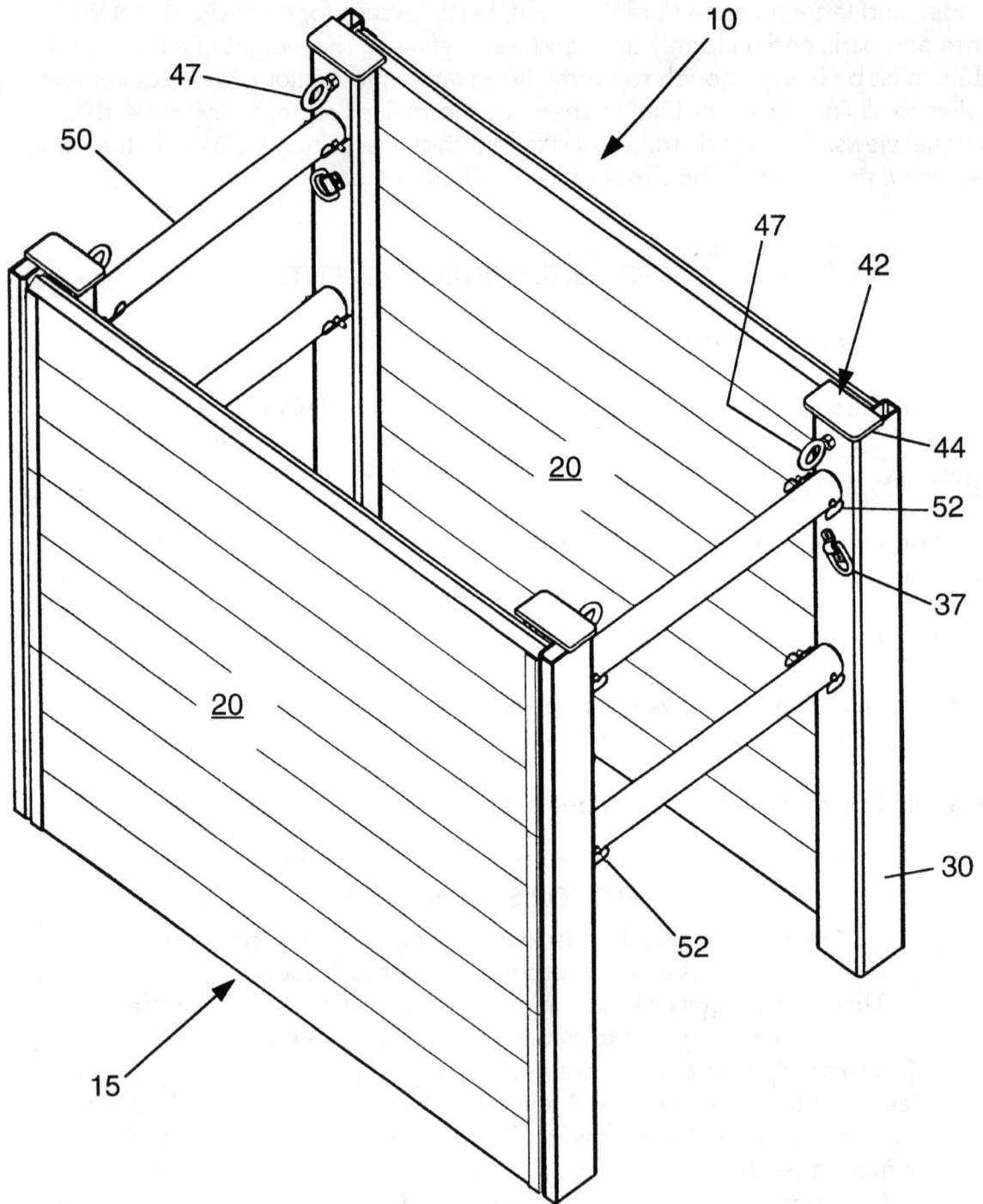

37 CFR 1.84(l) Character of lines, numbers and letters.

37 CFR 1.84(l) Character of lines, numbers and letters

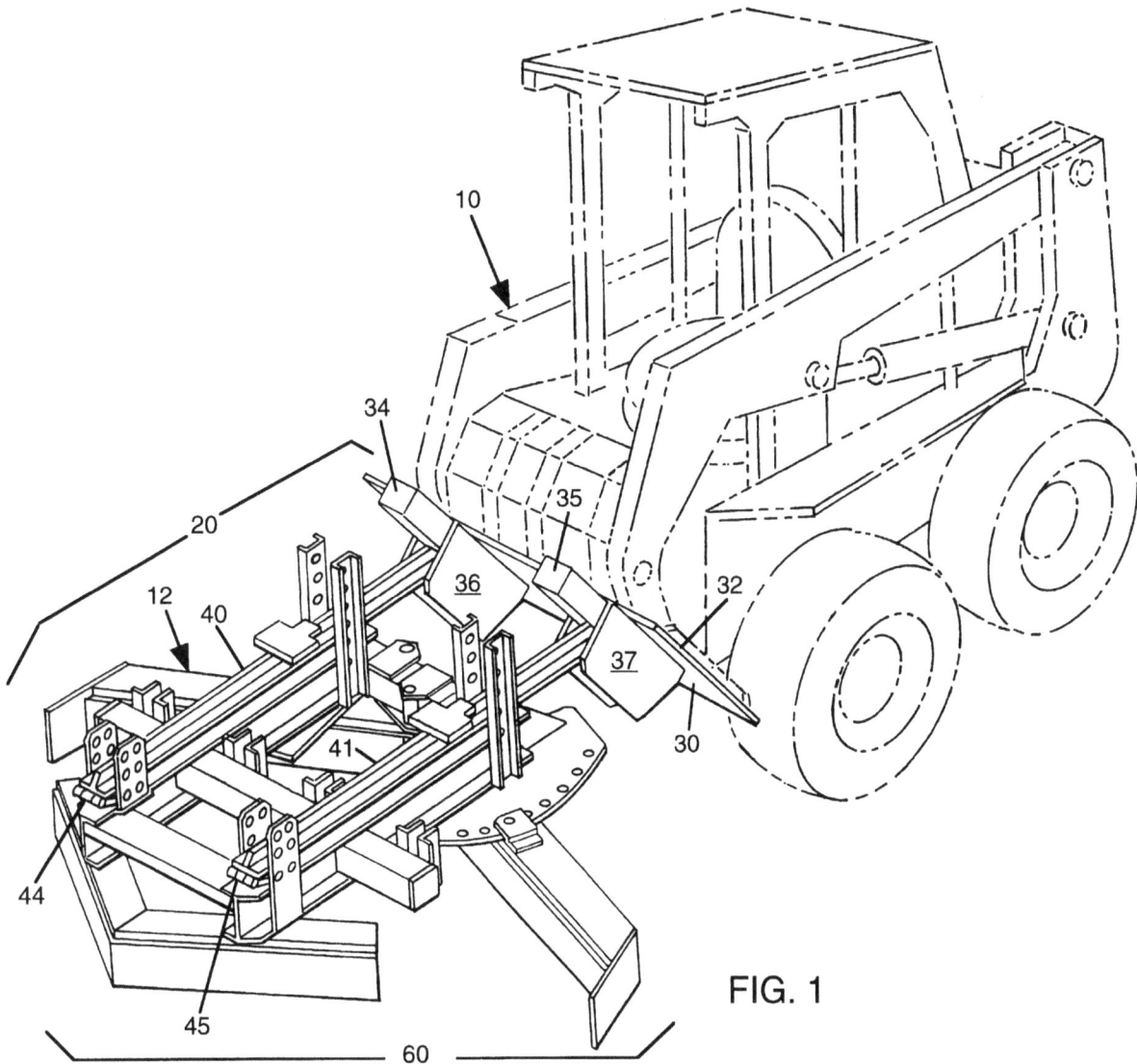

FIG. 1

Character of lines, numbers and letters. All drawings must be made by a process, which will give them satisfactory reproduction characteristics. Every line, number, and letter must be durable, clean, black (except for color drawings), sufficiently dense and dark, and uniformly thick and well-defined. The weight of all lines and letters must be heavy enough to permit adequate reproduction.

Use a **thin broken line made up of short dashes** for hidden edges and contours. (Phantom line).

37 CFR 1.84(l) Character of lines, numbers and letters.

37 CFR 1.84(m) Shading

(m) Shading. The use of shading in views is encouraged if it aids in understanding the invention and if it does not reduce legibility. Shading is used to indicate the surface or shape of spherical, cylindrical, and conical elements of an object. Flat parts may also be lightly shaded. Such shading is preferred in the case of parts shown in perspective, but not for cross sections. See paragraph (h)(3) of this section. Spaced lines for shading are preferred. These lines must be thin, as few in number as practicable, and they must contrast with the rest of the drawings. As a substitute for shading, heavy lines on the shade side of objects can be used except where they superimpose on each other or obscure reference characters. Light should come from the upper left corner at an angle of 45°. Surface delineations should preferably be shown by proper shading. Solid black shading areas are not permitted, except when used to represent bar graphs or color.

---

37 CFR 1.84(m) USPTO COMMENTS

Shading as described in 37 CFR 1.84(m) and hatching as described in 37 CFR 1.84(h)(3) are not the same technique:

• **Shading** is used in perspective views to indicate the "surface or shape" of an element. Spaced lines (see example on page 98) are preferred for shading, although stippling (see example on page 114) and other techniques may be used. (See examples on pages 113 through 117).

• **Hatching** (see Pages 99 through 103) is used in cross-sectional views to show "section portions of an object" and consists of "regularly spaced oblique parallel lines." Sometimes a particular form of hatching (see Appendix) denotes the material of which a section portion is made.

AUTHOR'S COMMENTS
See the next five pages for examples of shading and hatching.
Also see the Annex for hatching, coding and shading.

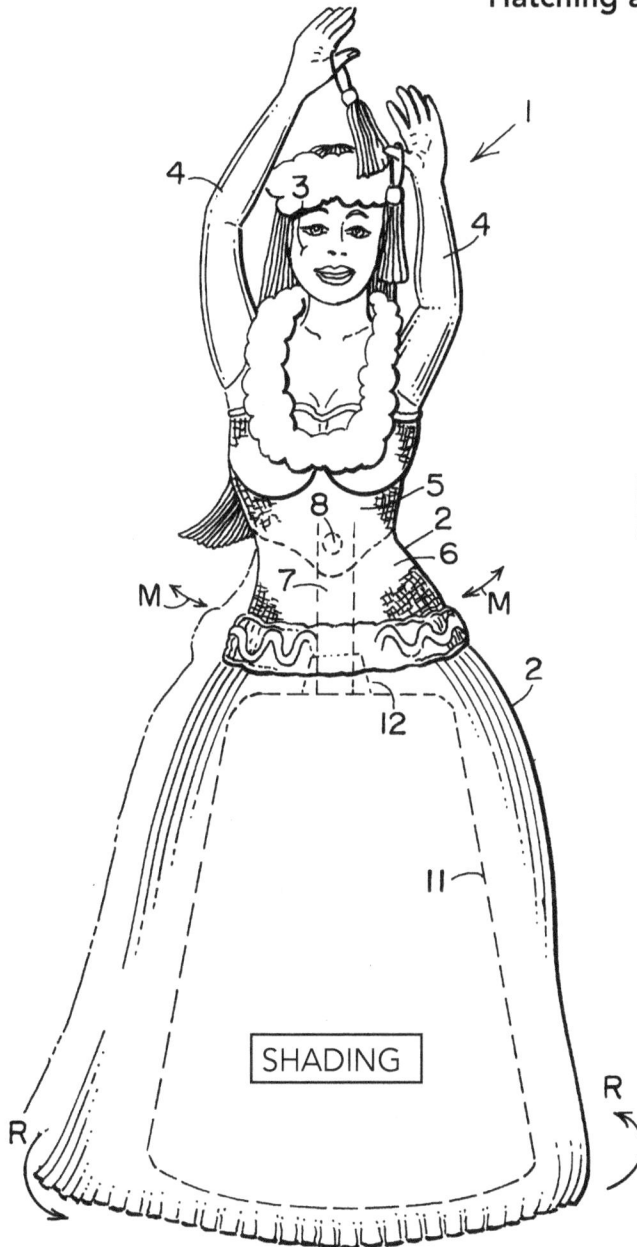

FIG. 1

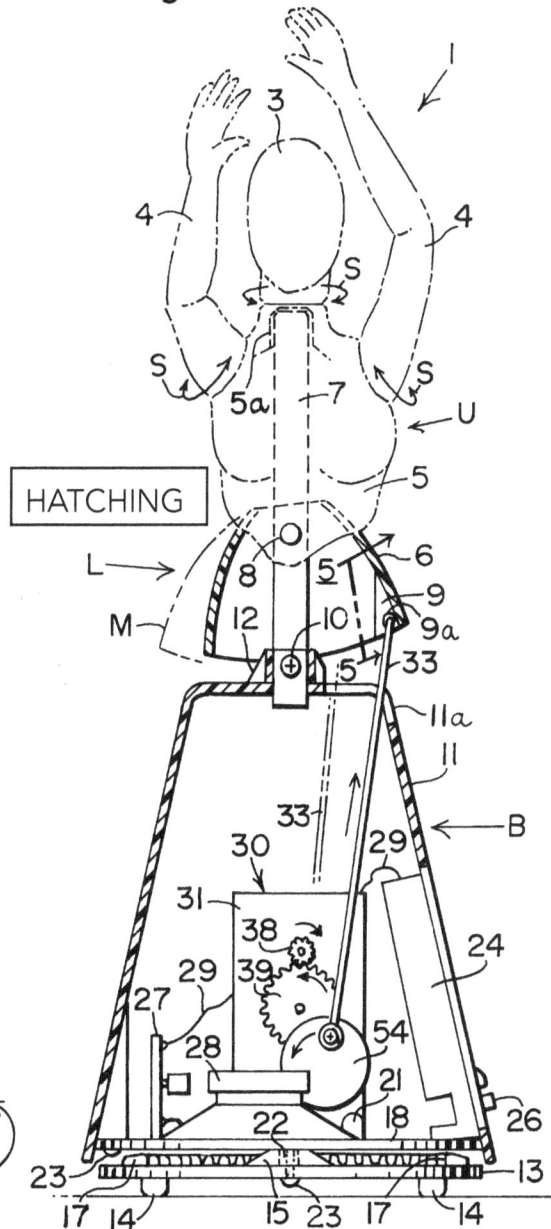

FIG. 2

Hatching as described in **37 CFR 1.84(h)(3)** and **shading** as described in **37 CFR 1.84(m)** are not the same technique:

Hatching is used in cross-sectional views to show "section portions of an oject" and consists of "regularly spaced oblique parallel lines." Sometimes a particular form of hatching (see related pages) denotes the material of which a section portion is made.

Shading is used in perspective views to indicate the "surface or shape of spherical, cylindrical, and conical elements of an object," although "flat parts may also be lightly shaded." Spaced lines are preferred for shading, although stippling and other techniques may be used. (See following pages, samples of shading.)

37 CFR 1.84(m) Shading

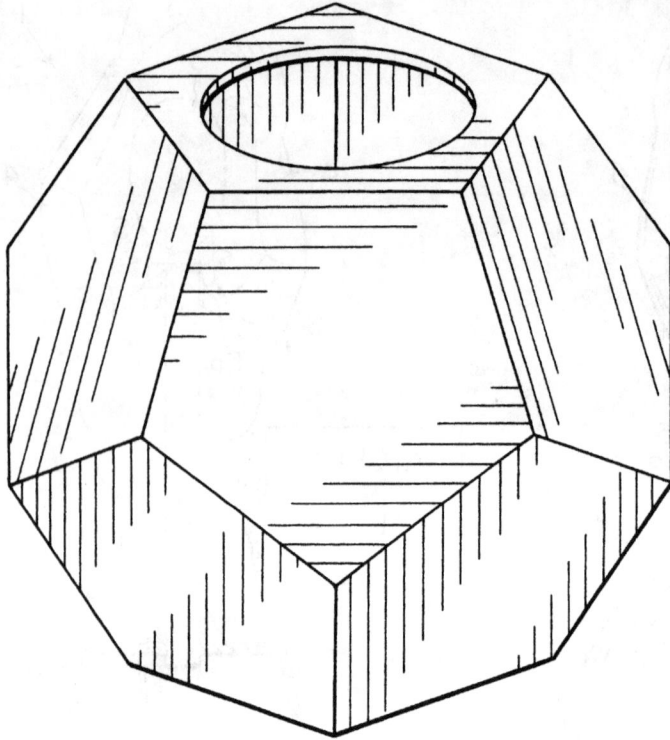

(a) Ink line shading.

(b) Ink stipple shading.

37 CFR 1.84(m) Shading, examples showing line shading and stipple shading.

37 CFR 1.84(m) Shading

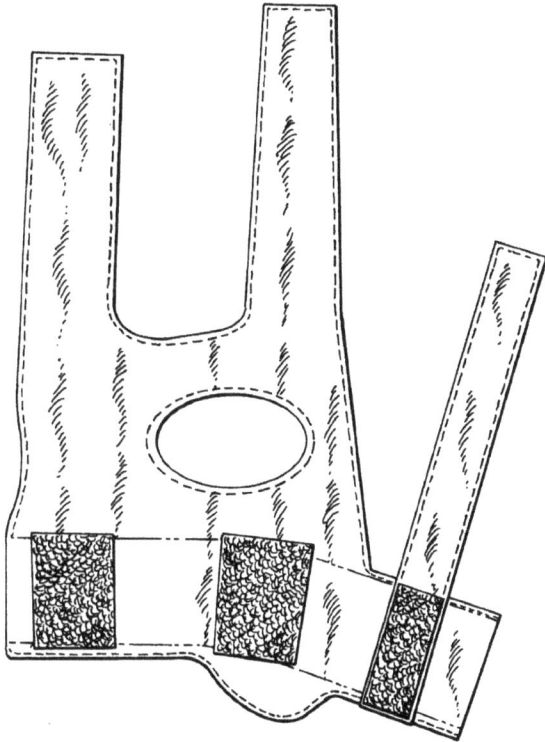

Leather material with stitched edges
and loop padding as one-half of
hook & loop.

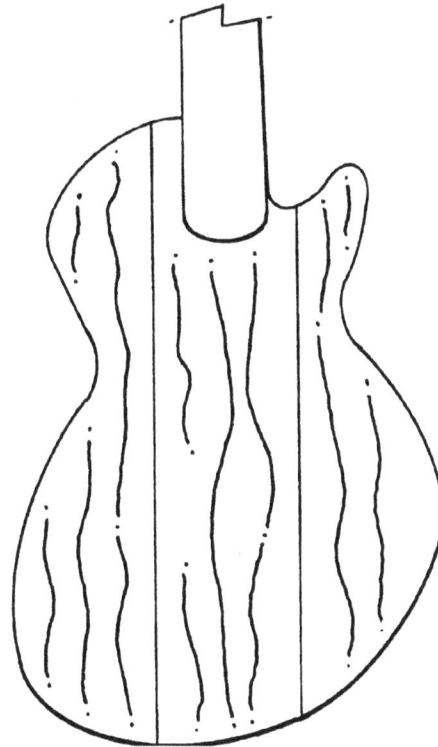

Simple wood material.

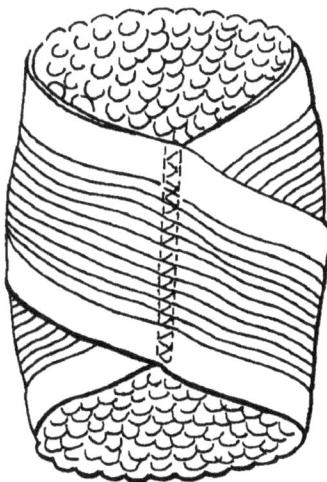

Showing sheepskin in a
medical elbow pad.

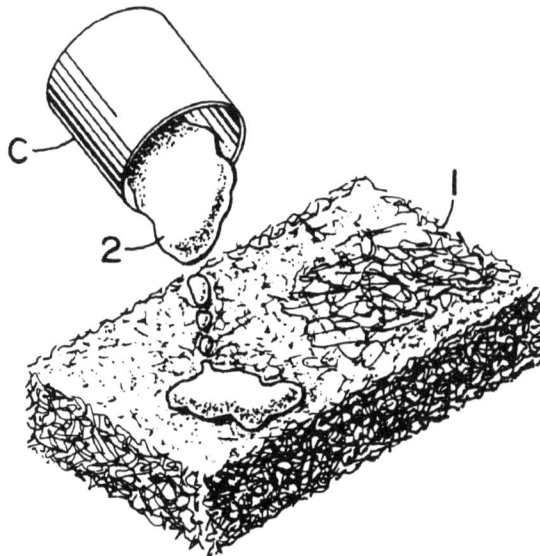

Illustrating: 1) a cellulose material; 2) a sealing
compound; and C) a container.

37 CFR 1.84(m) Shading, examples of non-metalic materials.

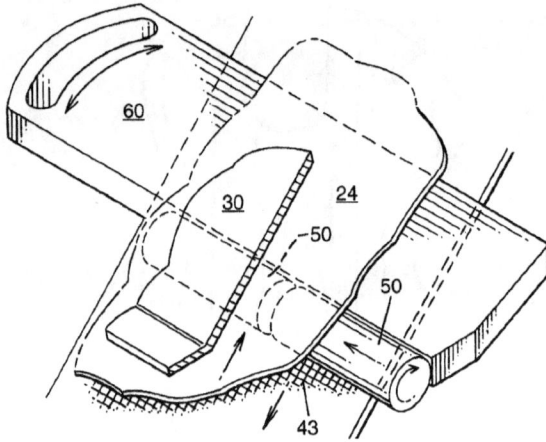

Shading on metal machine parts
and at the bottom belt material.

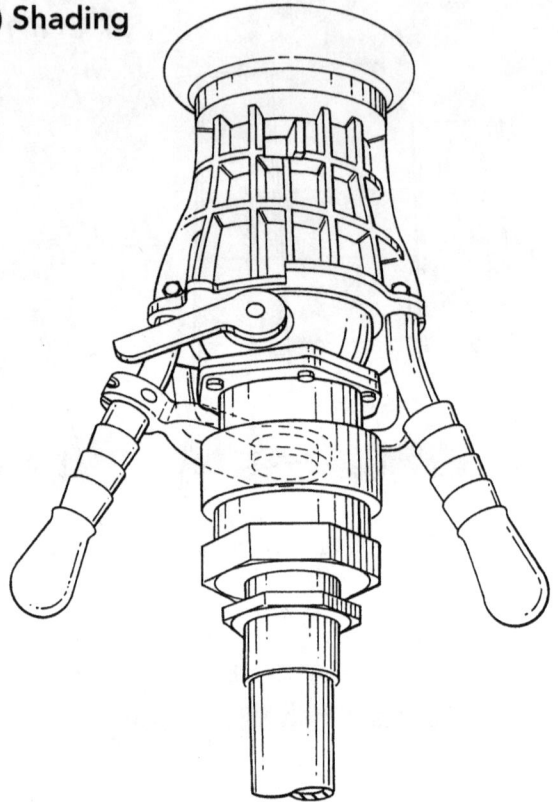

Shading on cast metal parts and
rubber grip handles.

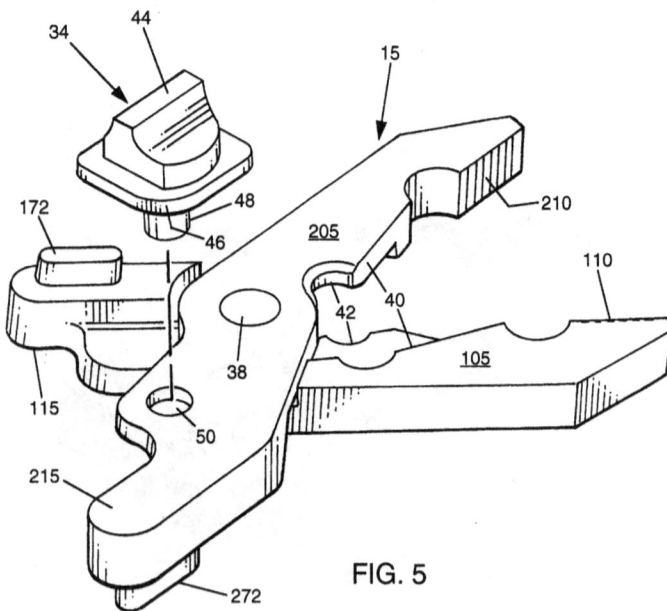

FIG. 5

Shading on metal parts on
a hand tool jaw set.

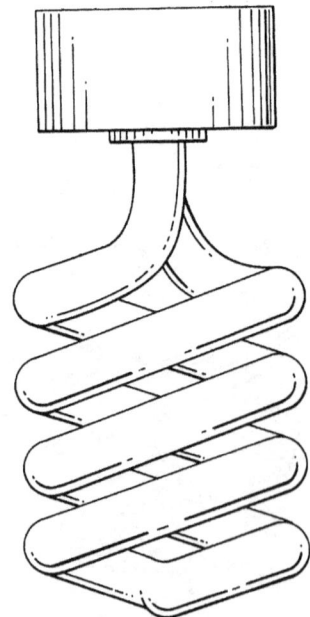

Shading light bulb's glass
tubing with plastic base.

37 CFR 1.84(m) Shading, examples on glass tubing, metal and plastic.

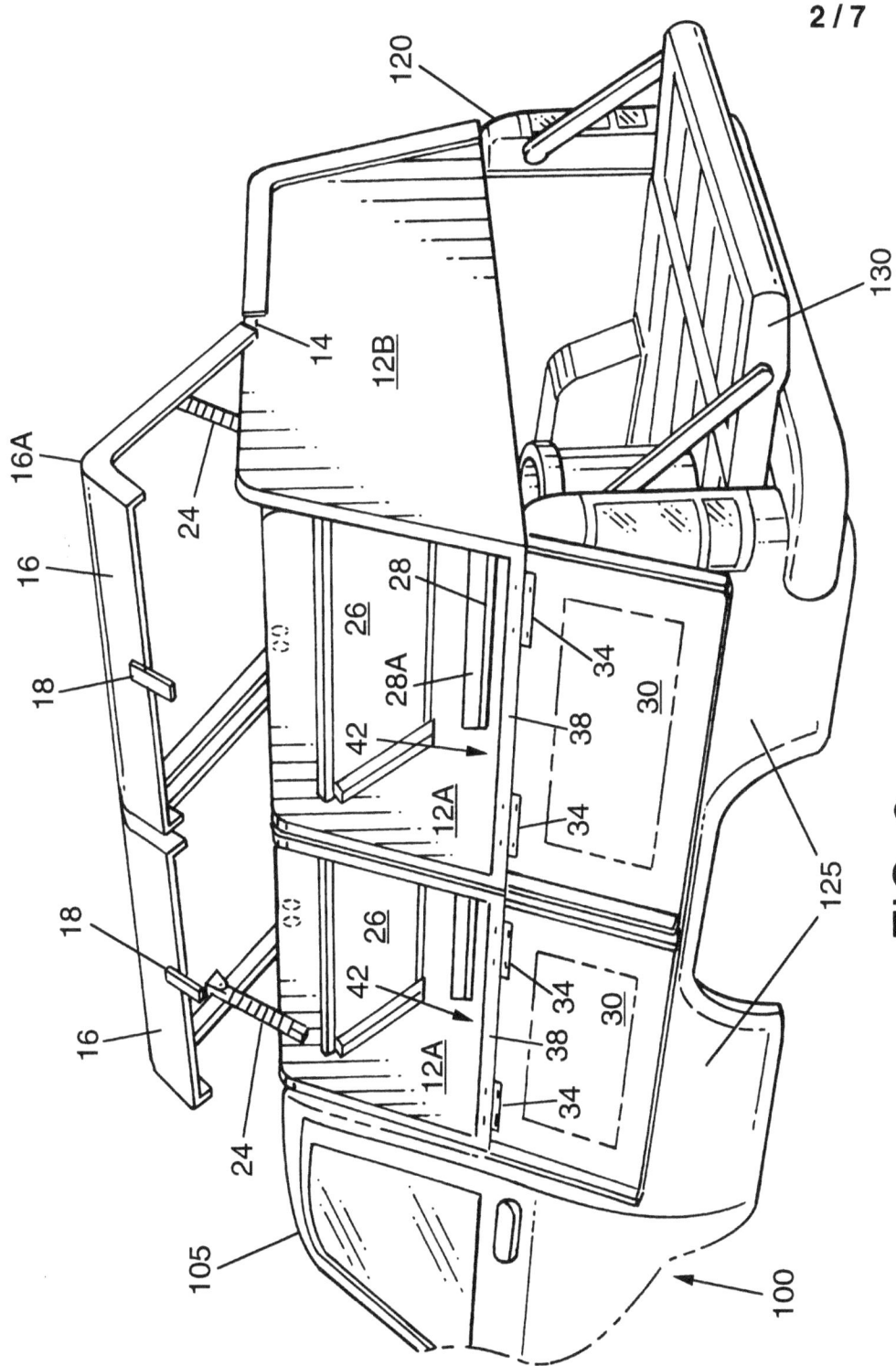

FIG. 2

37 CFR 1.84(m) Shading, example of surface shading on glass window and truck bulkheads.

37 CFR 1.84(n) Symbols

(n) Symbols. Graphical drawing symbols may be used for conventional elements when appropriate. The elements for which such symbols and labeled representations are used must be adequately identified in the specification. Known devices should be illustrated by symbols which have a universally recognized conventional meaning and are generally accepted in the art. Other symbols which are not universally recognized may be used, subject to approval by the Office, if they are not likely to be confused with existing conventional symbols, and if they are readily identifiable.

---

37 CFR 1.84(n) Symbols USPTO COMMENTS

Graphical drawing symbols, as indicated in **37 CFR 1.84(n)**, may be used for the conventional elements when appropriate. The elements for which such symbols and labeled representations are used must be adequately identified in the specification.

Known devices should be illustrated by symbols that have a universally recognized conventional meaning and are generally accepted in the art, provided no further detail is essential for understanding the subject matter of the claimed invention. Other symbols may be used on condition that they are not likely to be confused with existing conventional symbols, and that they are readily identifiable.

In general, in lieu of a symbol, a conventional element, combination, or circuit may be shown by an appropriately labeled rectangle, square, or circle; abbreviations should not be used unless their meanings are evident and not confusing with the abbreviations used in the suggested symbols. In electrical symbols, an arrow through an element indicates variability thereof; dotted-line connection of arrows indicates ganging thereof; and inherent property (as resistance) may be indicated by showing symbol (for resistor) in dotted lines.

AUTHOR'S COMMENTS
With technology changing and being added to daily,
new graphic symbols are coming onboard rapidly.
Fortunately, these new symbols are easy to locate with a Web search.
(See some general USPTO symbols in the Annex.)

---

37 CFR 1.84(n) Symbols, see following pages.

2 / 3

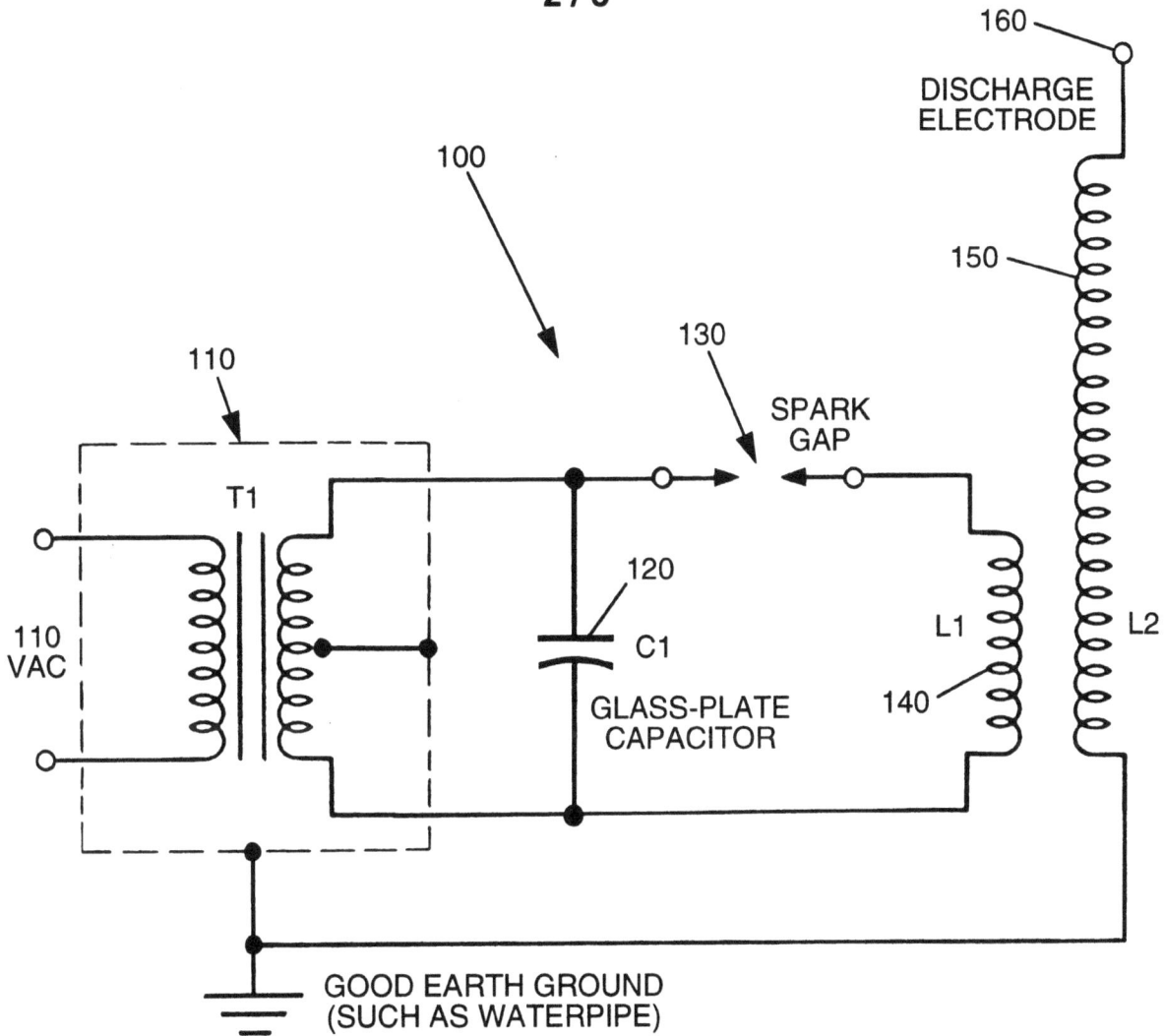

FIG. 2 <u>PRIOR ART</u>

AUTHOR'S COMMENTS

Example of how FIG. 2 is identified
as PRIOR ART with the words
in all capitals underlined.

---

37 CFR 1.84(n) Symbols and 37 CFR 1.84(o) legends.

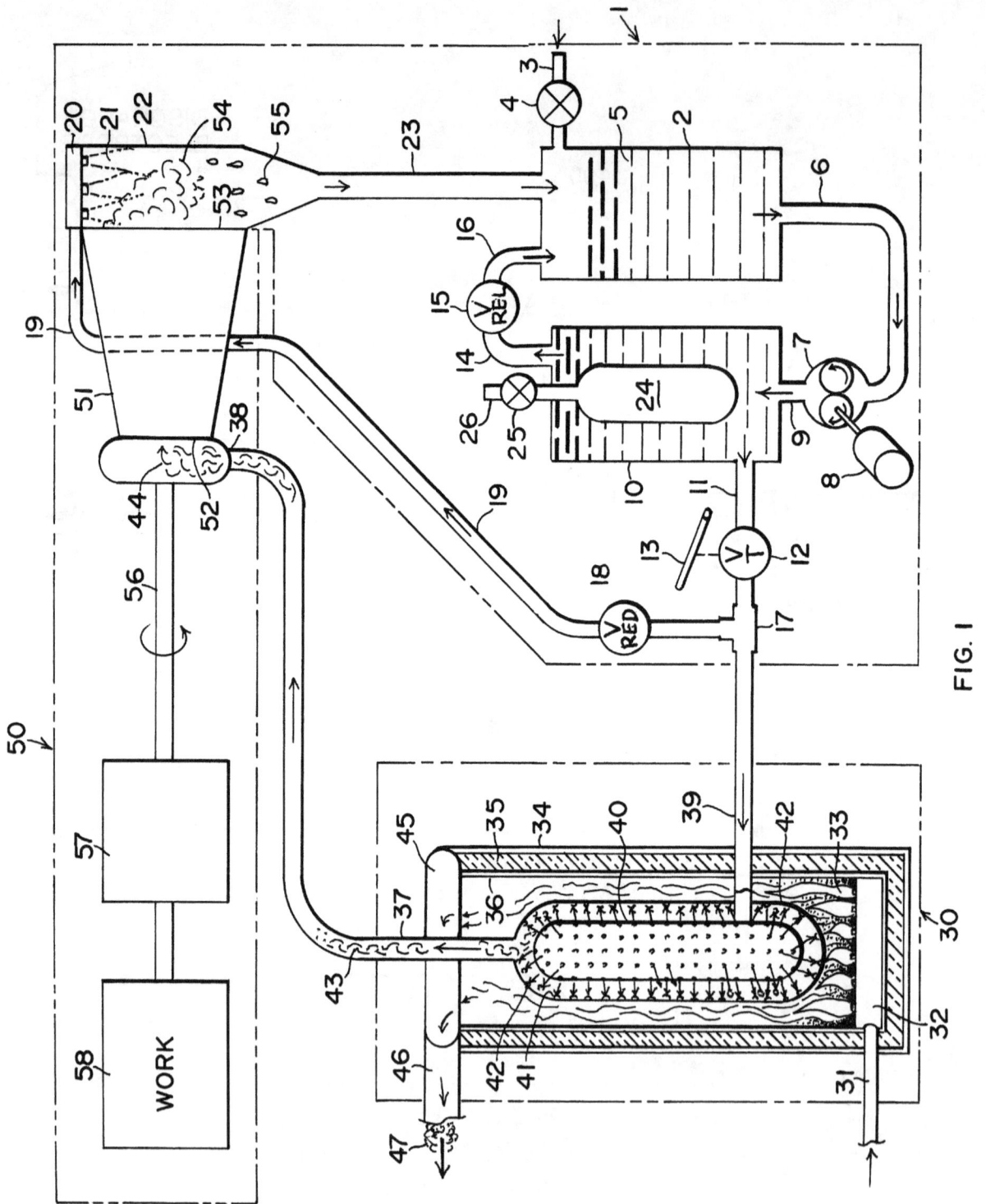

FIG. I

37 CFR 1.84(n) Symbols, example illustrating pictorial and block symbols.

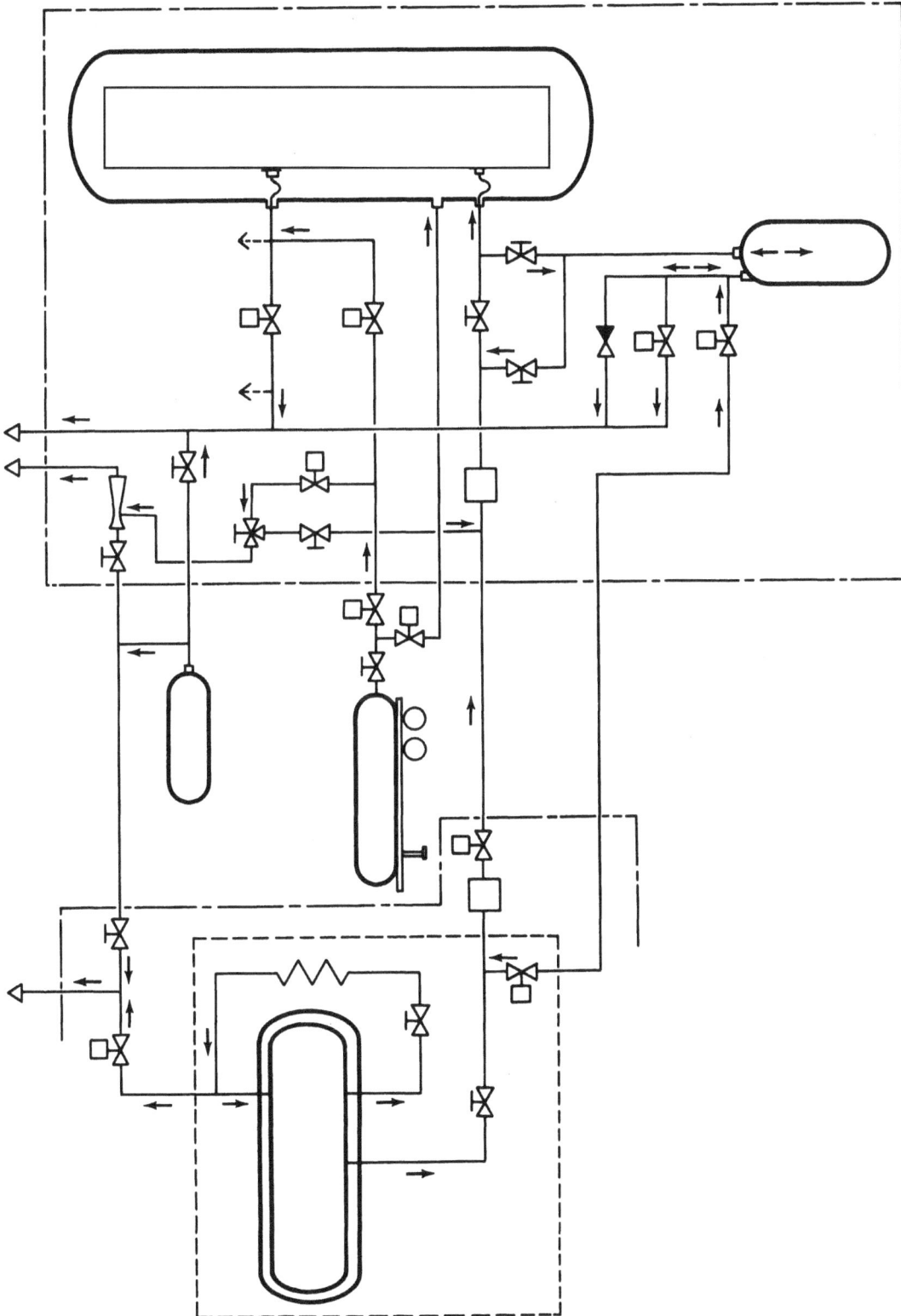

37 CFR 1.84(n) Symbols

37 CFR 1.84(n) Symbols, example of liquid and gas plumbing symbols.

37 CFR 1.84(o) Legends

(o) Legends. Suitable descriptive legends may be used subject to approval by the Office, or may be required by the examiner where necessary for understanding of the drawing. They should contain as few words as possible.

---

37 CFR 1.84(o) USPTO COMMENTS

Words should not be used to describe the figure itself, such as "This is a bar graph." All text legends must be approved by the Office.

The elements for which such labeled representations are used must be adequately identified in the specification.

Drawings cannot contain the following:

• Expressions or depictions contrary to morality.

• Expressions or depictions contrary to public order.

• Trademarks and service marks unless the applicant is shown to have a proprietary interest in the mark.

• Any statement or other matter obviously irrelevant or unnecessary under the circumstances.

The "as few words as possible" guideline does not apply when the drawing is a computer screen image.

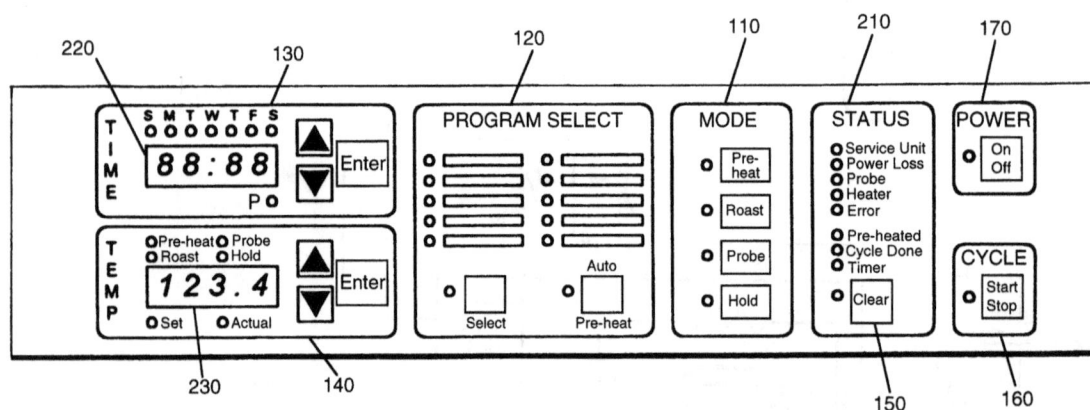

AUTHOR'S COMMENTS

In reference to "when the drawing is a computer screen image":
This generally is because all of the words, characters and images
on the computer screen are included in the patent application.
This rule also applies to other "screens," such as:
smart phones, hand-held devices, screens on household
appliances and transportation vehicle instrument panels.

37 CFR 1.84(o) Legends, example of an Appliance Screen Image.

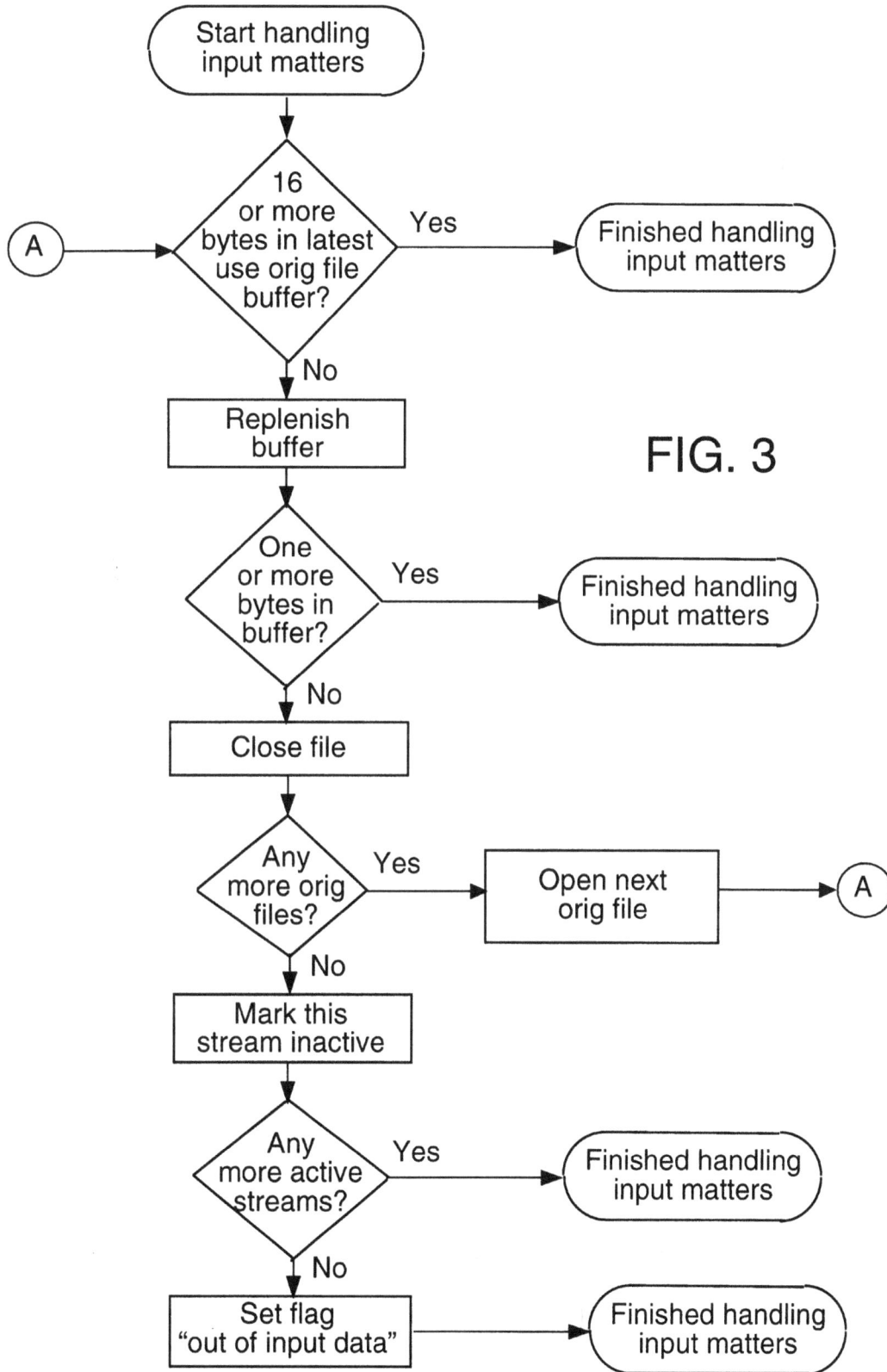

37 CFR 1.84(o) Legends, example of illustrating a computer software flow chart.

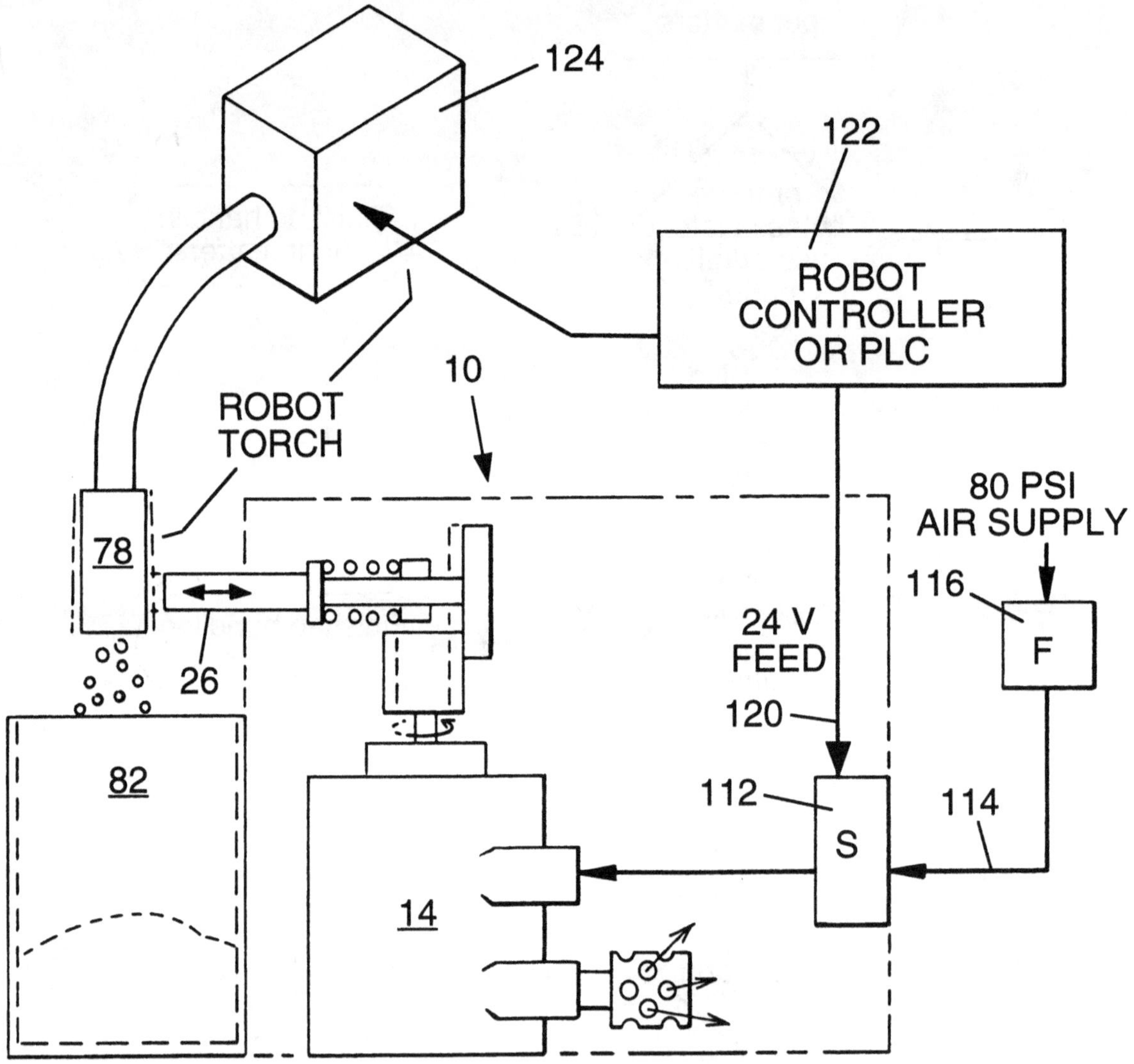

FIG. 7

AUTHOR'S COMMENTS
If you are going to file for a PCT application later, it is best to choose words for "Legends," that are internationally or technically acceptable.

37 CFR 1.84(o) Legends.

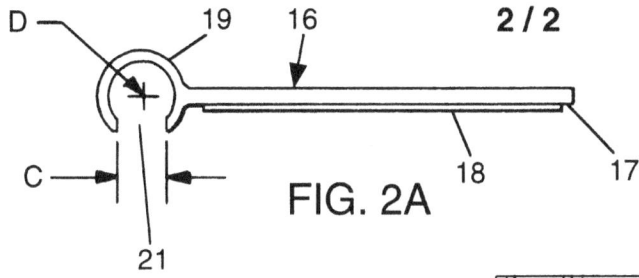

FIG. 2A

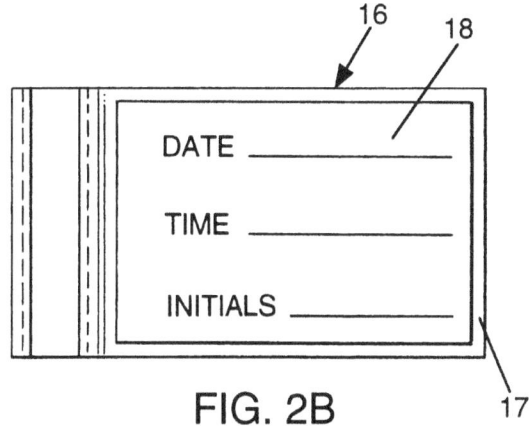

FIG. 2B

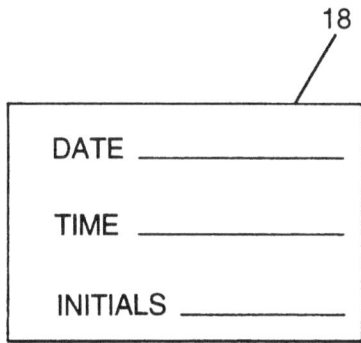

FIG. 3A

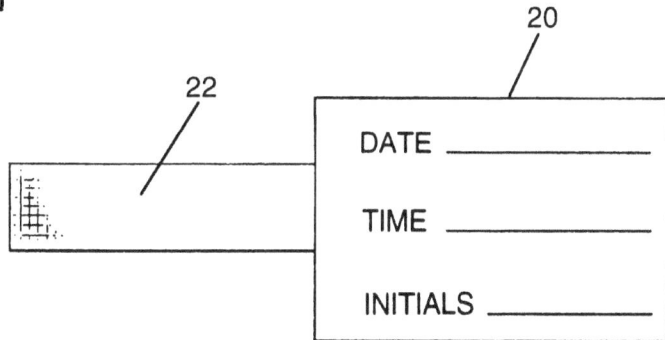

FIG. 3B

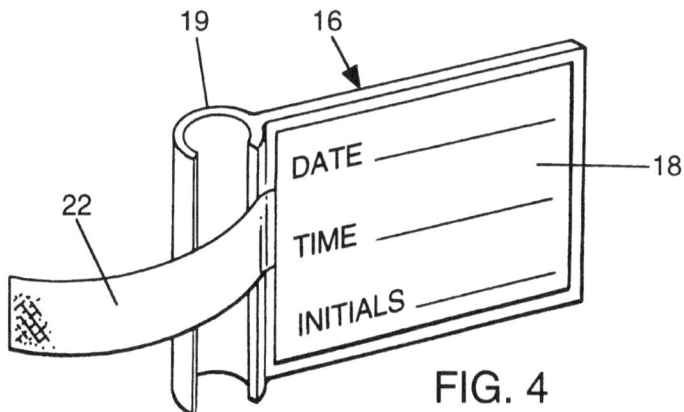

FIG. 4

37 CFR 1.84(o) Legends, example of illustrating a simple medical tagging device.

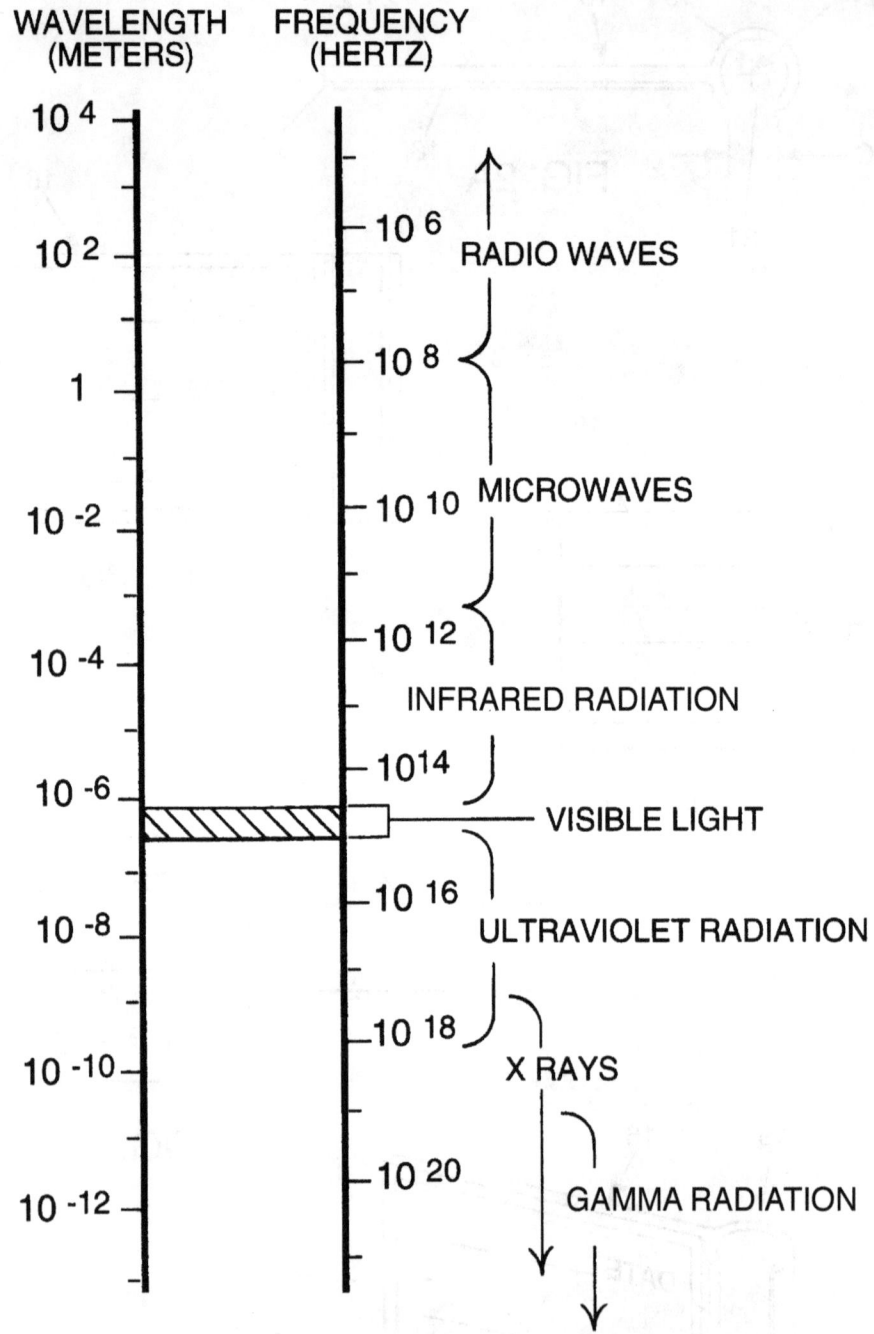

WAVELENGTH
(METERS)

FREQUENCY
(HERTZ)

10^4

10^2

10^6 — RADIO WAVES

10^8

1

10^{10} MICROWAVES

10^{-2}

10^{12}

10^{-4}

INFRARED RADIATION

10^{14}

10^{-6} — VISIBLE LIGHT

10^{16}

10^{-8} ULTRAVIOLET RADIATION

10^{18}

10^{-10} X RAYS

10^{-12} 10^{20} GAMMA RADIATION

TYPES OF ELECTROMAGNETIC RADIATION

FIG. 3

37 CFR 1.84(o) Legends, example of illustrating an electromagnetic spectrum.

CALCULATED INCREASE IN ARC LENGTH
DUE TO DEFLECTION
(EAVES TO ANCHOR)

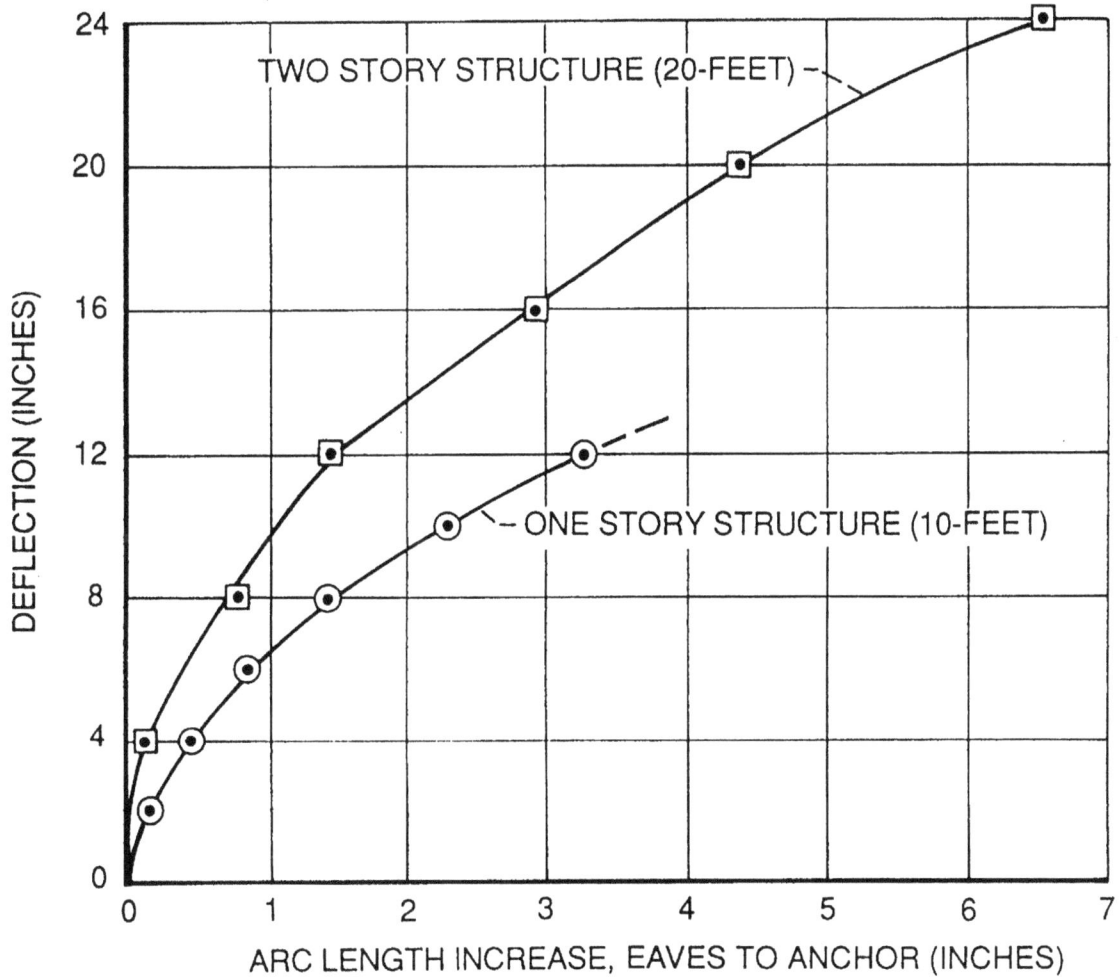

FIG. 10

37 CFR 1.84(o) Legends, example of illustrating a graphic chart.

37 CFR 1.84(p)

(p) Numbers, letters, and reference characters

(1) Reference characters (numerals are preferred), sheet numbers, and view numbers must be plain and legible, and must not be used in association with brackets or inverted commas, or enclosed within outlines, e.g., encircled. They must be oriented in the same direction as the view so as to avoid having to rotate the sheet. Reference characters should be arranged to follow the profile of the object depicted.

(2) The English alphabet must be used for letters, except where another alphabet is customarily used, such as the Greek alphabet to indicate angles, wavelengths, and mathematical formulas.

(3) Numbers, letters, and reference characters must measure at least .32 cm. (1/8 inch) in height. They should not be placed in the drawing so as to interfere with its comprehension. Therefore, they should not cross or mingle with the lines. They should not be placed upon hatched or shaded surfaces. When necessary, such as indicating a surface or cross section, a reference character may be underlined and a blank space may be left in the hatching or shading where the character occurs so that it appears distinct.

(4) The same part of an invention appearing in more than one view of the drawing must always be designated by the same reference character, and the same reference character must never be used to designate different parts.

(5) Reference characters not mentioned in the description shall not appear in the drawings. Reference characters mentioned in the description must appear in the drawings.

---

37 CFR 1.84(p) USPTO COMMENTS

Each element on a view must be identified by a reference number, except on design drawings.

While the rules do not specifically prohibit such practices, the use of **primed reference characters should be kept to a minimum.** Single primed characters for designating the same element in different embodiments, if used sparingly, can aid in easily understanding the invention and its different embodiments, but the overuse of primed numbers tends to obfuscate the drawings and should be avoided. The same holds for subscript and superscript numbers. Although the rules do not specifically prohibit the use of subscripts and superscripts, such use tends to obfuscate the drawing and should be avoided. **(See following pages for Author's comments.)**

126

AUTHOR'S COMMENTS

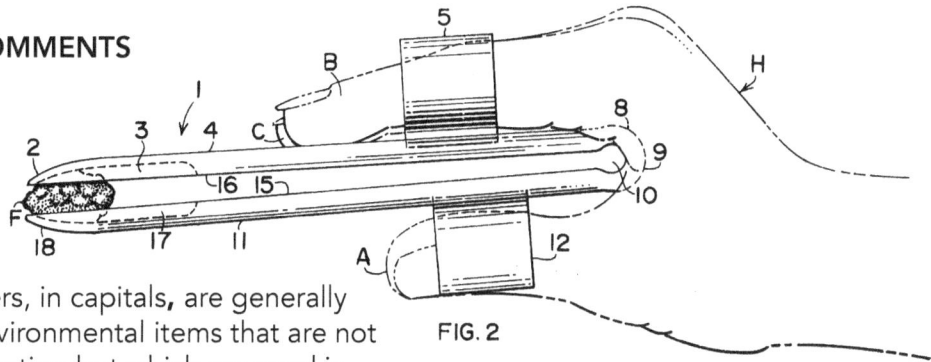

FIG. 2

Reference letters, in capitals, are generally assigned to environmental items that are not part of the invention but which are used in conjunction with it.

A good rule to follow when assigning reference numbers is to **start your part numbering with a number higher than your highest figure number.** This way there is less chance of confusion by having a part number and a section number the same.

Another example in numbering a complicated invention is to separate the components into categories such as; machine parts, electrical and hydraulic systems. Assign machine parts 100 series numbers, electrical 200, and hydraulic 300, etc,.

32　45　27a　27b　27c

Use 12-point Helvetica, or equivalent on U.S. Patents.

32　45　27a　27b　27c

Use 14-point Helvetica, or equivalent on PCT Patents.

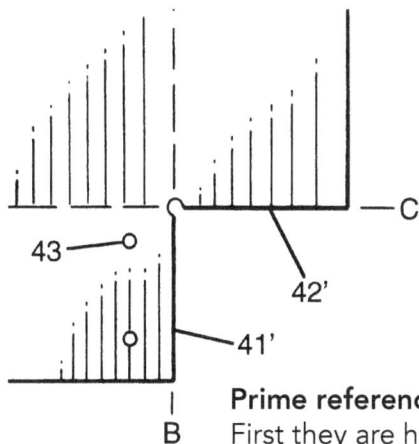

FIG. 23

Use 18 / 24 point Helvetica or equivalent on FIG. Numbers.

FIG. 6A

FIG. 5 PRIOR ART

Prime reference on numbers and letters have a few problems. First they are hard to see, and second they do not give you enough range. It is better to use "lower case" letters because they are easier to locate on the drawing and you have a larger variety to use.

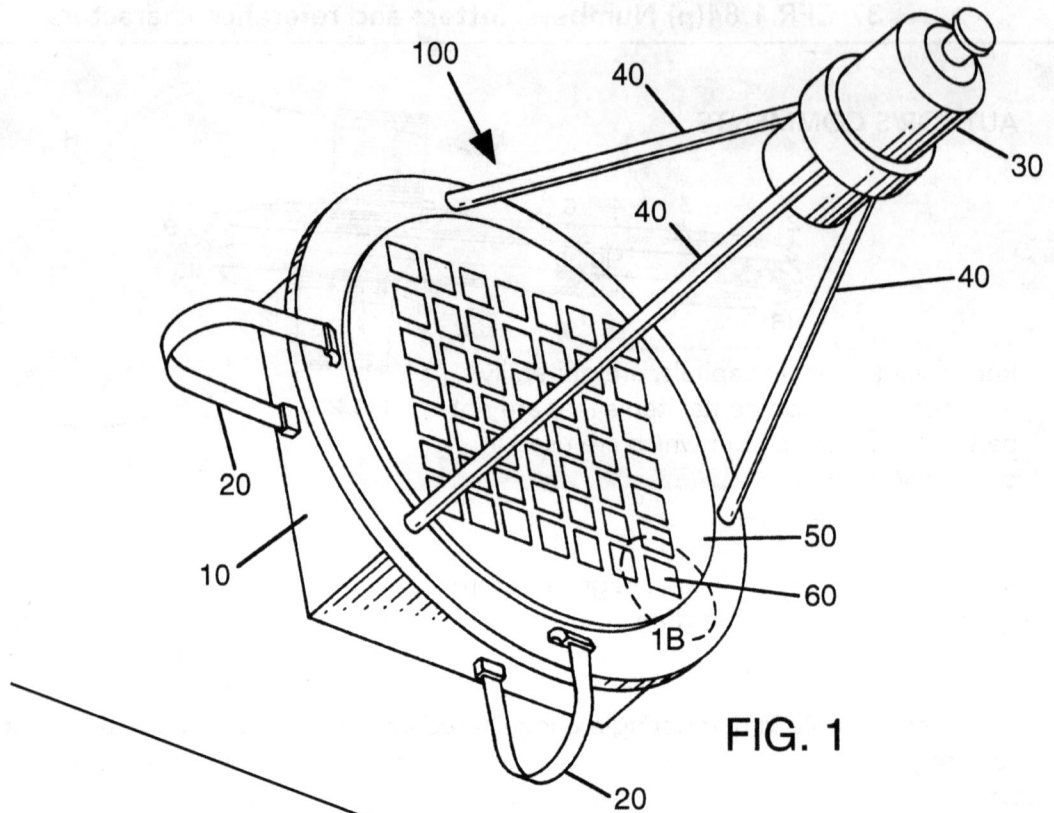

FIG. 1

100

40

40

40

30

20

10

50

60

1B

20

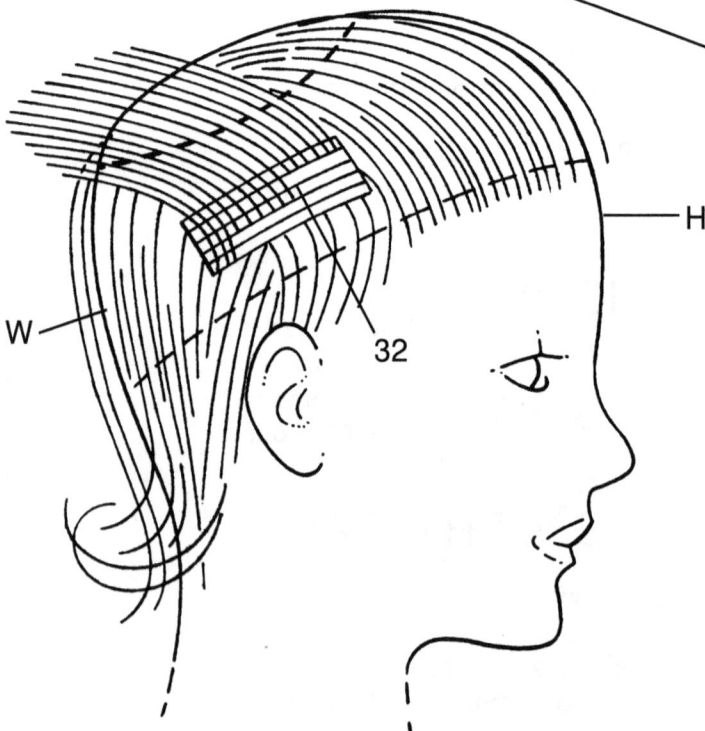

W

32

H

FIG. 2 <u>PRIOR ART</u>

37 CFR 1.84(p) Numbers, letters and reference characters.

The page shows diagrams only with labels.

37 CFR 1.84(q) Lead lines

(q) Lead lines. Lead lines are those lines between the reference characters and the details referred to. Such lines may be straight or curved and should be as short as possible. They must originate in the immediate proximity of the reference character and extend to the feature indicated. Lead lines must not cross each other. Lead lines are required for each reference character except for those, which indicate the surface or cross section on which they are placed. **Such a reference character must be underlined to make it clear that a lead line has not been left out by mistake.** Lead lines must be executed in the same way as lines in the drawing. See examples below.

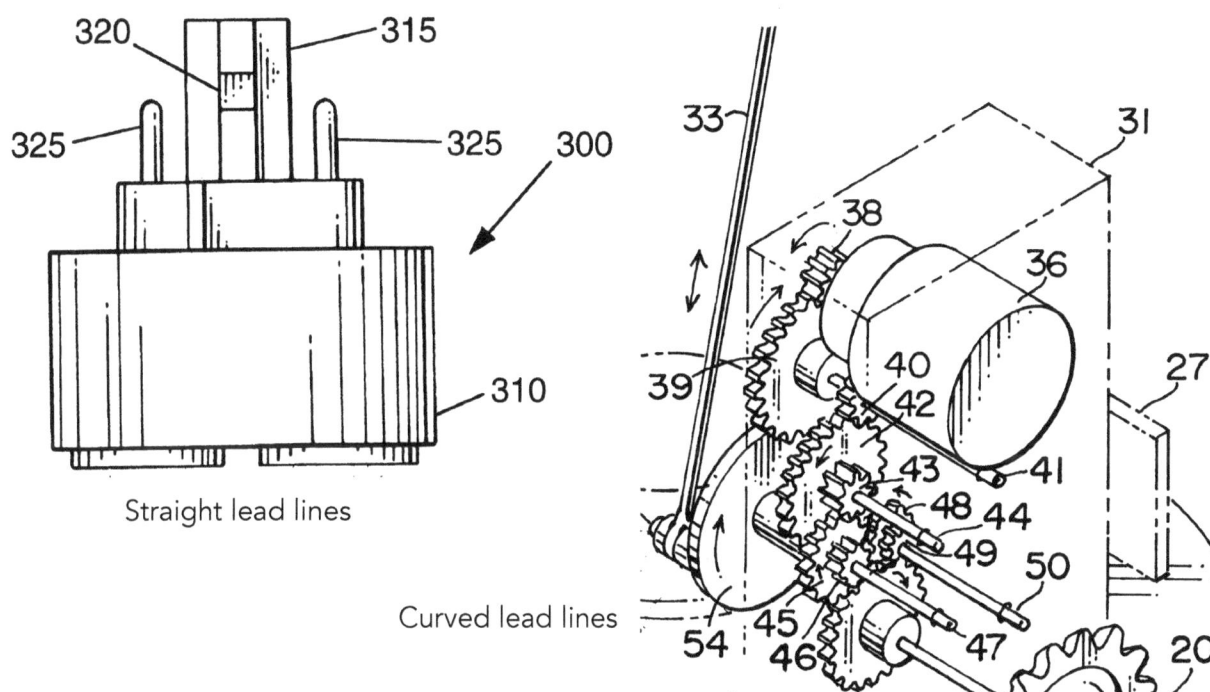

Straight lead lines

Curved lead lines

AUTHOR'S COMMENTS:
The example on the left shows straight lead lines and numbers done on a computer. The example on the right shows curved lead lines and numbers that were done by hand using drawing guides.

Example of reference character underlined to show whole part as a sub-assembly and that the lead line was not left out.

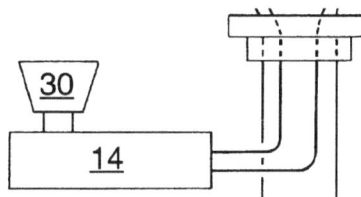

37 CFR 1.84(q) Lead lines.

129

(r) Arrows. Arrows may be used at the ends of lines, provided that their meaning is clear, as follows:

(1) On a lead line, a freestanding arrow to indicate the entire section towards which it points; (70)

(2) On a lead line, an arrow touching a line to indicate the surface shown by the line looking along the direction of the arrow; (22) or

(3) To show the direction of movement.

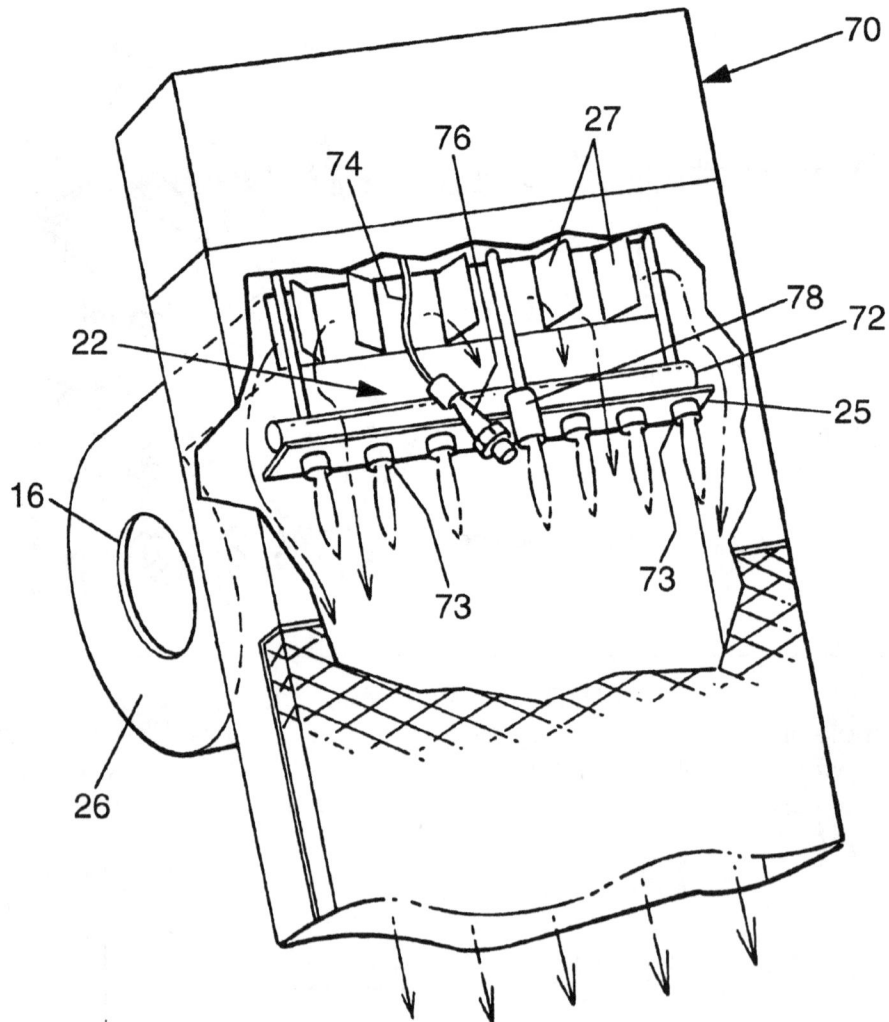

Sample Figure showing use of arrows.

37 CFR 1.84(r) Arrows, also see 37 CFR 1.84(h) for arrows used in sectional views, page 1-26.

130

(s) Copyright or Mask Work Notice. A copyright or mask work notice may appear in the drawing, but must be placed within the sight of the drawing immediately below the figure representing the copyright or mask work material and be limited to letters having a print size of .32 cm. to .64 cm. (1/8 to 1/4 inches) high. The content of the notice must be limited to only those elements provided for by law. For example, "©1983 John Doe" (17 U.S.C. 401) and "*M* John Doe" (17 U.S.C. 909) would be properly limited and, under current statutes, legally sufficient notices of copyright and mask work, respectively. Inclusion of a copyright or mask work notice will be permitted only if the authorization language set forth in **§ 1.71(e)** is included at the beginning **(preferably as the first paragraph) of the specification.**

USPTO COMMENTS

§ 1.71(d) and § 1.71(e) are reproduced below:

37 CFR 1.71 Detailed description and specification of the invention.

(d) A copyright or mask work notice may be placed in a design or utility patent application adjacent to copyright and mask work material contained therein. The notice may appear at any appropriate portion of the patent application disclosure. For notices in drawings, see § 1.84(s). The content of the notice must be limited to only those elements provided for by law. For example, "©1983 John Doe (17 U.S.C. 401) and "*M* John Doe" (17 U.S.C. 909) would be properly limited and, under current statutes, legally sufficient notices of copyright and mask work, respectively. Inclusion of a copyright or mask work notice will be permitted only if the authorization language set forth in paragraph (e) of this section is included at the beginning (preferably as the first paragraph) of the specification.

(e) The authorization shall read as follows:

A portion of the disclosure of this patent document contains material, which is subject to (copyright or mask work) protection. The (copyright or mask work) owner has no objection to the facsimile reproduction by anyone of the patent document or the patent disclosure, as it appears in the Patent and Trademark Office patent file or records, but otherwise reserves all (copyright or mask work) rights whatsoever.

AUTHOR'S COMMENTS
For details on Mask Work Notice see 17 USC 909.
See next page for example of copyright used in conjunction with a patent drawing.
---

37 CFR 1.84(s) Copyright or Mask Work Notice.

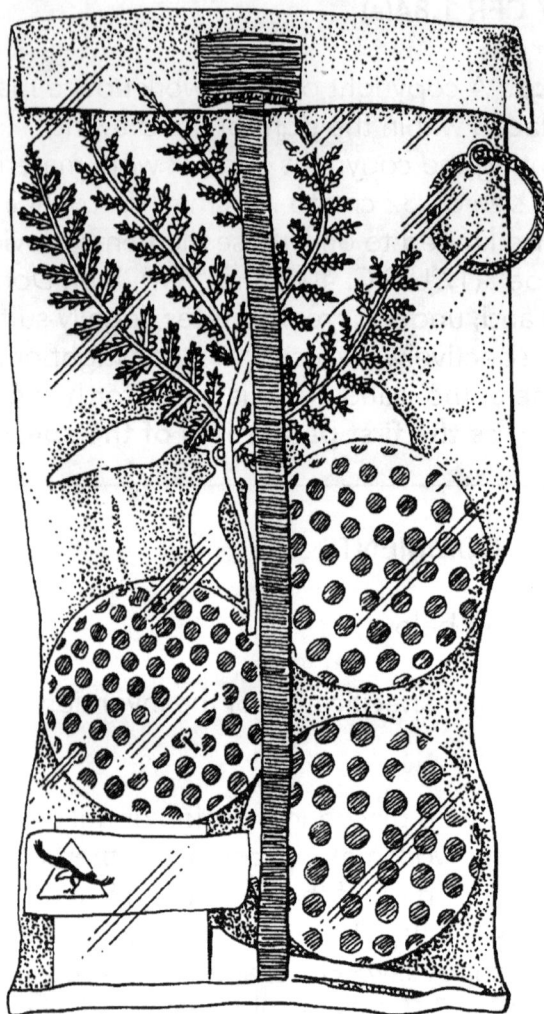
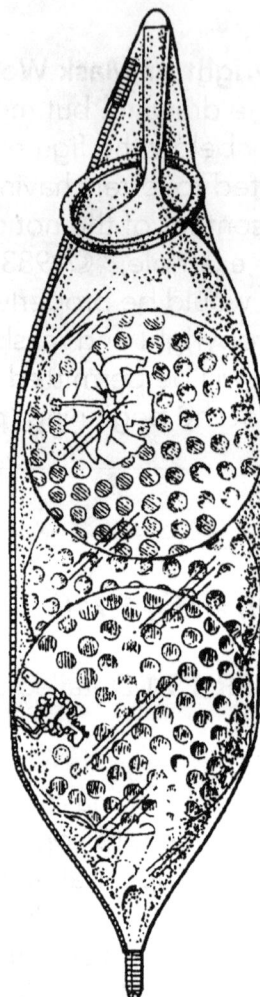

FIG. 2   FIG. 3

© 1989, Theresa Carrillo
dba First Class USA

Inventor: Carrillo, Theresa J. (Honolulu, HI) Patent: D335,255 May 4, 1993
Primary Examiner: Ansher, Bernard
Assistant Examiner: Siegel, Mitchell
Attorney, Agent or Firm: Reiss, Seth M.

Example of two figures from a design patent that has a copyright notice.

37 CFR 1.84(s) Copyright or Mask Work Notice.

37 CFR 1.84(t)

(t) Numbering of sheets of drawings. The sheets of drawings should be numbered in consecutive Arabic numerals, starting with 1, within the sight as defined in paragraph (g) of this section. These numbers, if present, must be placed in the middle of the top of the sheet, but not in the margin. The numbers can be placed on the right-hand side if the drawing extends too close to the middle of the top edge of the usable surface. The drawing sheet numbering must be clear and larger than the numbers used as reference characters to avoid confusion. The number of each sheet should be shown by two Arabic numerals placed on either side of an oblique line, with the first being the sheet number and the second being the total number of sheets of drawings, with no other marking. (see examples at the bottom of the page)

11.7 Numbering of Sheets (WIPO PCT Rule 11, Ref.)

(a) All the sheets contained in the international application shall be numbered in consecutive Arabic numerals.

(b) The numbers shall be centered at the top or bottom of the sheet, but shall not be placed in the margin.

139. Arrangement of Elements and Numbering of Sheets. The elements of the international application must be placed in the following order: the request, the description (if applicable, including the sequence listing free text referred to in Rule 5.2(b) but excluding the sequence listing part of the description), the claim(s), the abstract, the drawings (if any), and, where applicable, the sequence listing part of the description. All sheets constituting the international application must be numbered in consecutive Arabic numerals **with the following separate series of numbering:** the first applying to the request only and commencing with the first sheet of the request; the second series commencing with the first sheet of the description and continuing through the claims until the last sheet of the abstract; if applicable, **a third series applying to the sheets of the drawings only**; and, if applicable, a further series applying to the sequence listing part of the description commencing with the first sheet of that part. The number of each sheet of the drawings must consist of two sets of Arabic numerals separated by a slant, the first set being the sheet number and the second set being the total number of sheets of drawings (for example, 1/3, 2/3, 3/3); see Rule 11.7 and Section 207.

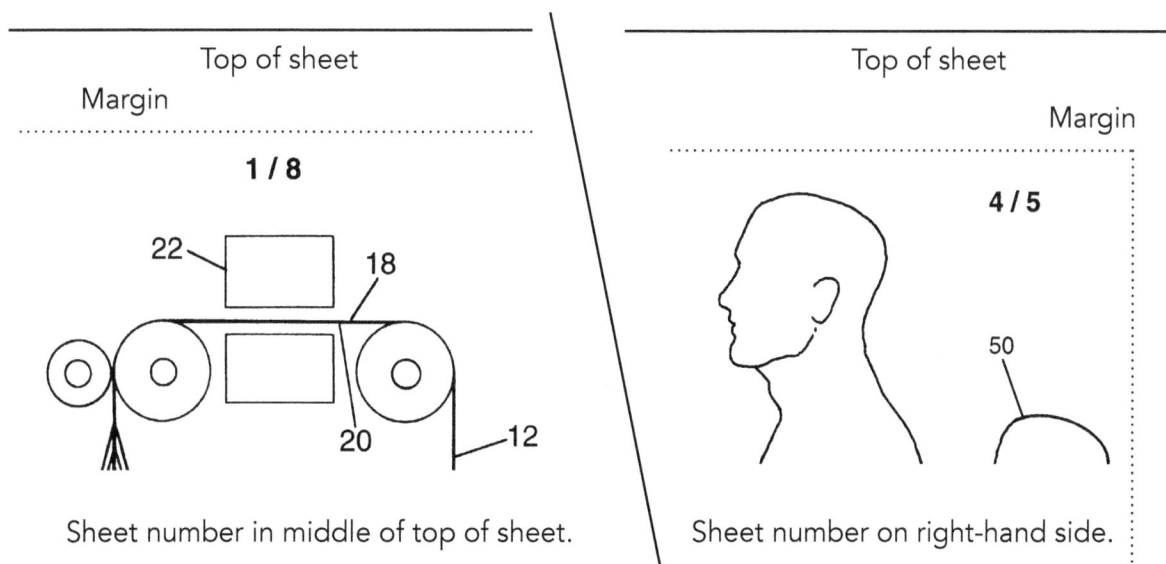

Sheet number in middle of top of sheet.

Sheet number on right-hand side.

37 CFR 1.84(t) Numbering of sheets of drawings.

(u) Numbering of views

(1) The different views must be numbered in consecutive Arabic numerals, starting with 1, independent of the numbering of the sheets and, if possible, in the order in which they appear on the drawing sheet(s). Partial views intended to form one complete view, on one or several sheets, must be identified by the same number **followed by a capital letter.** View numbers must be preceded by the abbreviation **"FIG." Where only a single view is used in an application to illustrate the claimed invention, it must not be numbered and the abbreviation "FIG." must not appear.**

(2) Figure numbers and letters identifying the views must be simple and clear and must not be used in association with brackets, circles, or inverted commas. The view numbers must be larger than the numbers used for reference characters.

AUTHOR'S COMMENTS

I generally used 18/24 point Hevetica regular for numbering of views as FIGs.

FIG. 1, 2, 3, etc.

FIG. 6A, 6B, 6C etc.

FIG. 8 PRIOR ART

There are a few occasions where you are required to add specific words after the FIG. number, such as PRIOR ART.

Capital Letters are generally used in three forms:
1) partial views intended to form one complete view on one of several pages (see page 94);

2) wave-form drawings where sections are aligned with a dashed time line (see page 83); and

3) where an applicant is required to add an additional figure required by a patent examiner.

NOTE: Under recent USPTO rules your patent examiner may request additional identification words, such as CORRECTION, ADDITION or REPLACEMENT after the FIG. number, or imprinted at the top of drawing sheet in the margin area. Other than PRIOR ART, which is mandatory, I would not recommend inserting the other words until instructed by the patent examiner.

---

37 CFR 1.84(u) Numbering of views.

37 CFR 1.84(v) Security markings

(v) Security markings. Authorized security markings may be placed on the drawings provided they are outside the sight, preferably centered in the top margin.

---

37 CFR 1.84(v) USPTO COMMENTS

Security markings are primarily the responsibility of the Office; however, the applicant might identify the drawings with the security designations such as NATO, TS, S, or C.

AUTHOR'S COMMENTS

My experiences with security markings were with some of the patent drawings I did for the U.S. Air Force, NATO and NASA.
In each case I did not put the authorized security markings on the patent drawings; it was done by their own Office of Patent Council.

I remember working on just one civilian patent application where the inventor's patent application was classified by the U.S. Navy and because the inventor was not, at that time, an American citizen, he was told he no longer could work on his own invention.
He later received his American citizenship and was hired by the Navy to complete the invention.

I worked in three research centers where I did scientific illustrations and patent drawings and it was always a battle between the academics who wanted to get published and the attorneys who wanted to apply for patents first.

37 CFR 1.84(v) Security markings.

(w) **Corrections.** Any corrections on drawings submitted to the Office must be durable and permanent.

1.85   Corrections to drawings.

(a) **A utility or plant application will not be placed on the files for examination** until objections to the drawings have been corrected. Except as provided in § 1.215(c), any patent application publication will not include drawings filed after the application has been placed on the files for examination. Unless applicant is otherwise notified in an Office action, objections to the drawings in a utility or plant application will not be held in abeyance, and a request to hold objections to the drawings in abeyance will not be considered a bona fide attempt to advance the application to final action (§ 1.135(c)). If a drawing in a design application meets the requirements of § 1.84(e), (f), and (g), and is suitable for reproduction but is not otherwise in compliance with § 1.84, the drawing may be admitted for examination.

(b) **The Office will not release drawings for purposes of correction.** If corrections are necessary, new corrected drawings must be submitted within the time set by the Office.

(c) **If a corrected drawing is required** or if a drawing does not comply with § 1.84 or an amended drawing submitted under § 1.121(d) in a nonprovisional international design application does not comply with § 1.1026 at the time an application is allowed, the Office may notify the applicant in a notice of allowability and set a three-month period of time from the mail date of the notice of allowability within which the applicant must file a corrected drawing in compliance with § 1.84 or 1.1026, as applicable, to avoid abandonment. This time period is not extendable under § 1.136 (see § 1.136(c)).

AUTHOR'S COMMENTS

See Chapter 5 for Patent Drawing Corrections
for both USPTO and WIPO PCT

Chapter Three
Section 2

**Drawing & Reproduction Rules For
WIPO PCT Nonprovisional (Utility) Patents**
Location:
MPEP 9th Edition November 2015
Laws, Rules & Index
**Appendix T - Patent Cooperation Treaty
Article 7 - The Drawings, Rule 11 through 11.14**

Applicant

Receiving Office (RO)

United States Patent and Trademark Office (USPTO)
Nonprovisional (Utility) Patent Application
Domestic and/or International Filing

1
Provisional
Application for Patent

2
Nonprovisional
Patent Application

Select

Domestic
Application

5

Domestic
....
International

3
World Intellectual Property Organization
(WIPO) Patent Cooperation Treaty (PCT)
International Patent Application

148
Contracting
Parties

Select

5

4
European Patent Office (EPO)
Designated Office

Select

40
Member
States

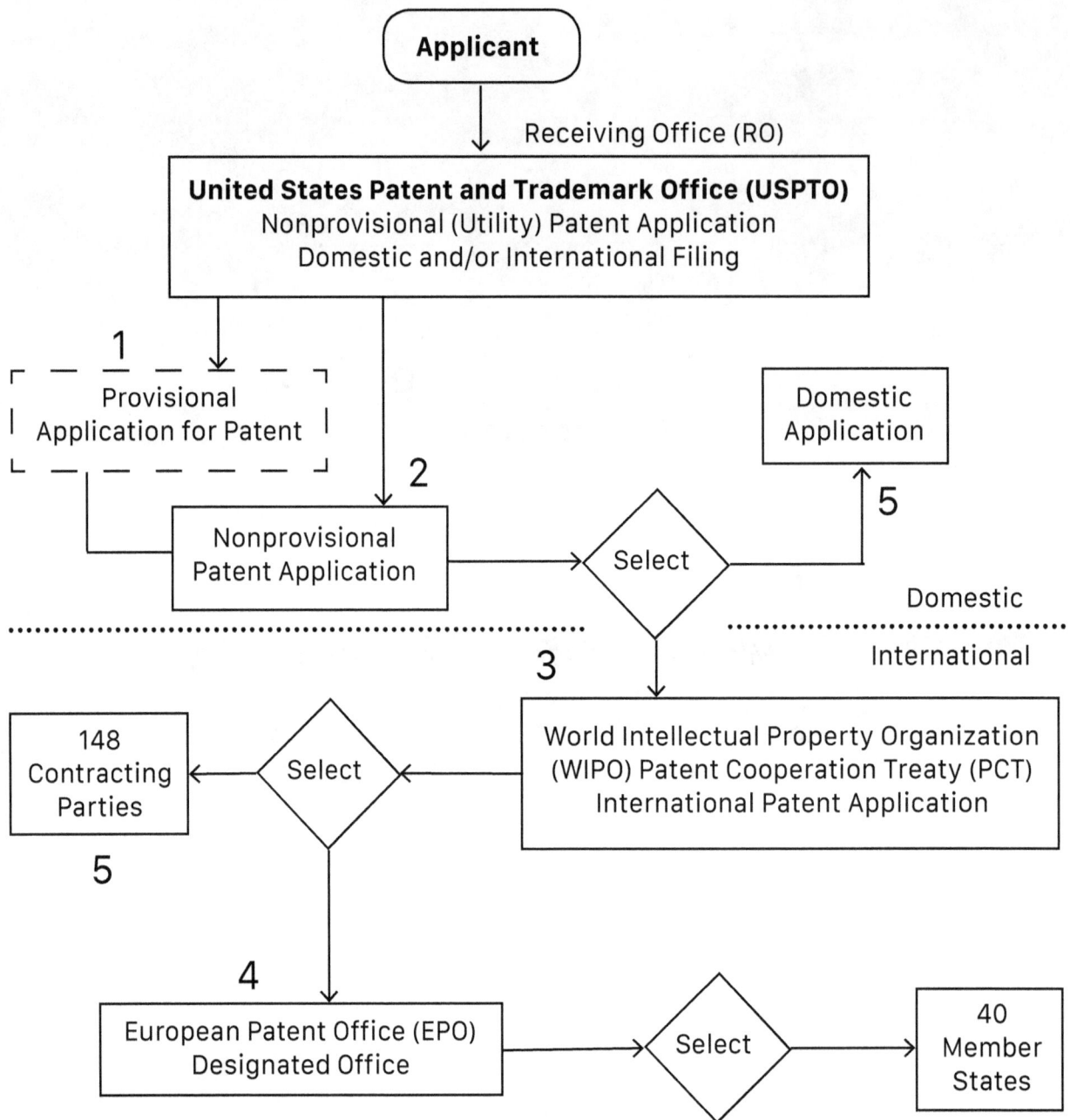

NOTE: APPLIED DRAWING RULES:
1) - 35 U.S.C. § 113 Provisional Applications (see Chapter Six)
2) - 37 CFR 1.84 Nonprovisional Applications (see Chapter Three)
3) - PCT Rule 11 [R-6] MPEP PCT Applications (see Chapter Three)
4) - Rule 46 Form of Drawings & Rule 48 Technical Prep for Publishing
5) - (US) Domestic and/or International PCT filing

General remarks on the PCT system (1)

The PCT system is a patent "filing" system, not a patent "granting" system. There is no "PCT patent"

The PCT system provides:

- An international phase comprising:
    - filing of the international application;
    - international search and written opinion of the ISA;
    - international publication;
    - international preliminary examination; and
    - a national/regional phase before designated Offices

The decision on granting patents is taken exclusively by national or regional Offices in the national phase

General remarks on the PCT system (2)

- Only inventions may be protected via the PCT by applying for patents, utility models and similar titles.

- Design and trademark protection cannot be obtained via the PCT. There are separate international conventions dealing with these types of industrial property protection (the Hague Agreement and the Madrid Agreement and Protocol, respectively).

- The PCT is administered by WIPO as are other international treaties in the field of industrial property, such as the Paris Convention.

Source: WIPO PCT Seminar Presentation July 1, 2015

Rule 11
Physical Requirements of the International Application

11.2 Fitness for Reproduction

(a) All elements of the international application (i.e., the request, the description, the claims, the drawings, and the abstract) shall be so presented as to admit of direct reproduction by photography, electrostatic processes, photo offset and microfilming, in any number of copies.

(b) All sheets shall be free from creases and cracks; they shall not be folded.

(c) Only one side of each sheet shall be used.

(d) Subject to Rule 11.10(d) and Rule 11.13(j), each sheet shall be used in an upright position (i.e., the short sides at the top and bottom).

4. Further elaboration of these requirements appears in paragraphs 143 to 175 of the Applicant's Guide. Of particular note are paragraphs 173 and 174, concerning shading and photographs:

173. Is the use of shading permitted? The use of shading in figures is allowed provided this assists in their understanding and is not so extensive as to impede legibility. Shading may, for instance, be used to indicate the shape of spherical, cylindrical, conical elements, etc. Flat parts may also be lightly shaded. Such shading is allowed in the case of parts shown in perspective but not for cross-sections. Only spaced lines may be used for shading, not fully blacked out areas. These lines must be thin, as few in number as possible and they must contrast with the rest of the drawings.

174. May a photograph be presented instead of a drawing? The PCT makes no provision for photographs. Nevertheless, they are allowed where it is impossible to present in a drawing what is to be shown (for instance, crystalline structures). Where, exceptionally, photographs are submitted, they must be black and white, must be on sheets of A4 size, and must respect the minimum margins (see paragraph 148) and admit of direct reproduction. Color photographs are not accepted, nor are color drawings. Photographs are retained by the International Bureau as part of the record copy.

FACTORS AFFECTING USABILITY OF DRAWINGS

11. A failure to meet the requirements of Rule 11 will not necessarily affect the ability of International Authorities to conduct a proper international search and preliminary examination. Obviously, the main requirement is that the drawings must be sufficiently clear for the examiner to be able to easily determine the working and scope of the invention in conjunction with the description.

12. National phase processing of the international application by designated Offices is generally done on the basis of the international application as published. While designated Offices during national phase processing will generally have needs equivalent to those of the International Authorities during the international phase, those Offices may also need to consider certain issues to a greater extent than is required solely for the purpose of conducting a high-quality search, for example, issues such as clarity and sufficiency of the disclosure. Furthermore, designated Offices may, for national phase processing, decide to require stricter compliance with the requirements of Rule 11, beyond the "reasonably uniform publication" standard applied under Rule 26 during the international phase. Consequently, high quality drawings in the international publication may be important for the applicant to avoid the need to furnish replacement drawings to multiple individual designated Offices during national phase processing. This would imply that, for international publication, the quality standard for drawings is likely to be higher than might be necessary for the purposes of the international search.

13. Some issues to consider include the following:

(a) The receiving Office only conducts a brief formal examination of the drawings rather than evaluating them carefully in conjunction with the description. The formalities examiner does not need to be familiar with the technology involved. It may not be apparent from a formalities examination whether important details in drawings can be seen clearly, particularly in the case of photographs or drawings which are shaded in a way which does not comply with Rule 11.13(a).

(b) Drawings (especially photographs and greyscales) that appear clear in an international application filed on paper may not reproduce well in photocopies or in scanned electronic versions. This factor may be difficult to evaluate by the receiving Office where the record copy and the search copy are forwarded in paper form and subsequently scanned by the International Bureau and/or the International Searching Authority. On the other hand, where the applicant has filed the international application in multiple copies as may be required under Rule 11.1(b), the search copy as so filed may in fact be of a significantly higher quality than the international application as published (in the form of a scanned image later produced by the International Bureau).

(c) In general, photographs and grayscale drawings contained in international applications filed in electronic form are more likely to be clear when printed since there is no additional scanning step involved.

(d) Even where the clarity of a drawing affects the quality of the disclosure and the question whether the claimed invention is fully supported, this may sometimes be of little significance to the ability to conduct a high-quality international search.

(e) If an originally filed drawing is so poorly presented that it significantly reduces the ability to conduct a high-quality search, it may not be possible for the defect to be corrected since to do so would be likely to add subject matter. This contrasts with the case where scanning by the receiving Office or by the International Searching Authority has reduced the quality of the drawing that is seen by the examiner as compared to the clear copy originally filed by the applicant.

15. The scanning process referred to in paragraph 13(b), above, is a new factor which adds significantly to the difficulties of ensuring that receiving Offices are able to apply a consistent, appropriate standard of test for whether a drawing is adequate "for the purpose of reasonably uniform international publication," particularly in view of the increasing use of photographs and grayscale drawings. It might be desirable to provide for the International Bureau to notify the applicant directly (at the same time informing the receiving Office) where the original drawings are found not to be suitable for publication.   Source: WIPO PCT Union February 5, 2015

See Author's Comments on the following page.

Rule 11 Reference to Drawings
from
MPEP-9 Laws, Rules & Index
Appendix T - Patent Cooperation Treaty

Rule 11 Physical Requirements of the International Application

11.1 Number of Copies

(a) Subject to the provisions of paragraph (b), the international application and each of the documents referred to in the check list (Rule 3.3(a)(ii)) shall be filed in one copy.

(b) Any receiving Office may require that the international application and any of the documents referred to in the check list (Rule 3.3(a)(ii)), except the receipt for the fees paid or the check for the payment of the fees, be filed in two or three copies. In that case, the receiving Office shall be responsible for verifying the identity of the second and the third copies with the record copy.

11.2 Fitness for Reproduction

(a) All elements of the international application (i.e., the request, the description, the claims, the drawings, and the abstract) shall be so presented as to admit of direct reproduction by photography, electrostatic processes, photo offset, and microfilming, in any number of copies.

(b) All sheets shall be free from creases and cracks; they shall not be folded.

(c) Only one side of each sheet shall be used.

(d) Subject to Rule 11.10(d) and Rule 11.13(j), each sheet shall be used in an upright position (i.e., the short sides at the top and bottom).

11.3 Material to Be Used (Paper Filing)

All elements of the international application shall be on paper which shall be flexible, strong, white, smooth, non-shiny, and durable.

11.4 Separate Sheets, Etc.

(a) Each element (request, description, claims, drawings, abstract) of the international application shall commence on a new sheet.

(b) All sheets of the international application shall be so connected that they can be easily turned when consulted, and easily separated and joined again if they have been separated for reproduction purposes

11.5 Size of Sheets

The size of the sheets shall be A4 (29.7 cm x 21 cm). However, any receiving Office may accept international applications on sheets of other sizes **provided that the record copy, as transmitted to the International Bureau, and, if the competent International Searching Authority so desires, the search copy, shall be of A4 size.**

11.6   Margins

(a) The minimum margins of the sheets containing the description, the claims, and the abstract, shall be as follows:

- top: 2 cm
- left side: 2.5 cm
- right side: 2 cm
- bottom: 2 cm

(b) The recommended maximum, for the margins provided for in paragraph (a), is as follows:

- top: 4 cm
- left side: 4 cm
- right side: 3 cm
- bottom: 3 cm

(c) On sheets containing drawings, the surface usable shall not exceed 26.2 cm x 17.0 cm. The sheets shall not contain frames around the usable or used surface. The minimum margins shall be as follows:

- **top: 2.5 cm**
- **left side: 2.5 cm**
- **right side: 1.5 cm**
- **bottom: 1 cm.**

(d) The margins referred to in paragraphs (a) to (c) apply to A4-size sheets, so that, even if the receiving Office accepts other sizes, the A4-size record copy and, when so required, the A4-size search copy shall leave the aforesaid margins.

(e) Subject to paragraph (f) and to Rule 11.8(b), the margins of the international application, when submitted, must be completely blank.

(f) The top margin may contain in the left-hand corner an indication of the applicant's file reference, provided that the reference appears within 1.5 cm from the top of the sheet. The number of characters in the applicant's file refer ence shall not exceed the maximum fixed by the Administrative Instructions.
    (Author's Comment: only used on paper filing).

11.7   Numbering of Sheets

(a) All the sheets contained in the international application shall be numbered in consecutive Arabic numerals.

(b) The numbers shall be centered at the top or bottom of the sheet, but shall not be placed in the margin.

AUTHOR'S COMMENTS

Numbering of sheets in PCT Applications has been confusing in regard to the drawing sheet numbers. See page 154 for "207 Arrangement of Elements and Numbering of Sheets of the International Application."

PCT Rule 11.6 Margins, DIN size A4.

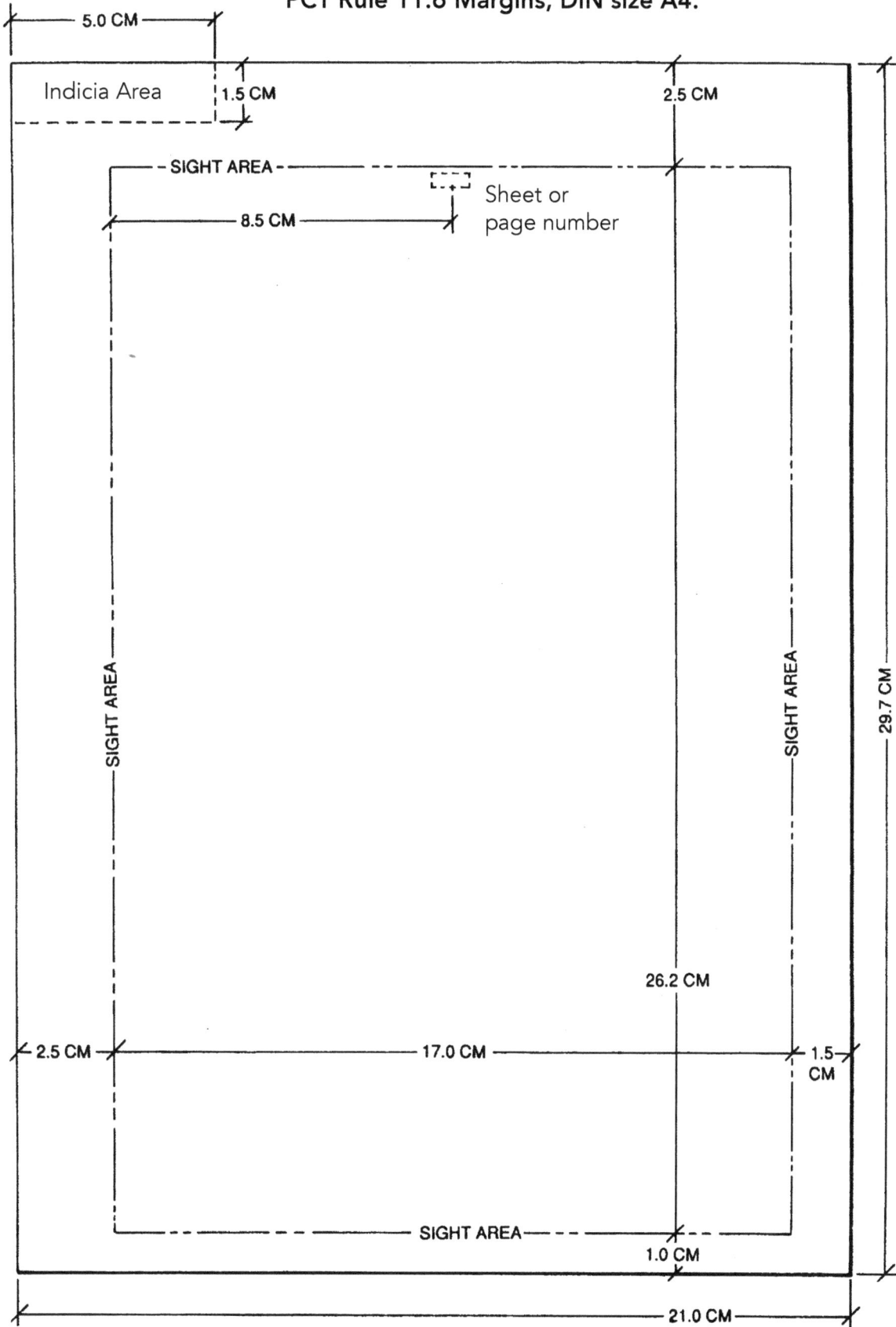

5.0 CM

Indicia Area

1.5 CM

2.5 CM

SIGHT AREA

8.5 CM

Sheet or
page number

SIGHT AREA

SIGHT AREA

29.7 CM

26.2 CM

2.5 CM

17.0 CM

1.5 CM

SIGHT AREA

1.0 CM

21.0 CM

PCT Rule 11.6 Margins, DIN Size A4 drawing sheet.

11.10 Drawings, Formulae, and Tables, in Text Matter

(a) The request, the description, the claims and the abstract shall not contain drawings.

(b) The description, the claims and the abstract may contain chemical or mathematical formulae.

(c) The description and the abstract may contain tables; any claim may contain tables only if the subject matter of the claim makes the use of tables desirable.

(d) Tables and chemical or mathematical formulae may be placed sideways on the sheet if they cannot be presented satisfactorily in an upright position thereon; sheets on which tables or chemical or mathematical formulae are presented sideways shall be so presented that the tops of the tables or formulae are at the left side of the sheet.

11.11 Words in Drawings

(a) The drawings shall not contain text matter, except a single word or words, when absolutely indispensable, such as "water," "steam," "open," "closed," "section on AB," and, in the case of electric circuits and block schematic or flow sheet diagrams, a few short catchwords indispensable for understanding.

(b) Any words used shall be so placed that, if translated, they may be pasted over without interfering with any lines of the drawings (see example on the following page).

11.12 Alterations, Etc.

Each sheet shall be reasonably free from erasures and shall be free from alterations, overwritings, and interlineations. Non-compliance with this Rule may be authorized if the authenticity of the content is not in question and the requirements for good reproduction are not in jeopardy.

§ 11.11 Words in Drawings

(a) The drawings shall not contain text matter, except a single word or words, when absolutely indispensable, such as "water," "steam," "open," "closed," "section on AB," and, in the case of electric circuits and block schematic or flow sheet diagrams, a few short catchwords indispensable for understanding.

(b) Any words used shall be so placed that, if translated, they may be pasted over without interfering with any lines of the drawings.

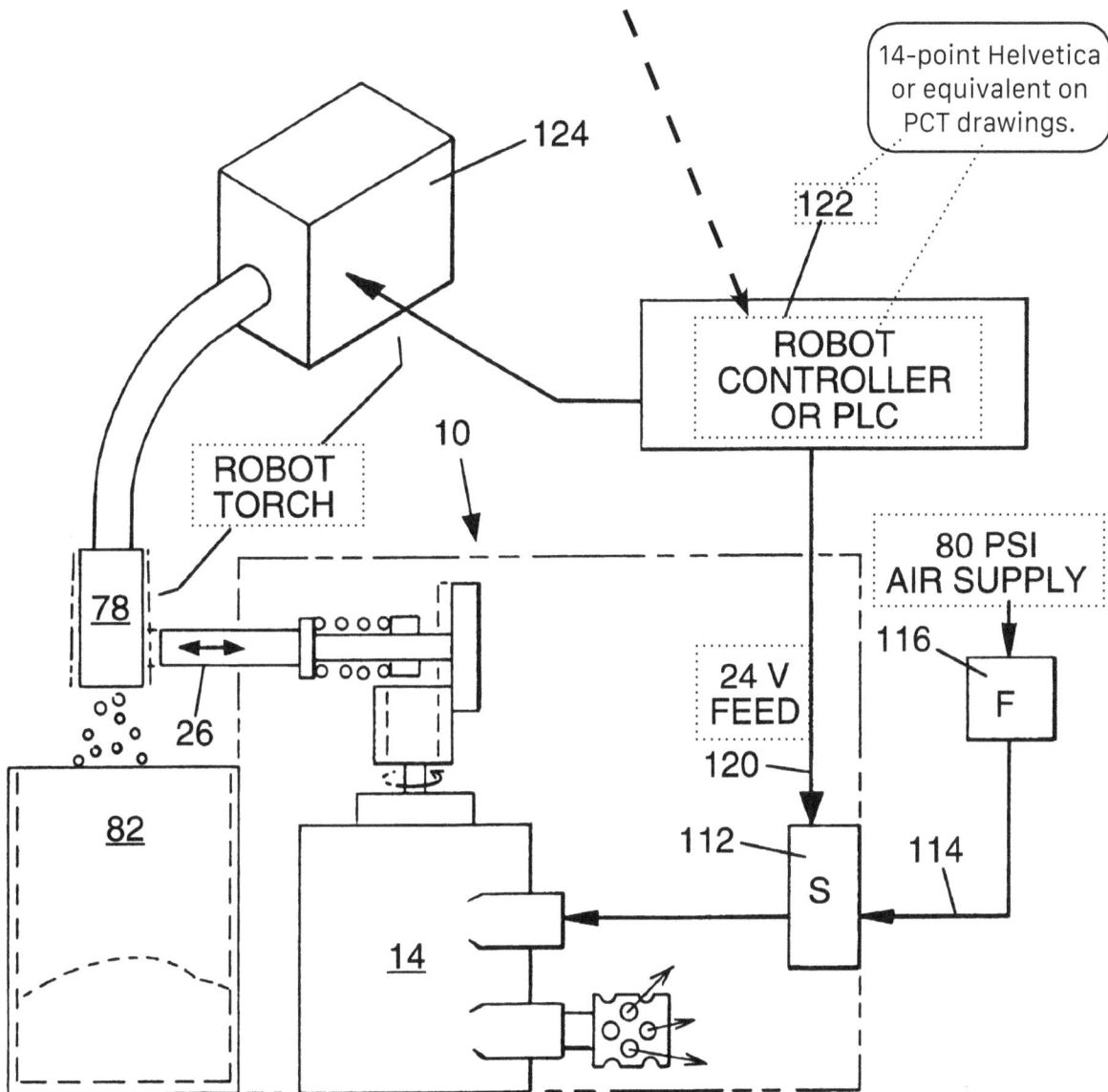

Example of words in drawings, PCT Rule 11 [R-6] Drawings.

11.13 Special Requirements for Drawings

(a) Drawings shall be executed in durable, black, sufficiently dense and dark, uniformly thick and well-defined, lines and strokes without colorings.

(b) Cross-sections shall be indicated by oblique hatching that should not impede the clear reading of the reference signs and leading lines.

(c) The scale of the drawings and the distinctness of their graphical execution shall be such that a photographic reproduction with a linear reduction in size to two-thirds would enable all details to be distinguished without difficulty.

(d) When, in exceptional cases, the scale is given on a drawing, it shall be represented graphically.

(e) All numbers, letters and reference lines, appearing on the drawings, shall be simple and clear. Brackets, circles or inverted commas shall not be used in association with numbers and letters.

(f) All lines in the drawings shall, ordinarily, be drawn with the aid of drafting instruments.

(g) Each element of each figure shall be in proper proportion to each of the other elements in the figure, except where the use of a different proportion is indispensable for the clarity of the figure.

(h) The height of the numbers and letters shall not be less than 0.32 cm. For the lettering of drawings, the Latin and, where customary, the Greek alphabets shall be used.

(i) The same sheet of drawings may contain several figures. Where figures on two or more sheets form in effect a single complete figure, the figures on the several sheets shall be so arranged that the complete figure can be assembled without concealing any part of any of the figures appearing on the various sheets.

(j) The different figures shall be arranged on a sheet or sheets without wasting space, preferably in an upright position, clearly separated from one another. Where the figures are not arranged in an upright position, they shall be presented sideways with the top of the figures at the left side of the sheet.

(k) The different figures shall be numbered in Arabic numerals consecutively and independently of the numbering of the sheets.

(l) Reference signs not mentioned in the description shall not appear in the drawings, and vice versa.

(m) The same features, when denoted by reference signs, shall, throughout the international application, be denoted by the same signs.

(n) If the drawings contain a large number of reference signs, it is strongly recommended to attach a separate sheet listing all reference signs and the features denoted by them.

USPTO Code of Federal Regulations:	UTILITY PATENT DRAWING RULES: SUBJECT:	WIPO PCT RULE:	WIPO PCT Paragraph:
37 CFR 1.84(a)	Drawings	7.1, 11.10	5.128
37 CFR 1.84(a)(1)	Black ink (black line)	11.13(a)	
37 CFR 1.84(a)(2)	Color	No	
37 CFR 1.84(b)	Photographs		
37 CFR 1.84(b)(1)	Black & white (grayscale)	10.11(e)	5.159
37 CFR 1.84(b)(2)	Color	No	No
37 CFR 1.84(c)	Identification of drawings (paper filing)	11.6(t)	
37 CFR 1.84(d)	Graphic forms in drawings	11.9(b), 11.10	5.107, 8
37 CFR 1.84(e)	Type of paper	11.2, 3, 5	5.133
37 CFR 1.84(f)	Size of paper (sheets)	11.5	5.133
37 CFR 1.84(f)(1)	DIN Size A4	11.2(a)	5.133
37 CFR 1.84(f)(2)	Letter 8-1/2 x 11 inches	No	No
37 CFR 1.84(g)	Margins	11.6(c)	5.133
37 CFR 1.84(g)(1)	DIN Size A4	11.2(a)	5.133
37 CFR 1.84(g)(2)	Letter 8-1/2 x 11 inches	No	No
37 CFR 1.84(h)	Views (plan, elevation or perspective)	7.1	
37 CFR 1.84(h)(1)	Exploded views	7.1	5.129
37 CFR 1.84(h)(2)	Partial views		
37 CFR 1.84(h)(3)	Sectional views	7.1, 11.13(b)	5.129, 5.147
37 CFR 1.84(h)(4)	Alternate position		
37 CFR 1.84(h)(5)	Modified forms		
37 CFR 1.84(i)	Arrangement of views	11.10(d)	5.134, 5
37 CFR 1.84(j)	Front-page view (abstract)	3.3(a), 8.2	5.170, 1, 2
37 CFR 1.84(k)	Scale	11.13(c)(g)	5.150
37 CFR 1.84(l)	Character of lines, numbers and letters	11.13(e)	5.143
37 CFR 1.84(m)	Shading	10.1	5.158
37 CFR 1.84(n)	Symbols	10.1(d)(e)	5.157
37 CFR 1.84(o)	Legends (text matter)	11.11	5.156
37 CFR 1.84(p)	Numbers, letters and reference characters	11.13(e)(h)	5.152
37 CFR 1.84(q)	Lead lines	11.13	5.145
37 CFR 1.84(r)	Arrows	11.13	5.146
37 CFR 1.84(s)	Copyright or Mask Work Notice		
37 CFR 1.84(t)	Numbering of sheets of drawings	11.7(a)	5.140
37 CFR 1.84(u)	Numbering of views	11.13(k)	
37 CFR 1.84(v)	Security markings		
37 CFR 1.84(w)	Corrections (also see Chapter Five) and §1.85	91	5.161
37 CFR 1.58	Tables	11.10(c)(d)	5.109
	List of reference signs	11.13(n)	5.160

Reference table: 37 CFR 1.84 Drawing Rules to WIPO PCT Drawing Rules

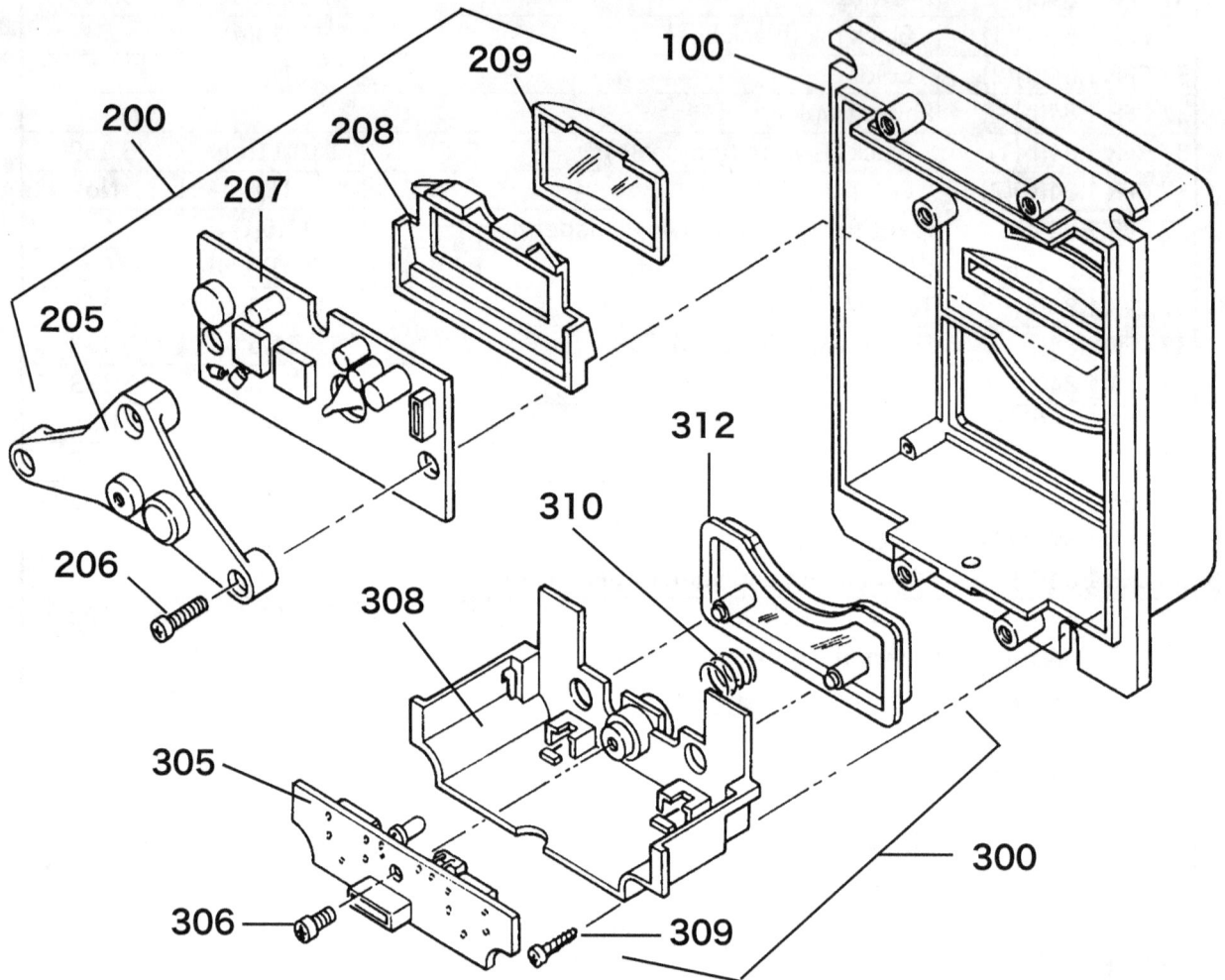

FIG. 5

NOTES:
1 – Sheet number 3 of 8 made with 14/18 point
    san serif type.
2 – Reference numbers 12/14 point.
3 – Figure number 18/24 point.
4 – Sub-assemblies with brackets 200 and 300.
5 – Complete exploded view does not need bracket
    when it is the only figure on the sheet.

Example of exploded view figure with part, FIG. and sheet numbering.

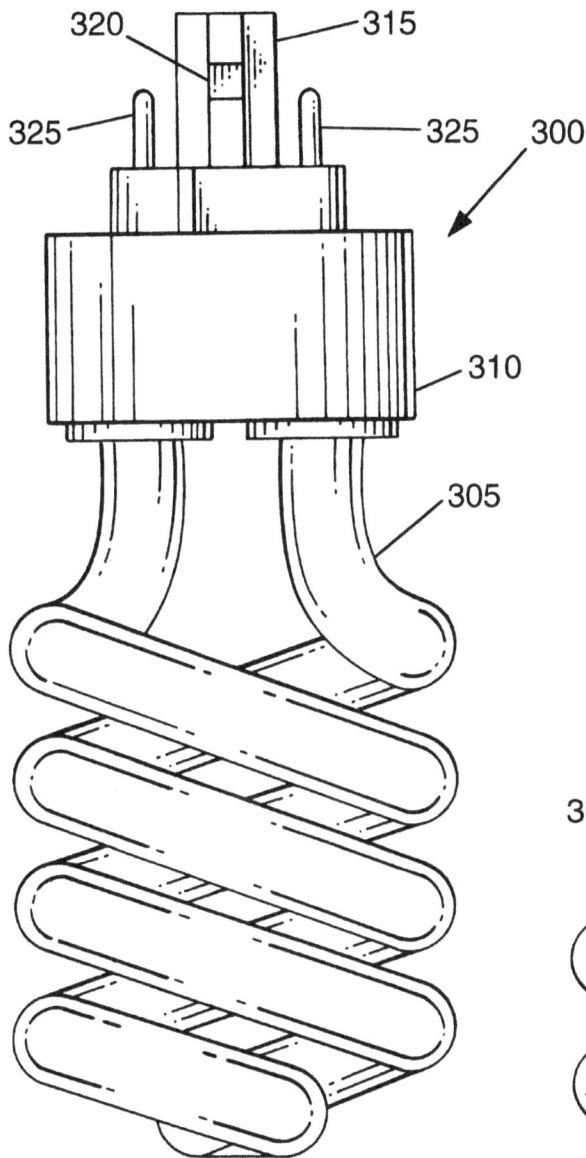

FIG. 11

AUTHOR'S NOTE:
Part identification numbers done
in 14-point Helvetica, or equivalent,
to hold up to PCT size reductions.

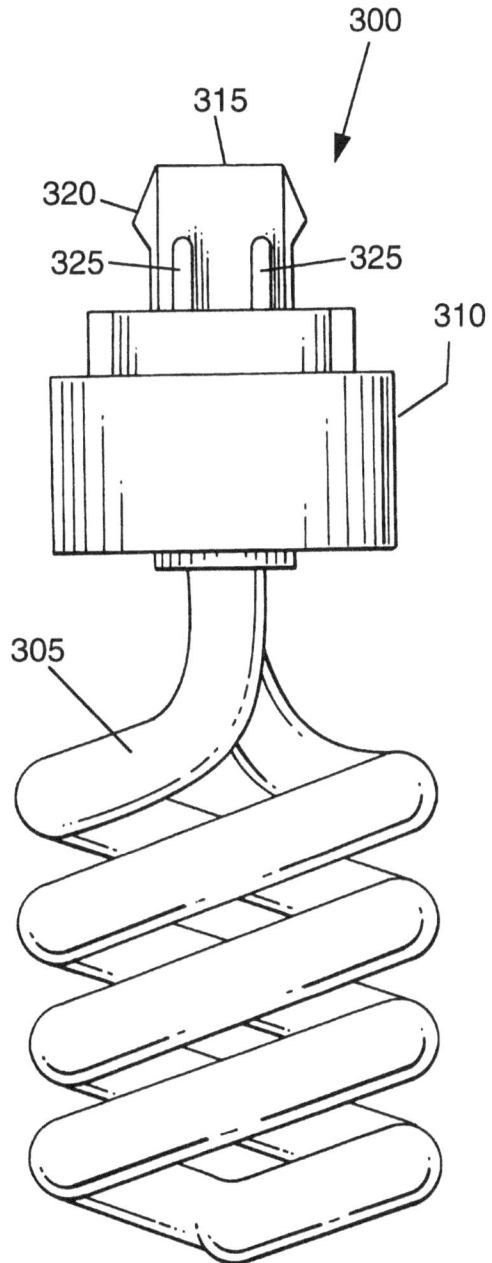

FIG. 12

Example of shading, numbers and FIG. numbers, PCT Rule 11 Drawings.

PCT PATENT FILING PROCEDURE
The PCT system is a patent "filing" system,
not a patent "granting" system.
There is no "PCT patent."

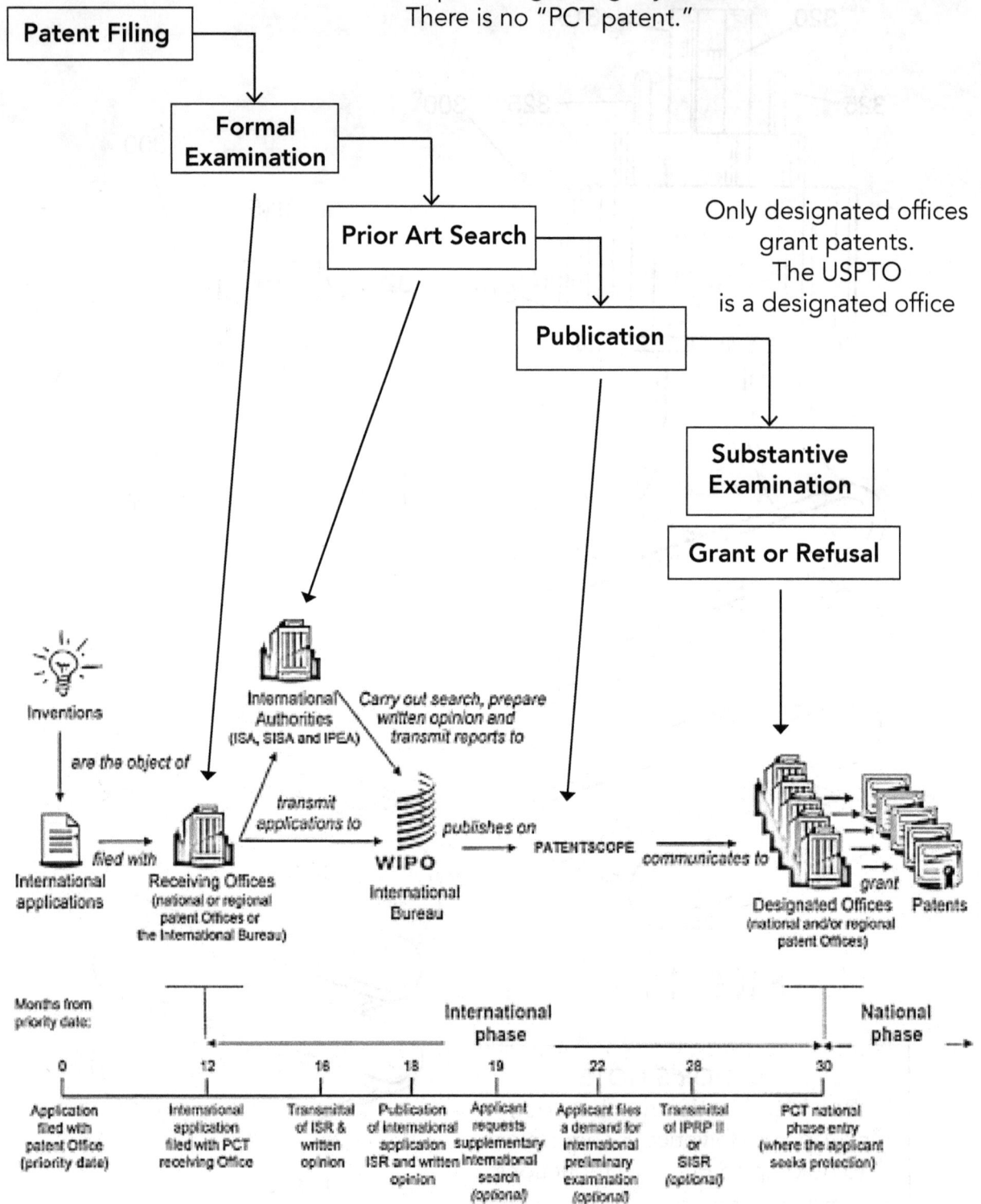

Patent Filing

Formal
Examination

Prior Art Search

Only designated offices
grant patents.
The USPTO
is a designated office

Publication

Substantive
Examination

Grant or Refusal

Inventions

are the object of

International
applications

filed with

Receiving Offices
(national or regional
patent Offices or
the International Bureau)

International
Authorities
(ISA, SISA and IPEA)

*Carry out search, prepare
written opinion and
transmit reports to*

*transmit
applications to*

WIPO
International
Bureau

publishes on

PATENTSCOPE

communicates to

Designated Offices
(national and/or regional
patent Offices)

grant

Patents

Months from priority date:		International phase						National phase
0	12	16	18	19	22	28	30	
Application filed with patent Office (priority date)	International application filed with PCT receiving Office	Transmittal of ISR & written opinion	Publication of international application ISR and written opinion	Applicant requests supplementary international search (optional)	Applicant files a demand for international preliminary examination (optional)	Transmittal of IPRP II or SISR (optional)	PCT national phase entry (where the applicant seeks protection)	

Source: WIPO, lower chart

What is the Patent Cooperation Treaty (PCT)?

The PCT is an international treaty with more than 145 Contracting States. The PCT makes it possible to seek patent protection for an invention simultaneously in a large number of countries by filing a single "international" patent application instead of filing several separate national or regional patent applications. The granting of patents remains under the control of the national or regional patent Offices in what is called the "national phase."

General Description of Formal and Substantive Examinations

Formal Examination WIPO IB

An international application shall contain, as specified in this Treaty and the Regulations, a request, a description, one or more claims, one or more drawings (where required), and an abstract.

The abstract merely serves the purpose of technical information and cannot be taken into account for any other purpose, particularly not for the purpose of interpreting the scope of the protection sought.

The "international" application shall: [filing system]
- be in a prescribed language;
- comply with the prescribed physical requirements;
- comply with the prescribed requirement of unity of invention; and
- be subject to the payment of the prescribed fees.

Substantive Examination USPTO RO or other Designated Offices

Examination by the Offices of the Designated Contracting Parties following publication of the international registration by the International Bureau, the offices of the designated Contracting Parties proceed with examination if required under their respective laws. As a result of that examination, the office may notify the International Bureau of a refusal of protection for its territory.

The "national phase" application shall: [granting system]
- be examined for technical expertise in the inventions subject matter;
- be examined for legal aspects in patent law, novelty, claim wording . . . ;
- all the parts from the "Formal Examination";
- go through a comprehensive search for prior art;
- be subject to the payment of the prescribed fees; and
- grant patent.

AUTHOR'S COMMENTS
In either the Formal and/or Substantive Examination the drawing submitted can be subjected to examination for technical and/or reproduction corrections.

207   Arrangement of Elements and Numbering of Sheets of the International Application   Source: USPTO MPEP-9

(a) In effecting the sequential numbering of the sheets of the international application in accordance with Rule 11.7, the elements of the international application shall be placed in the following order:

(i) the request;

(ii) the description (if applicable, including the sequence listing free text referred to in Rule 5.2(b) but excluding the sequence listing part of the description referred to in item (vi) of this paragraph):

(iii) the claims;

(iv) the abstract;

(v) if applicable, the drawings; and

(vi) if applicable, the sequence listing part of the description.

(b) The sequential numbering of the sheets shall be effected by using the following separate series of numbering:

(i) the first series applying to the request only and commencing with the first sheet of the request;

(ii) the second series commencing with the first sheet of the description (as referred to in paragraph (a)(ii)) and continuing through the claims until the last sheet of the abstract;

(iii) if applicable, a further series applying to the sheets of the drawings only and commencing with the first sheet of the drawings; the number of each sheet of the drawings shall consist of two Arabic numerals separated by a slant, the first being the sheet number and the second being the total number of sheets of drawings (for example, 1/3, 2/3, 3/3); and

(iv) if applicable, a further series applying to the sequence listing part of the description, commencing with the first sheet of that part.

AUTHOR'S COMMENTS

Because of confusion about numbering sheets in PCT applications I have included the above text from the USPTO's MPEP-9.
Some applicants thought they had to number their complete application starting with the first page requiring renumbering the patent drawing sheets.
See Rule 11.7 on page 144.

Chapter Four

DRAWING & REPRODUCTION RULES FOR
Design Patents & International Registration
of Industrial Designs:

Section 1 - USPTO Design Patent Drawing Rules (Chap.16)

Section 2 - U.S. Design Patents Drawing Rules
under the Hague Agreement (MPEP Chap.2900)

Section 3 - Reproduction (Drawing) Rules under the
WIPO Hague Agreement for the registration
of industrial designs (Rule 9 / A.I. Part 4)

Application

DESIGN PATENT APPLICATION
through
USPTO Receiving Office (RO)

U.S. Classification

Section 1

U.S. Design Patent
Chap. 16 Application
Drawing Rules:
MPEP-9 Chap.1500

Section 2

International Design Registration
WIPO Hague Agreement
Via USPTO-RO
MPEP-9 Chap.2900

Locarno Classification
of Industrial Designs

Registration

WIPO-Hague System of
Industrial Design Registration
Drawing Rules: WIPO-Hague
Rule 9 Reproductions of
the Industrial Designs

WIPO-Hague
Industrial Design Search
Hague Express Database

Section 3

Publish & Search

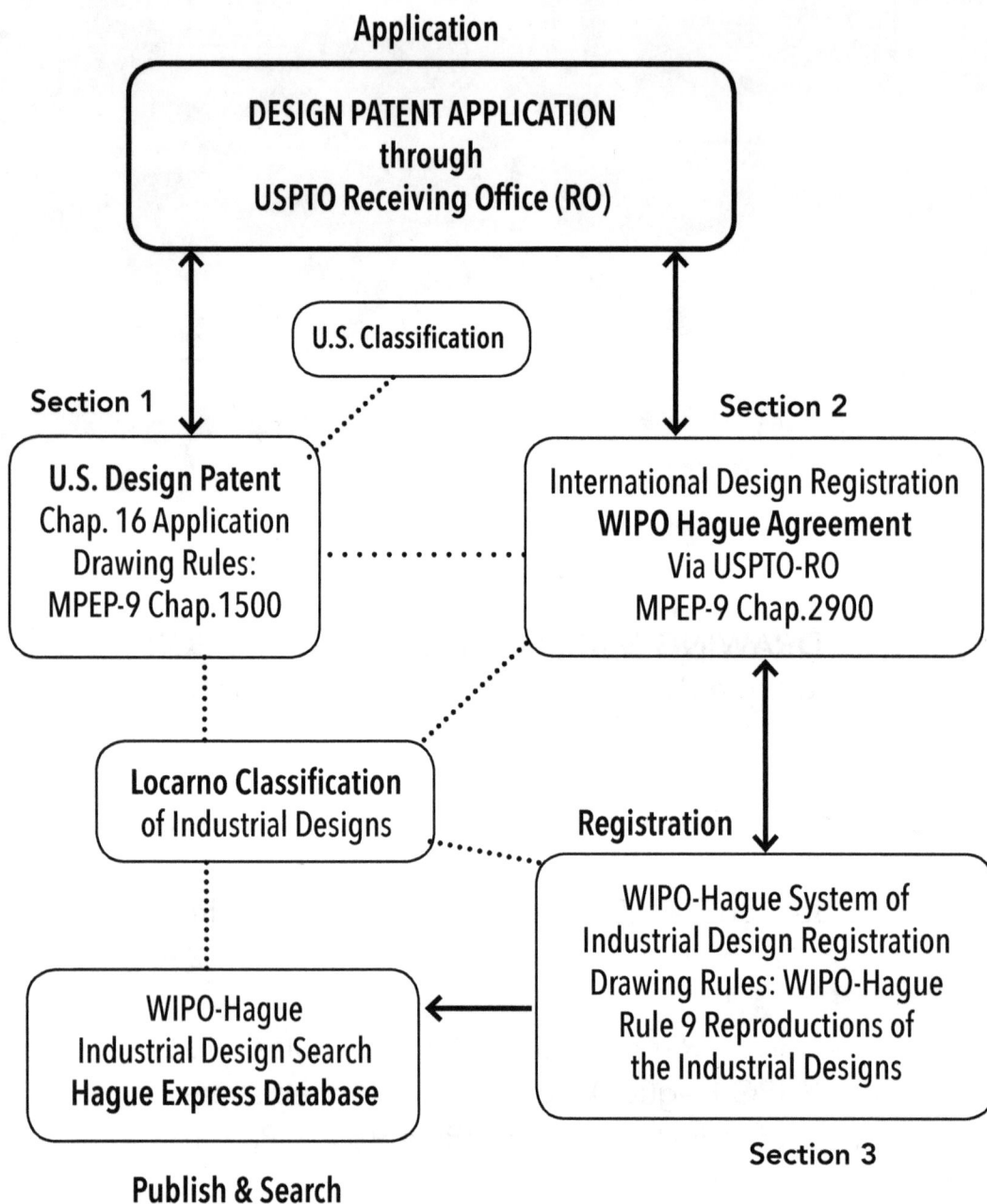

Section1: USPTO Design Patent Domestic Chap.16 Rules.

Section 2: USPTO Design Patent under WIPO Hague International Rules.

Section 3: WIPO Hague Agreement of Industrial Design Registrations.

Chart of U.S. Domestic Design Patent Applications & Hague Agreement Registration.

Differences in Design Drawing and Reproduction Rules between the USPTO and the WIPO Hague Agreement on Industrial Design Registrations

Subject Number:	Subject:	USPTO Design Patent:	USPTO Design Hague Agreement:	WIPO Hague Agreement:
1	Drawing sheet size	Letter/A-4	A-4	A-4
2	Maximum image area	16 x 24 cm	16 x 16 cm	16 x 16 cm
3	Black line drawing	Yes	Yes	Yes
4	Grayscale drawing (image)	Yes	Yes	Yes
5	Black & white photograph	Yes	Yes	Yes
6	Color drawing	Yes	Yes	Yes
7	Color Photograph	Yes	Yes	Yes
8	Mix of drawings & photographs	No	Yes	Yes
9	Figures in scale with each other	Yes	No	No
10	Maximum number of 2-D Figures	1	1	1
11	Maximum number of 3-D Figures	6 +	6	6
12	Figure numbering	FIG. 1 . . .	1.1 . . .	1.1 . . .
13	Multiple design protection	No	No	Yes-100
14	Maximum number of reproductions	None Req.	None Req.	None Req.
15	Specimens of design	No	No	Yes
16	Technical application examination	Yes-Chap16	Yes	No
17	E-Filing requirements	PDF	PDF/JPG	JPG/TIF
18	Design Classification	US/Locarno	Locarno	Locarno
19	Issuance of Patent	Yes	Yes	No

Section 1   Section 2   Section 3

Source: Studio 94

Author's Comments:
At the time of publication, industrial design protection in the United States was in transition with the melding of the USPTO's domestic drawing rules and WIPO's International rules used in the Hague Agreement on the registration of industrial designs.

Manual of Patent Examining Procedure (MPEP)
Ninth Edition, November 2015
Table of Contents

1503.02 Drawing [R-07.2015]
37 CFR 1.152 Design drawings

The design must be represented by a drawing that complies with the requirements of § 1.84 and must contain a sufficient number of views to constitute a complete disclosure of the appearance of the design. Appropriate and adequate surface shading should be used to show the character or contour of the surfaces represented. Solid black surface shading is not permitted except when used to represent the color black as well as color contrast. Broken lines may be used to show visible environmental structure, but may not be used to show hidden planes and surfaces that cannot be seen through opaque materials. Alternate positions of a design component, illustrated by full and broken lines in the same view are not permitted in a design drawing. Photographs and ink drawings are not permitted to be combined as formal drawings in one application. Photographs submitted in lieu of ink drawings in design patent applications must not disclose environmental structure but must be limited to the design claimed for the article.

Every design patent application must include either a drawing or a photograph of the claimed design. As the drawing or photograph constitutes the entire visual disclosure of the claim, it is of utmost importance that the drawing or photograph be clear and complete, and that nothing regarding the design sought to be patented is left to conjecture. **(Author's emphasis, also see chart on page 157).**

When inconsistencies are found among the views, the examiner should object to the drawings and request that the views be made consistent. Ex parte Asano, 201 USPQ 315, 317 (Bd. Pat. App. & Inter. 1978); Hadco Products, Inc. v. Lighting Corp. of America Inc., 312 F. Supp. 1173, 1182, 165 USPQ 496, 503 (E.D. Pa. 1970), vacated on other grounds, 462 F.2d 1265, 174 USPQ 358 (3d Cir. 1972). When the inconsistencies are of such magnitude that the overall appearance of the design is unclear, the claim should be rejected under 35 U.S.C. 112(a) and (b), (or for applications filed prior to September 16, 2012, 35 U.S.C. 112, first and second paragraphs), as nonenabling and indefinite. See MPEP § 1504.04, subsection I.A.

Chapter Four
Section 1
USPTO Design Patent Drawing Rules (Chap.16)

Chapter 1500
Design Patents

1504.01(a)   Computer-Generated Icons [R-07.2015]

To be directed to statutory subject matter, design applications for computer-generated icons must comply with the "article of manufacture" requirement of 35 U.S.C. 171.

I. GUIDELINES FOR EXAMINATION OF DESIGN PATENT APPLICATIONS FOR COMPUTER-GENERATED ICONS

The following guidelines have been developed to assist USPTO personnel in determining whether design patent applications for computer-generated icons comply with the "article of manufacture" requirement of 35 U.S.C. 171.

A. General Principle Governing Compliance With the "Article of Manufacture" Requirement Computer-generated icons, such as full screen displays and individual icons, are 2-dimensional images which alone are surface ornamentation. See, e.g., Ex parte Strijland, 26 USPQ2d 1259 (Bd. Pat. App. & Int. 1992) (computer-generated icon alone is merely surface ornamentation). The USPTO considers designs for computer-generated icons embodied in articles of manufacture to be statutory subject matter eligible for design patent protection under 35 U.S.C. 171. Thus, if an application claims a computer-generated icon shown on a computer screen, monitor, other display panel, or a portion thereof, the claim complies with the "article of manufacture" requirement of 35 U.S.C. 171. Since a patentable design is inseparable from the object to which it is applied and cannot exist alone merely as a scheme of surface ornamentation, a computer-generated icon must be embodied in a computer screen, monitor, other display panel, or portion thereof, to satisfy 35 U.S.C. 171. See MPEP § 1502.

"We do not see that the dependence of the existence of a design on something outside itself is a reason for holding it is not a design 'for an article of manufacture.'" See In re Hruby, 373 F.2d 997, 1001, 153 USPQ 61, 66 (CCPA 1967) (design of water fountain patentable design for an article of manufacture). The dependence of a computer-generated icon on a central processing unit and computer program for its existence itself is not a reason for holding that the design is not for an article of manufacture.

B. Procedures for Evaluating Whether Design Patent Applications Drawn to Computer-Generated Icons Comply With the "Article of Manufacture" Requirement
USPTO personnel shall adhere to the following procedures when reviewing design patent applications drawn to computer-generated icons for compliance with the "article of manufacture" requirement of 35 U.S.C. 171.

(A) Read the entire disclosure to determine what the applicant claims as the design and to determine whether the design is embodied in an article of manufacture.

Since the claim must be in formal terms to the design "as shown, or as shown and described," the drawing provides the best description of the claim. 37 CFR 1.153 or 1.1025.

(1) Review the drawing to determine whether a computer screen, monitor, other display panel, or a portion of any of those articles, is shown. Although a computer-generated icon may be embodied in only a portion of a computer screen, monitor, or other display panel, the drawing must contain a sufficient number of views to constitute a complete disclosure of the appearance of the article.

(2) Review the title to determine whether it clearly refers to the claimed subject matter. 37 CFR 1.153 or 1.1067. The following titles do not adequately describe a design for an article of manufacture under 35 U.S.C. 171: "computer icon;" or "icon." On the other hand, the following titles do adequately describe a design for an article of manufacture under 35 U.S.C. 171: "computer screen with an icon;" "display panel with a computer icon;" "portion of a computer screen with an icon image;" "portion of a display panel with a computer icon image;" or "portion of a monitor displayed with a computer icon image."

(3) Review the specification to determine whether a characteristic feature statement is present. If a characteristic feature statement is present, determine whether it describes the claimed subject matter as a computer-generated icon embodied in a computer screen, monitor, other display panel, or portion thereof. (See McGrady v. Aspenglas Corp., 487 F.2d 859, 208 USPQ 242 (S.D.N.Y. 1980) – (descriptive statement in design patent application narrows claim scope).

(B) If the drawing does not depict a computer-generated icon embodied in a computer screen, monitor, other display panel, or a portion thereof, in either solid or broken lines, reject the claimed design under 35 U.S.C. 171 for failing to comply with the article of manufacture requirement.

(1) If the disclosure as a whole does not suggest or describe the claimed subject matter as a computer-generated icon embodied in a computer screen, monitor, other display panel, or portion thereof, indicate that:

(a) The claim is fatally defective under 35 U.S.C. 171; and

(b) Amendments to the written description, drawings and/or claim attempting to overcome the rejection will ordinarily be entered, however, any new matter will be required to be canceled from the written description, drawings and/or claims. If new matter is added, the claim should be rejected under 35 U.S.C. 112(a).

(2) If the disclosure as a whole suggests or describes the claimed subject matter as a computer-generated icon embodied in a computer screen, monitor, other display panel, or portion thereof, indicate that the drawing may be amended to overcome the rejection under 35 U.S.C. 171. Suggest amendments that would bring the claim into compliance with 35 U.S.C. 171.

(C) Indicate all objections to the disclosure for failure to comply with the requirements of the Rules of Practice in Patent Cases. See, e.g., 37 CFR 1.71, 1.81-1.85, and 1.152-1.154. Suggest amendments that would bring the disclosure into compliance with the requirements of the Rules of Practice in Patent Cases.

(D) Upon reply by applicant:
    (1) enter any amendments; and
    (2) review all arguments and the entire record, including any amendments, to determine whether the drawing, title, and specification clearly disclose a computer-generated icon embodied in a computer screen, monitor, other display panel, or portion thereof.

(E) If, by a preponderance of the evidence (see In re Oetiker, 977 F.2d 1443, 1445, 24 USPQ2d 1443, 1444 (Fed. Cir. 1992) ("After evidence or argument is submitted by the applicant in response, patentability is determined on the totality of the record, by a preponderance of evidence with due consideration to persuasiveness of argument."), the applicant has established that the computer-generated icon is embodied in a computer screen, monitor, other display panel, or portion thereof, withdraw the rejection under 35 U.S.C. 171.

II. EFFECT OF THE GUIDELINES ON PENDING DESIGN APPLICATIONS DRAWN TO COMPUTER-GENERATED ICONS

USPTO personnel shall follow the procedures set forth above when examining design patent applications for computer-generated icons pending in the USPTO as of April 19, 1996.

III. TREATMENT OF TYPE FONTS

Traditionally, type fonts have been generated by solid blocks from which each letter or symbol was produced. Consequently, the USPTO has historically granted design patents drawn to type fonts. USPTO personnel should not reject claims for type fonts under 35 U.S.C. 171 for failure to comply with the "article of manufacture" requirement on the basis that more modern methods of typesetting, including computer-generation, do not require solid printing blocks.

IV. CHANGEABLE COMPUTER GENERATED ICONS

Computer-generated icons including images that change in appearance during viewing may be the subject of a design claim. Such a claim may be shown in two or more views. The images are understood as viewed sequentially, no ornamental aspects are attributed to the process or period in which one image changes into another.

A descriptive statement must be included in the specification describing the transitional nature of the design and making it clear that the scope of the claim does not include anything that is not shown. Examples of such a descriptive statement are as follows:

> "The subject matter in this patent includes a process or period in which an image changes into another image. This process or period forms no part of the claimed design;" or
>
> "The appearance of the transitional image sequentially transitions between the images shown in Figs. 1-8. The process or period in which one image transitions to another image forms no part of the claimed design;" or
>
> "The appearance of the transitional image sequentially transitions between the images shown in Figs. 1-8. No ornamental aspects are associated with the process or period in which one image transitions to another image."

Source: USPTO MPEP-9

NOTE: The reference to "Figs. 1-8" is for "descriptive statement" example only; there are no actual Figures illustrated here.

1504.01(b) Design Comprising Multiple Articles or Multiple Parts Embodied in a Single Article [R-08.2012]

While the claimed design must be embodied in an article of manufacture as required by 35 U.S.C. 171, it may encompass multiple articles or multiple parts within that article. See Ex parte Gibson, 20 USPQ 249 (Bd. App. 1933).

(a) When the design involves multiple articles, the title must identify a single entity of manufacture made up by the parts (e.g., set, pair, combination, unit, assembly). **A descriptive statement should be included in the specification making it clear that the claim is directed to the collective appearance of the articles shown.**

If the separate parts are shown in a single view, the parts must be shown embraced by a bracket "}".

(b) The claim also may involve multiple parts of a single article, where the article is shown in broken lines and various parts are shown in solid lines. In this case, no bracket is needed. See MPEP § 1503.01.

AUTHOR'S COMMENTS

In regard to U.S. Design Patent applications, you can claim only one design in each application, but one design may be on "Multiple Articles" or "Multiple Parts," for example:

(a) A single claimed design on a set of coffee utensils consisting of coffee cup, a coffee pot, cream and sugar bowls; a single design claimed on the handles of eating utensils; or

a three-dimensional puzzle that when assembled illustrates the design.

(b) A single design on a laptop computer with inlet and outlet ports in broken lines to identify the "different embodiments" on one claimed design.

NOTE: If you are going to produce patent design drawings that will be used in a Hague Agreement registration you may want to examine the requirements of the various member states, you select, on multiple parts.

CAUTION: If you are submitting multiple designs in a Hague registration and the multiple designs are published, and the US is one of your selected member states, you must only claim one design – the remaining published designs may become "Prior Art."

1512 Relationship Between Design Patent, Copyright, and Trademark [R-07.2015]

¶ 15.55 Design Patent-Copyright Overlap

There is an area of overlap between Copyright and Design Patent Statutes where an author/inventor can secure both a Copyright and a Design Patent. Thus, an ornamental design may be copyrighted as a work of art and also may be the subject matter of a Design Patent. The author/inventor may not be required to elect between securing a copyright or a design patent. See In re Yardley, 493 F. 2d 1389, 181 USPQ 331 (CCPA 1974). In Mazer v. Stein, 347 U.S. 201, 100 USPQ 325 (U.S. 1954), the Supreme Court noted the election of protection doctrine but did not express any view on it since a Design Patent had been secured in the case and the issue was not before the Court.

It is the policy of the Patent and Trademark Office to permit the inclusion of a copyright notice in a Design Patent application, and thereby any patent issuing therefrom, under the following conditions:

(1) A copyright notice must be placed adjacent to the copyright material and, therefore, may appear at any appropriate portion of the patent application disclosure including the drawing. However, if appearing on the drawing, the notice must be limited in print size from 1/8 inch to 1/4 inch and must be placed within the "sight" of the drawing immediately below the figure representing the copyright material. If placed on a drawing in conformance with these provisions, the examiner will not object to the notice as extraneous matter under 37 CFR 1.84.

(2) The content of the copyright notice must be limited to only those elements required by law. For example, "© 1983 John Doe" would be legally sufficient under 17 U.S.C. 401 and properly limited.

(3) Inclusion of a copyright notice will be permitted only if the following waiver is included at the beginning (preferably as the first paragraph) of the specification to be printed for the patent:

A portion of the disclosure of this patent document contains material to which a claim for copyright is made. The copyright owner has no objection to the facsimile reproduction by anyone of the patent document or the patent disclosure, as it appears in the Patent and Trademark Office patent file or records, but reserves all other copyrights whatsoever.

(4) Inclusion of a copyright notice after a Notice of Allowance has been mailed will be permitted only if the criteria of 37 CFR 1.312 have been satisfied.

Any departure from these conditions may result in a refusal to permit the desired inclusion. If the waiver required under condition (3) above does not include the specific language "(t)he copyright owner has no objection to the facsimile reproduction by anyone of the patent document or the patent disclosure, as it appears in the Patent and Trademark Office patent file or records...," the examiner will object to the copyright notice as improper.

The files of design patents D-243,821, D-243,824 and D-243,920 show examples of an earlier similar procedure.

¶ 15.55.01 Design Patent - Trademark Overlap

A design patent and a trademark may be obtained on the same subject matter. The Court of Customs and Patent Appeals, in In re Mogen David Wine Corp., 328 F.2d 925, 140 USPQ 575 (CCPA 1964), later reaffirmed by the same court at 372 F.2d 539, 152 USPQ 593 (CCPA 1967), has held that the underlying purpose and essence of patent rights are separate and distinct from those pertaining to trademarks, and that no right accruing from the one is dependent upon or conditioned by any right concomitant to the other.

IV. INCLUSION OF TRADEMARKS IN DESIGN PATENT APPLICATIONS

A. *Specification*

The use of trademarks in design patent application specifications is permitted under limited circumstances. See **MPEP § 608.01(v).** This section assumes that the proposed use of a trademark is a legal use under federal trademark law.

B. *Title*

It is improper to use a trademark alone or coupled with the word "type" (e.g., Band-Aid type Bandage) in the title of a design. Examiners must object to the use of a trademark in the title of a design application and require its deletion therefrom.

C. *Drawings*

When a trademark is used in the drawing disclosure of a design application, the specification must include a statement preceding the claim identifying the trademark material forming part of the claimed design and the name of the owner of the registered trademark. Form paragraph 15.76 may be used.

¶ 15.76 Trademark in Drawing

The [1] forming part of the claimed design is a registered trademark of [2]. The specification must be amended to include a statement preceding the claim identifying the trademark.

Examiner Note:
1. In bracket 1, identify the trademark material.
2. In bracket 2, identify the trademark owner.

AUTHOR'S COMMENTS

Examples of Trademark Design Patent Overlap:
1 – Sport shoes that contain the TM in the shoe design.
2 – Combination of TM and grill design on automobiles and trucks.
3 – The TM integrated into eatable food designs. (Class 1 Foodstuffs)

NOTES ON CONTENTS:
1 - Items boxed in with dotted lines are referenced to: additional subjects that are in a US-Hague registration.
2 - Items boxed in with solid lines are referenced to: Drawings, Drawing Rules or Laws.
3 - Boxed–numbered subject details are on the following pages.

U.S. Design Patent Application Guide - Contents

(1) - Definition of a Design (USPTO)

A design consists of the visual ornamental characteristics embodied in, or applied to, an article of manufacture. Since a design is manifested in appearance, the subject matter of a design patent application may relate to the configuration or shape of an article, to the surface ornamentation applied to an article, or to the combination of configuration and surface ornamentation. A design for surface ornamentation is inseparable from the article to which it is applied and cannot exist alone. It must be a definite pattern of surface ornamentation, applied to an article of manufacture.

In discharging its patent-related duties, the United States Patent and Trademark Office (USPTO or Office) examines applications and grants patents on inventions when applicants are entitled to them. The patent law provides for the granting of design patents to any person who has invented any new, original and ornamental design for an article of manufacture. A design patent protects only the appearance of the article and not structural or utilitarian features.

Source: United States Patent and Trademark Office

What is an industrial design? (WIPO)

In a legal sense, an industrial design constitutes the ornamental or aesthetic aspect of an article.

An industrial design may consist of three dimensional features, such as the shape of an article, or two dimensional features, such as patterns, lines or color.

Source: WIPO Hague Agreement on the Registration of Industrial Designs

---

AUTHOR'S COMMENTS

When a business has a successful product and their trademark image becomes synonymous with their products this generally leads to the close relationship between the trademark and the product design.

Examples:

a) **Vehicle rubber tires** – with the company's trademark and trade names embossed on the sidewall and the tire tread design patented/registered and all three are protected as intellectual property.

b) **Automotive grillwork and the company's trademark** – With the designs of automobiles and trucks getting more similar most companies put most of their distinctions in the design of their front-end grillwork (trade dress).

(2) - Types of Designs and Modified Forms

An ornamental design may be embodied in an entire article or only a portion of an article, or may be ornamentation applied to an article. If a design is directed to just surface ornamentation, it must be shown applied to an article in the drawings, and the article must be shown in broken lines, as it forms no part of the claimed design.

A design patent application may only have a single claim (37 CFR § 1.153). Designs that are independent and distinct must be filed in separate applications since they cannot be supported by a single claim. Designs are independent if there is no apparent relationship between two or more articles. For example, a pair of eyeglasses and a door handle are independent articles and must be claimed in separate applications. Designs are considered distinct if they have different shapes and appearances even though they are related articles. For example, two vases having different surface ornamentation creating distinct appearances must be claimed in separate applications. **However, modified forms, or embodiments of a single design** concept, may be filed in one application. For example, vases with only minimal configuration differences may be considered a single design concept and both embodiments may be included in a single application. *An example of modified forms appears at the bottom of Page 16.*

Design counts
"In an industrial design application, some IP offices allow applications to contain more than one design for the same good, or in the same class; *others* allow only one design per application. In order to capture the differences in filing application systems across offices, one needs to compare their respective application and registration design counts."
Source: WIPO 2015 Report

AUTHOR'S COMMENTS
The USPTO Design Patent rules are one of the "others" that allow only a single claim for each design application. There are other contracting states, but not many, that allow only a single claim. These contracting states, including the U.S. generally have larger IP Offices and have been in operation for a long time.

---

(9) - The Figure Descriptions

The Figure Descriptions indicate what each view of the drawings represents, i.e., front elevation, top plan, perspective view, etc.

Any description of the design in the specification, other than a brief description of the drawing, is generally not necessary since, as a general rule, the drawing is the design's best description. However, while not required, a special description is not prohibited. In addition to the figure descriptions, the following types of statements are permissible in the specification:

1. A description of the appearance of portions of the claimed design that are not illustrated in the drawing disclosure (i.e., "the right side elevational view is a mirror image of the left side").

2. Description disclaiming portions of the article not shown, that form no part of the claimed design.

3. Statement indicating that any broken line illustration of environmental structure in the drawing is not part of the design sought to be patented.

4. Description denoting the nature and environmental use of the claimed design, if not included in the preamble.

(10) - A Single Claim

A design patent application may include only a single claim. The specific wording of the claim must be in formal terms to the ornamental design for the article (the article that embodies the design or to which it is applied) as shown, or as shown and described. The description of the article in the claim should be consistent in terminology with the title of the invention. See MPEP § 2920.04(a), subsection I.

A descriptive statement in design patent application narrows the claim scope.

> **AUTHOR'S COMMENTS**
> In regard to "figure descriptions:" When I did drawings
> for patent attorney's I made a list of figure descriptions
> to send along with the completed drawings.
> I did this because I learned while working with IP attorneys
> that they knew the correct legal wording, but were generally
> less knowledgeable in the correct figure-view descriptions.
> This made for a good working relationship.

(11, 12) - Photographs and Color Drawings (Chap.16)

Drawings in design applications may be submitted in black & white or in color. See 37 CFR 1.84(a). Photographs, including photocopies of photographs, are not ordinarily permitted in utility and design patent applications. The Office will accept photographs in utility and design patent applications, however, if photographs are the only practicable medium for illustrating the claimed invention. See 37 CFR 1.84(b). See also 37 CFR 1.81(c) and 37 CFR 1.83(c), and MPEP § 608.02.

Where color drawings and color photographs are submitted, only one set of color drawings or color photographs are required if submitted via EFS-Web. Three sets of color drawings or color photographs are required if not submitted via EFS-Web. See 37 CFR 1.84(a)(2)(ii). In addition, the specification must contain, or be amended to contain, the following language as the first paragraph of the brief description of the drawings: **The file of this patent contains at least one drawing/photograph executed in color. Copies of this patent with color drawing(s)/photograph(s) will be provided by the Office upon request and payment of the necessary fee. See 37 CFR 1.84(a)(2)(iii) and MPEP § 608.02.**

If the photographs are not of sufficient quality so that all details in the photographs are reproducible, this will form the basis of subsequent objection to the quality of the photographic disclosure. No application will be issued until objections directed to the quality of the photographic disclosure have been resolved and acceptable photographs have been submitted and approved by the examiner. If the details, appearance and shape of all the features and portions of the design are not clearly disclosed in the photographs, this would form the basis of a rejection of the claim under 35 U.S.C. 112(a) and (b), (or for applications filed prior to September 16, 2012, 35 U.S.C. 112, first and second paragraphs), as nonenabling and indefinite.

Photographs and drawings must not be combined in a formal submission of the visual disclosure of the claimed design in one application. The introduction of both photographs and drawings in a design application would result in a high probability of inconsistencies between corresponding elements on the drawings as compared with the photographs.

When filing informal photographs or informal drawings with the original application, a disclaimer included in the specification or on the photographs themselves may be used to disclaim any surface ornamentation, logos, written matter, etc. which form no part of the claimed design. See also MPEP § 1504.04, subsection II.

AUTHOR'S COMMENTS
If you are filing a domestic Chap.16 Design Patent Application you still cannot file both photographs and drawings, see page 208 no mixing of reproductions in different forms.

(11, 12) - Photographs and Color Drawings (Continued)

Color drawings are permitted in design applications when filed in accordance with the requirements of 37 CFR 1.84(a)(2). Color also may be shown in pen-and-ink drawings by lining the surfaces of the design for color in accordance with the symbols in MPEP § 608.02. If the drawing in an application is lined for color, the following statement should be inserted in the specification for clarity and to avoid possible confusion that the lining may be surface treatment: **The drawing is lined for color**. However, lining entire surfaces of a design to show color(s) may interfere with a clear showing of the design as required by 35 U.S.C. 112(a) (or for applications filed prior to September 16, 2012, 35 U.S.C. 112, first paragraph), as surface shading cannot be used simultaneously to define the contours of those surfaces (see Annex for Color Code).

If color photographs or color drawings are filed with the original application, color will be considered an integral part of the disclosed and claimed design. The omission of color in later filed photographs or drawings will be permitted if it is clear from the application that applicant had possession of the underlying configuration of the basic design without the color at the time of filing of the application. See In re Daniels, 144 F.3d 1452, 1456-57, 46 USPQ2d 1788, 1790 (Fed. Cir. 1998) and MPEP § 1504.04, subsection II. Note also 37 CFR 1.152, which requires that photographs submitted in lieu of ink drawings in design patent applications must not disclose environmental structure but must be limited to the design claimed for the article.

Form paragraph 15.05.041 may be used when color drawing(s) or photograph(s) have been submitted.

AUTHOR'S COMMENTS
Use a professional experienced in photographing products that are mostly studio shots that can capture the detail of the subject without shadows and other environmental objects that are not part of the design.
Use black & white or color, whichever is acceptable in your particular application.

Be prepared to give the photographer precise instructions of exactly what needs to be photographed for the various views, or better yet, you may want to act as art director on the photo shoot. It is your job, or the attorney's, to instruct the photographer on what is required in the way of views. It is the photographer's job to take good, clean, background-free photographs that are color, or gray-scale correct.

It is better to take too many pictures than too few.

Remember to have the photographer sign an *"assignment of copyright for the photographs"* so the inventor is the owner of the copyright on the patent application photographs. This would also apply to artists, if you have them do color drawings.

(13) - The Views

The drawings or photographs should contain a sufficient number of views to completely disclose the appearance of the claimed design, i.e., front, rear, right and left sides, top and bottom. While not required, it is suggested that perspective views be submitted to clearly show the appearance and shape of three-dimensional designs. If a perspective view is submitted, the surfaces shown would normally not be required to be illustrated in other views if these surfaces are clearly understood and fully disclosed in the perspective.

Views that are merely duplicates of other views of the design or that are merely flat and include no ornamentality may be omitted from the drawing if the specification makes this explicitly clear. For example, if the left and right sides of a design are identical or a mirror image, a view should be provided of one side and a statement made in the drawing description that the other side is identical or a mirror image. If the bottom of the design is flat, a view of the bottom may be omitted if the figure descriptions include a statement that the bottom is flat and unornamented. The term "unornamented" should not be used to describe visible surfaces that include structure that is clearly not flat. In some cases, the claim may be directed to an entire article, but because all sides of the article may not be visible during normal use, it is not necessary to disclose them. A sectional view that more clearly brings out elements of the design is permissible, however a sectional view presented to show functional features, or interior structure not forming part of the claimed design, is neither required nor permitted.

AUTHOR'S COMMENTS
Sectional views generally are usefull to deterine
the shape of a portion of a view that is hard to illustrate
(see example on following page).

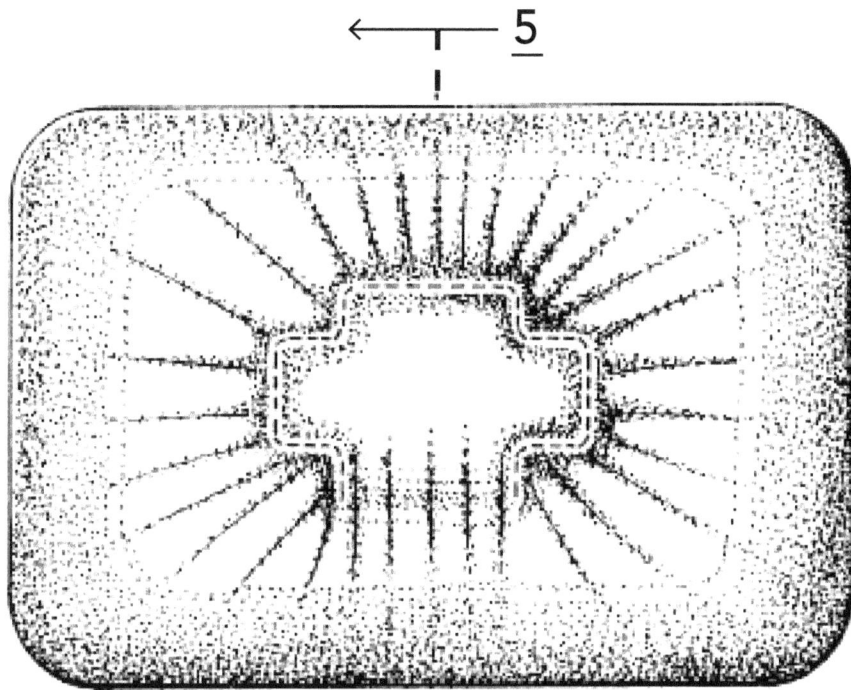

5

5

FIG. 2

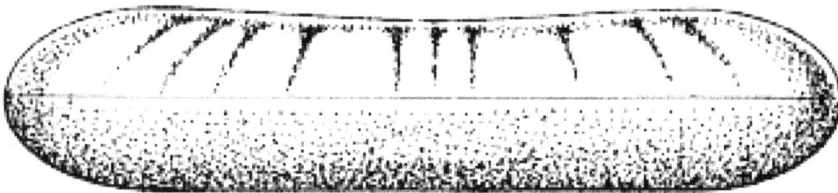

FIG. 3

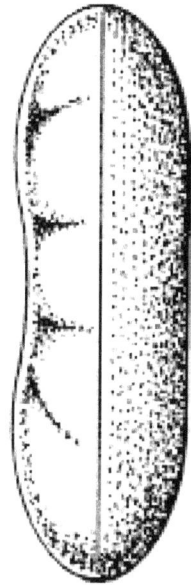

FIG. 4

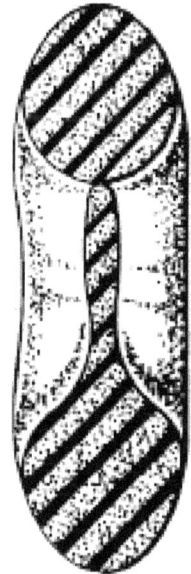

FIG. 5

NOTE:
For illustrative purposes only
not all figures shown.

Example of a U.S. Design Patent of an orthopedic pillow with ink stipple shading.
The patent examiner had **"requested a sectional view to clarify the construction."**

(14) - Surface Shading

The drawing should be provided with appropriate surface shading that clearly shows the character and contour of all surfaces of any three-dimensional aspects of the design. Surface shading also is necessary to distinguish between any open and solid areas of the design. Solid black surface shading is not permitted except when used to represent the color black as well as color contrast. Lack of appropriate surface shading in the drawing as filed may render the shape and contour of the design nonenabling under 35 U.S.C. 112, first paragraph. Additionally, if the shape of the design is not evident from the disclosure as filed, addition of surface shading after filing may be viewed as new matter. New matter is anything that is added to, or from, the claim, drawings or specification, that was neither shown nor suggested in the original application (see 35 U.S.C. 132 and 37 CFR § 1.121).

AUTHOR'S COMMENTS
If you are illustrating design line drawings, before adding the shading
I recommend saving the unshaded drawings as separate image files,
then add the shading for the final submission drawing files.
Some Contracting Parties do not allow "shading" in their design
drawing requirements so that way you have two options.

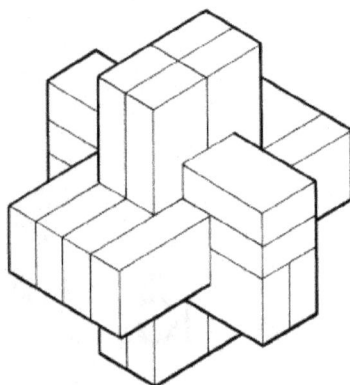

Unshaded, first DRW-file   Shaded, second DRW-file

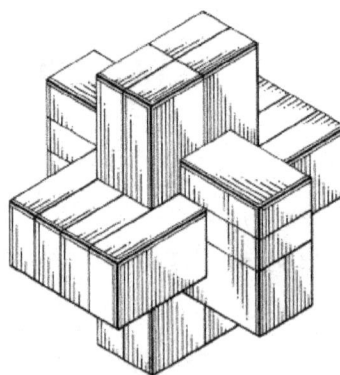

NOTE
Under present rules on shading
the front leading line illustrated
above is no longer required and
shading is held to a minimum.

(15) - Broken Lines

A broken line disclosure is understood to be for illustrative purposes only and forms no part of the claimed design. Structure that is not part of the claimed design, but is considered necessary to show the environment in which the design is used, may be represented in the drawing by broken lines. This includes any portion of an article in which the design is embodied or applied to that is not considered part of the claimed design. When the claim is directed to just surface ornamentation for an article, the article in which it is embodied must be shown in broken lines.

In general, when broken lines are used, they should not intrude upon or cross the showing of the claimed design and should not be of heavier weight than the lines used in depicting the claimed design. Where a broken line showing of environmental structure must necessarily cross or intrude upon the representation of the claimed design and obscures a clear understanding of the design, such an illustration should be included as a separate figure in addition to the other figures that fully disclose the subject matter of the design.

AUTHOR'S COMMENTS

Examples of the use of broken lines in design patent illustrations:

1) In automobile design illustrations where the wheels, exterior mirrors, etc. are not part of the design, they are represented by broken lines.
(Note: These objects generally have their own registered designs.)

2) Laptop computer design applications where the exterior design is in solid lines and the variation in input/output connections are in broken lines.

(Note: It is the variation in connectors in broken lines that generally are used to submit different embodiments of the same design claim.)

Design of child's toothbrush holder
illustrating in phantom line how
environment is used.
Figure is done in stipple
with India ink.

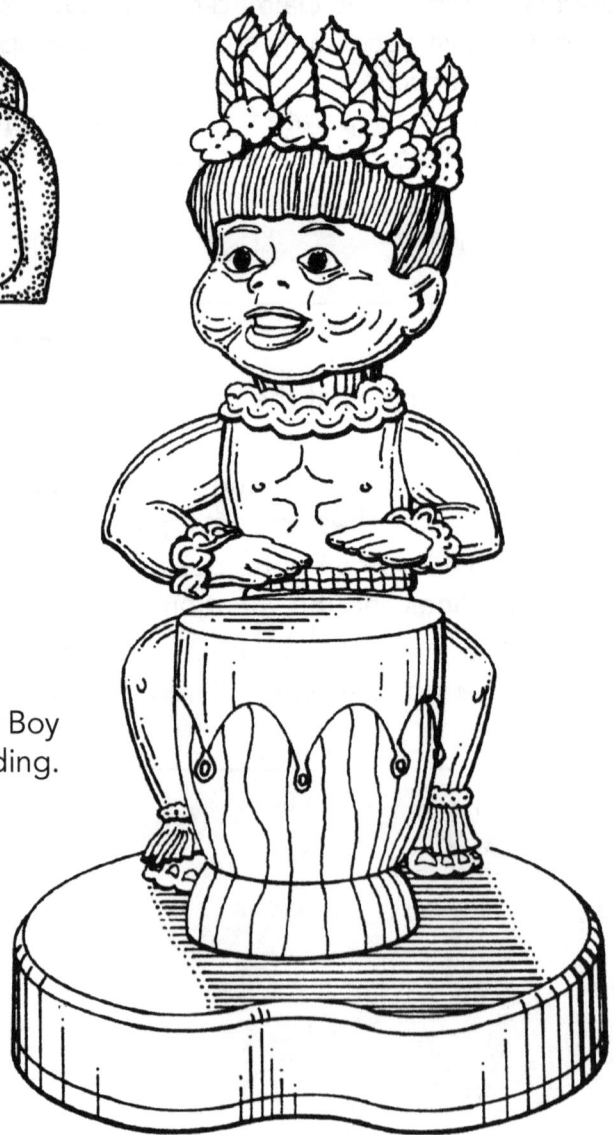

Design of Hawaiian Drummer Boy
illustrated in ink line with shading.

Example of Design Patent Drawings in stipple and ink line.

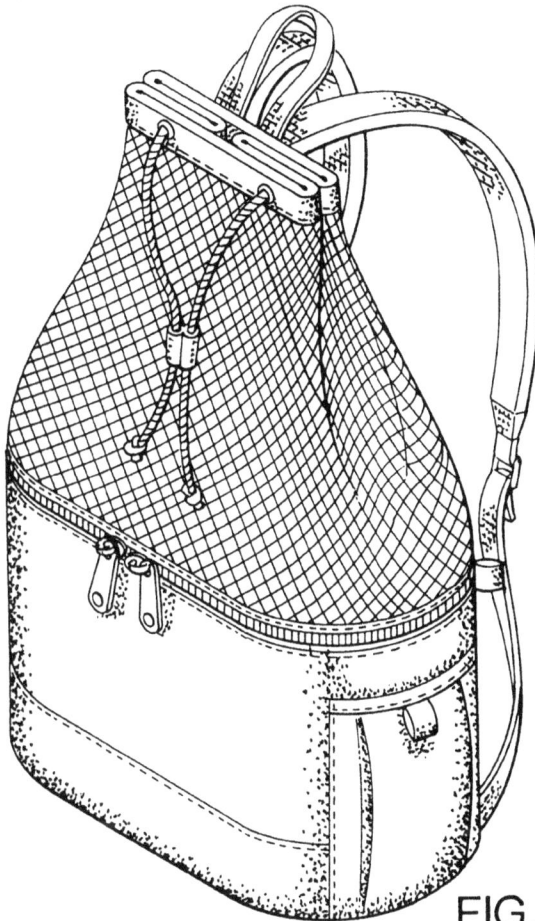

FIG. 1

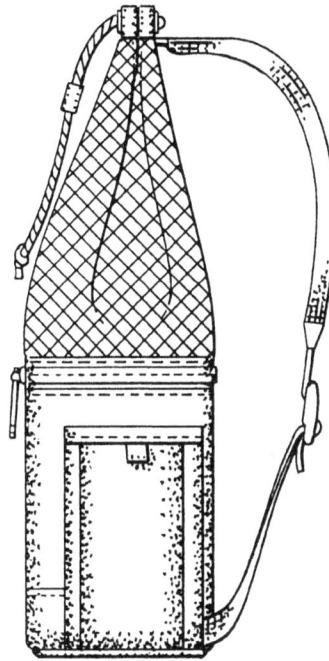

FIG. 2

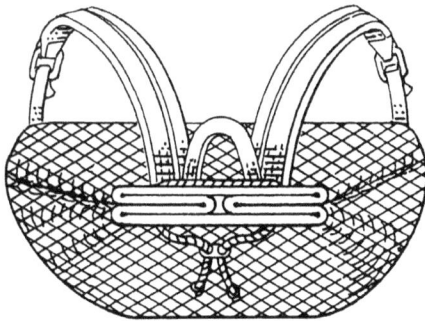

FIG. 3

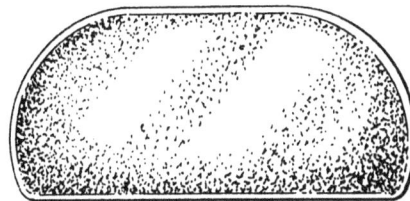

FIG. 4

AUTHOR'S COMMENTS

In the description of the figures it was described as:
FIG. 1 is an enlarged perspective view of a ... ; and
FIG. 4 is a bottom view illustrated without shoulder straps.

Example of Beach Bag Design Drawings in ink line and stipple shading.

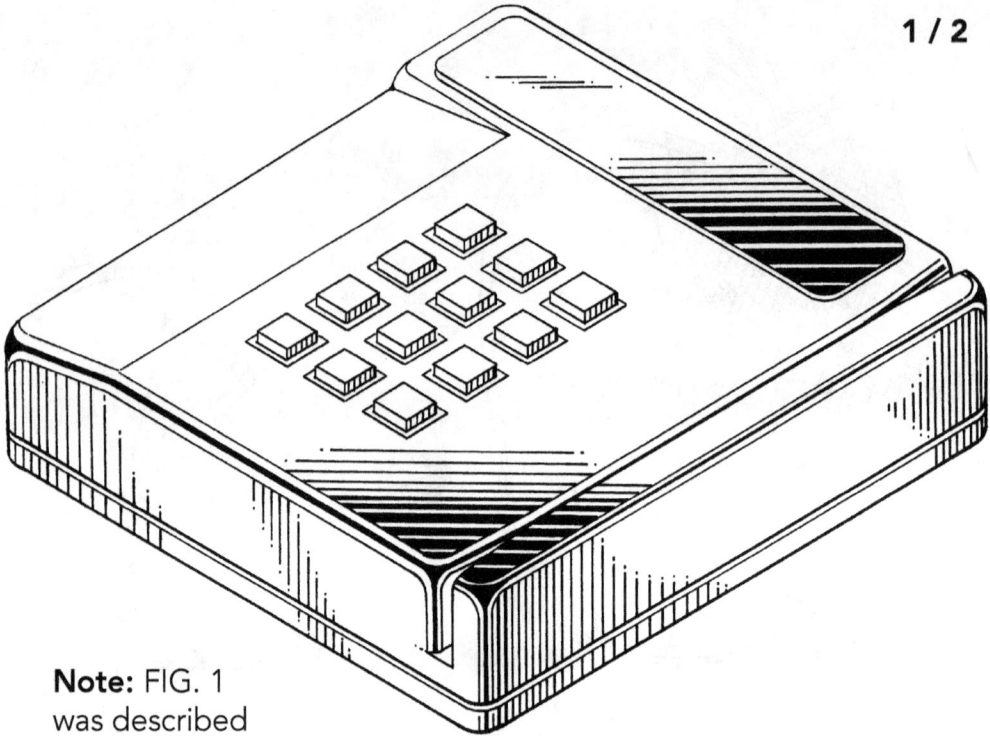

Note: FIG. 1 was described as an enlarged view in the patent description.

FIG. 1

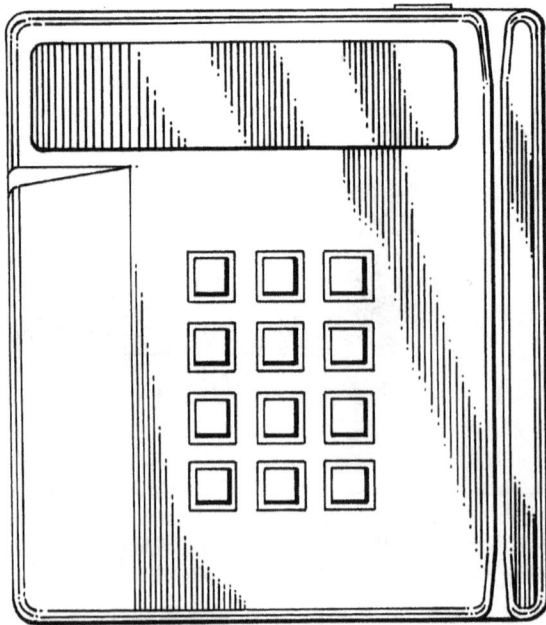

FIG. 2

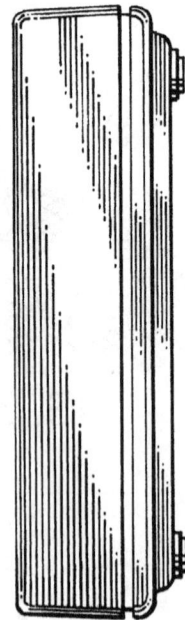

FIG. 3

Sheet 1 of Design Patent Drawings of a Credit Card Terminal.

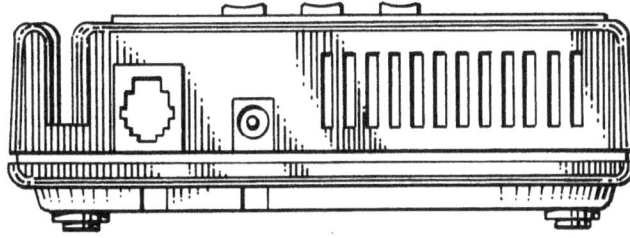

FIG. 4

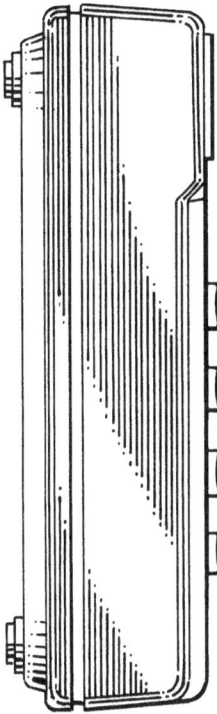

FIG. 5

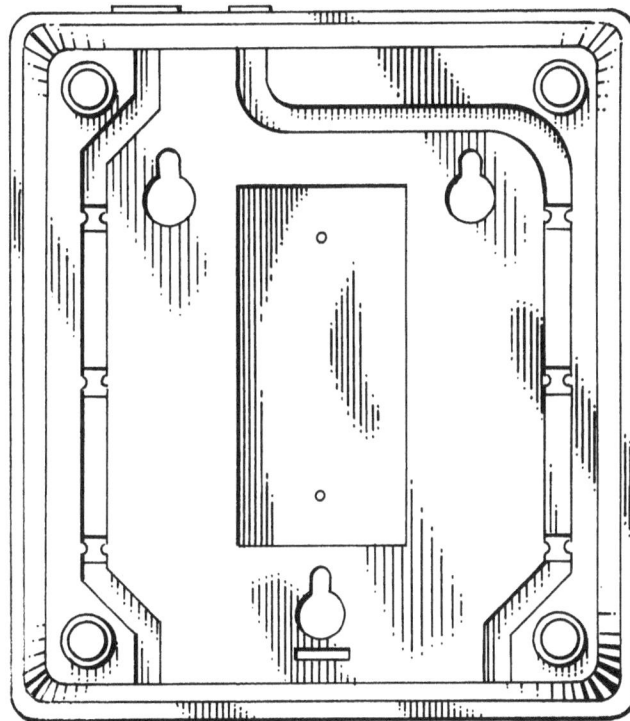

FIG. 6

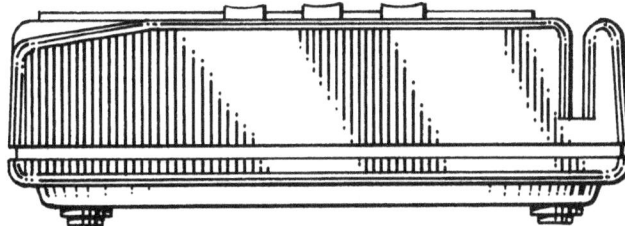

FIG. 7

Sheet 2 of Design Patent Drawings of a Credit Card Terminal.

12 / 16

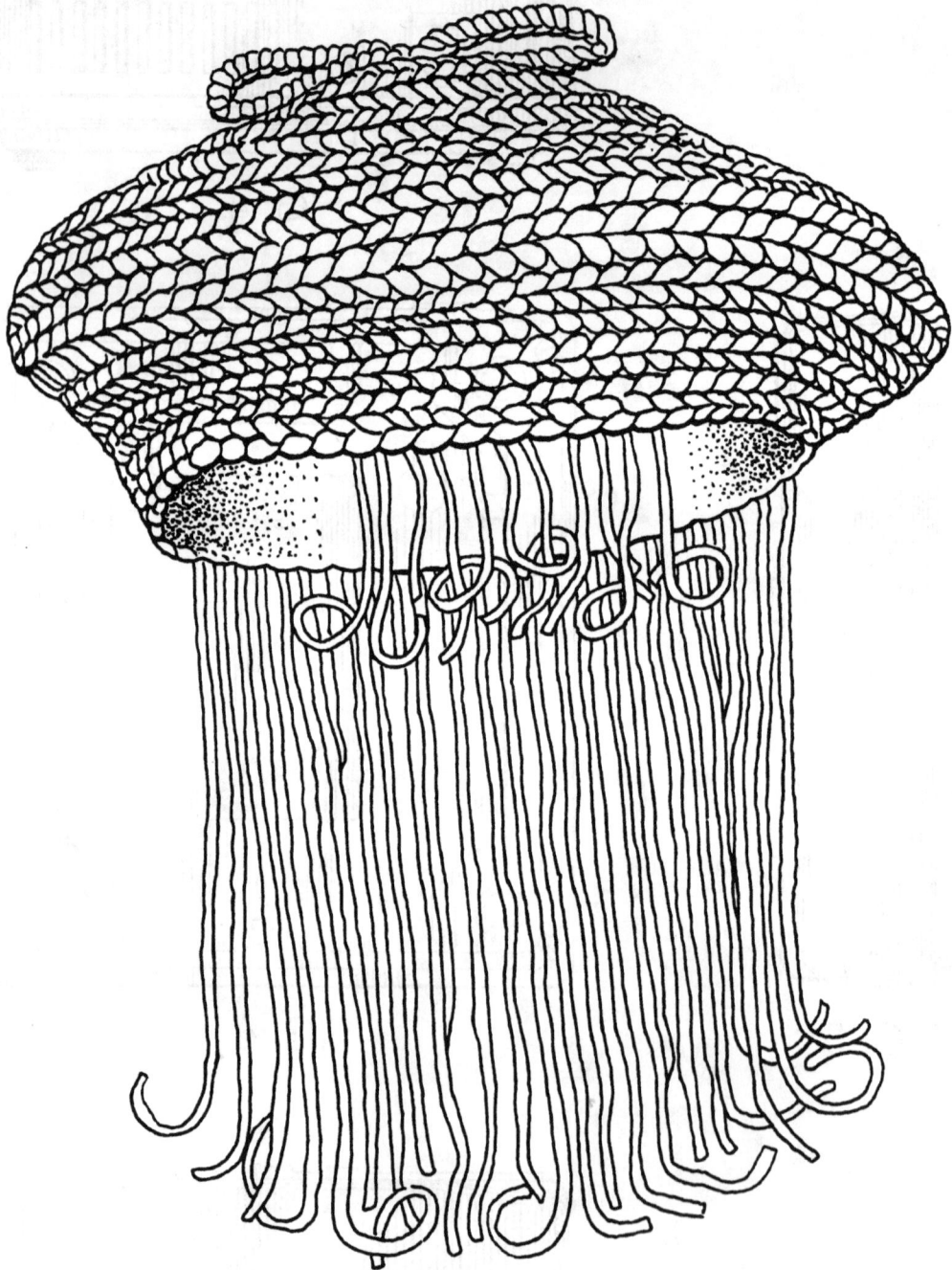

FIG. 14

Example of design patent drawing of a hair hat in ink line and stipple.

U.S. Design Classification Group IV Industrial Designs
(As of December 2012)

D1 *Edible Products*
D2 *Apparel and Haberdashery*
D3 Travel Goods, Personal Belongings, and Storage or Carrying Articles
D4 Brushware
D5 Textile or **Paper Yard Goods;** Sheet Material
D6 Furnishings
D7 Equipment for Preparing or Serving Food or Drink Not Elsewhere Specified
D8 Tools and Hardware
D9 Packages and Containers for Goods
D10 Measuring, **Testing** or Signaling Instruments
D11 *Jewelry, Symbolic Insignia, and Ornaments*
D12 Transportation
D13 Equipment for Production, Distribution, or Transformation of **Energy**
D14 Recording, Communication, or Information Retrieval Equipment
D15 Machines Not Elsewhere Specified
D16 *Photography and Optical Equipment*
D17 Musical Instruments
D18 Printing and Office Machinery
D19 *Office Supplies; Artists' and Teachers' Materials*
D20 Sales and Advertising Equipment
D21 Games, Toys and Sports Goods
D22 Arms, Pyrotechnics, Hunting and Fishing Equipment
D23 Environmental Heating and Cooling, Fluid Handling and Sanitary Equipment
D24 Medical and Laboratory Equipment
D25 Building Units and Construction Elements
D26 *Lighting*
D27 Tobacco and Smokers' Supplies
D28 *Cosmetic Products and Toilet Articles*
D29 *Equipment for Safety, Protection and Rescue*
D30 *Animal Husbandry*
      Reserved
D32 Washing, Cleaning or Drying Machines
D34 Material or Article Handling Equipment
D99 Miscellaneous

Notes on differences between the U.S. Design and the Locarno Classification:
1) Class indicated in *Italic* typeface are the same with differences in semantics.
2) Class indicated in **Bold** typeface are the same wording.
3) Class wording the same except for word(s) in **Bold** typeface.
4) Class completely or mostly different are in Regular typeface.
5) U.S. Class D7 is basically the same as Locarno Class 31.

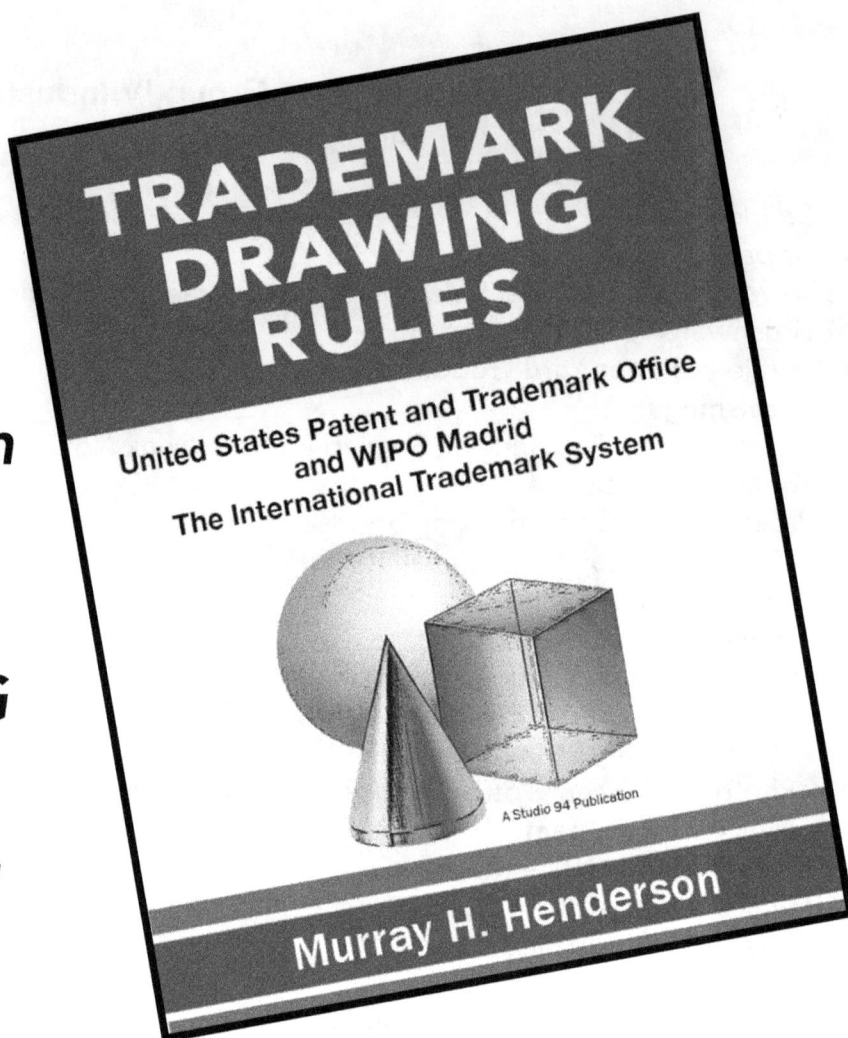

Chapter Four

Section 2
U.S. Design Patent Drawing Rules
under the Hague Agreement

Hague System Schematic
Filing with USPTO EFS-Web with US as a Designated Contracting Party

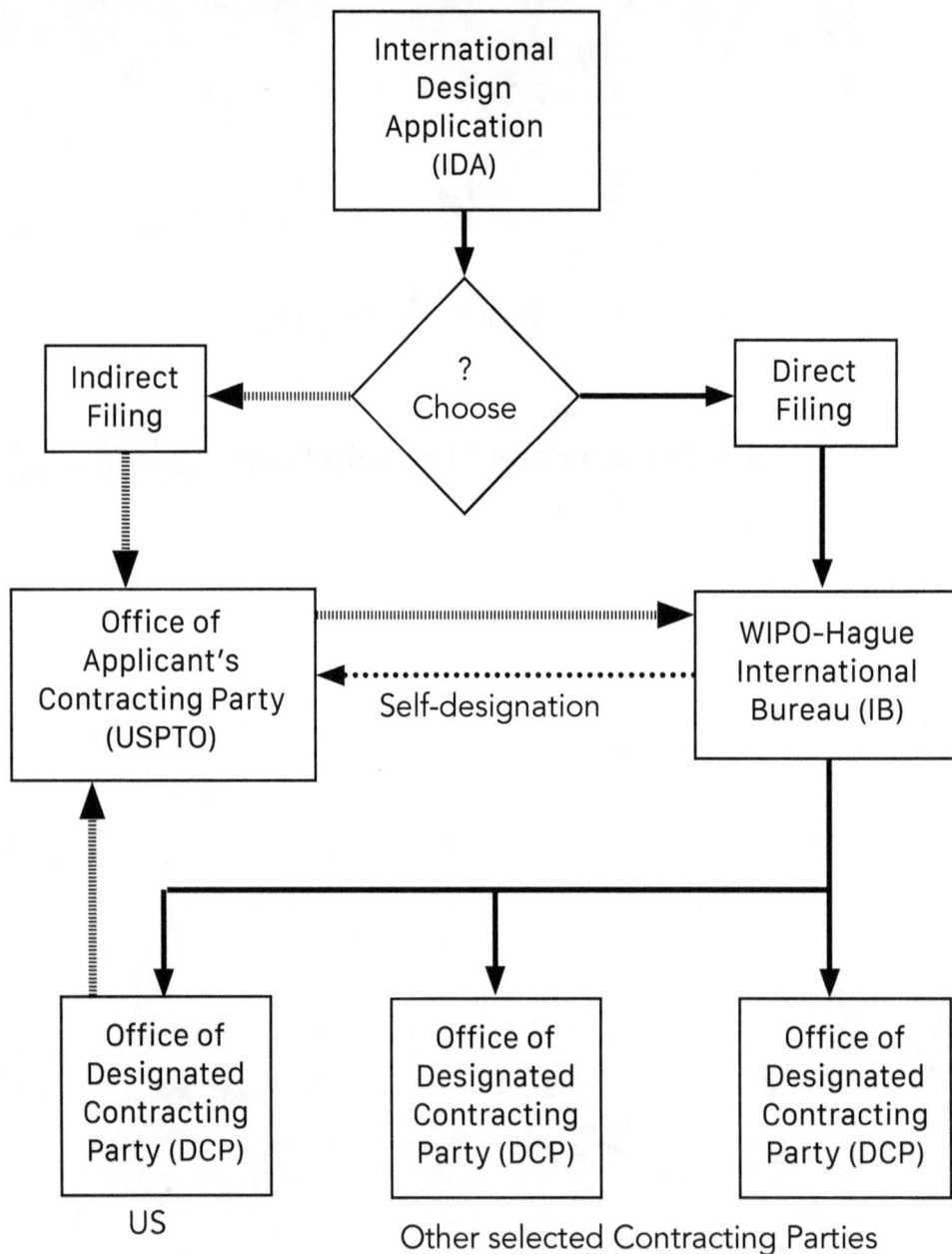

```
                    ┌─────────────────┐
                    │  International   │
                    │     Design       │
                    │  Application     │
                    │     (IDA)        │
                    └─────────────────┘
                             │
                             ▼
                           ◇ ?
                          Choose
              ┌───────────┘   └───────────┐
              ▼                           ▼
     ┌─────────────┐              ┌─────────────┐
     │  Indirect   │              │   Direct    │
     │   Filing    │              │   Filing    │
     └─────────────┘              └─────────────┘
              │                           │
              ▼                           ▼
     ┌─────────────────┐         ┌─────────────────┐
     │   Office of     │ ······▶ │  WIPO-Hague     │
     │  Applicant's    │         │ International    │
     │  Contracting    │ ◀······ │  Bureau (IB)    │
     │ Party (USPTO)   │ Self-designation         │
     └─────────────────┘         └─────────────────┘
              ▲                           │
              │             ┌─────────────┼─────────────┐
              │             ▼             ▼             ▼
     ┌─────────────┐ ┌─────────────┐ ┌─────────────┐
     │  Office of  │ │  Office of  │ │  Office of  │
     │ Designated  │ │ Designated  │ │ Designated  │
     │ Contracting │ │ Contracting │ │ Contracting │
     │ Party (DCP) │ │ Party (DCP) │ │ Party (DCP) │
     └─────────────┘ └─────────────┘ └─────────────┘
           US          Other selected Contracting Parties
```

2909.02 Reproductions (Drawings) [R-07.2015]
37 CFR 1.1026 Reproductions

Reproductions shall comply with the requirements of Rule 9 and Part Four of the Administrative Instructions.

Hague Rule 9
Reproductions of the Industrial Design

(1) [Form and Number of Reproductions of the Industrial Design]

(a) Reproductions of the industrial design shall, at the option of the applicant, be in the form of photographs or other graphic representations of the industrial design itself or of the product or products that constitute the industrial design. The same product may be shown from different angles; views from different angles shall be included in different photographs or other graphic representations.

(b) Any reproduction shall be submitted in the number of copies specified in the Administrative Instructions.

(2) [Requirements Concerning Reproductions]

(a) Reproductions shall be of a quality permitting all the details of the industrial design to be clearly distinguished and permitting publication.

(b) Matter that is shown in a reproduction but for which protection is not sought may be indicated as provided for in the Administrative Instructions.

(3) [Views Required]

(a) Subject to subparagraph (b), any Contracting Party bound by the 1999 Act which requires certain specified views of the product or products that constitute the industrial design or in relation to which the industrial design is to be used shall, in a declaration, so notify the Director General, specifying the views that are required and the circumstances in which they are required.

(b) No Contracting Party may require more than one view where the industrial design or product is two-dimensional, or more than six views where the product is three-dimensional.

(4) [Refusal on Grounds Relating to the Reproductions of the Industrial Design]

A Contracting Party may not refuse the effects of the international registration on the ground that requirements relating to the form of the reproductions of the industrial design that are additional to, or different from, those notified by that Contracting Party in accordance with paragraph (3)(a) have not been satisfied under its law. A Contracting Party may, however, refuse the effects of the international regis tration on the ground that the reproductions contained in the international regis tration are not sufficient to disclose fully the industrial design.

Administrative instructions concerning reproductions contained in Part Four of the Administrative Instructions for the Application of the Hague Agreement **("Administrative Instructions") are set forth on the following page(s):**

Hague Administrative Instructions Section 401:
Presentation of Reproductions

(a) One and the same international application may comprise both photographs and other graphic representations, in black & white or in color.

(b) Each reproduction accompanying an international application shall be submitted in a single copy.

(c) The photographs or other graphic representations accompanying an international application filed on paper shall be either pasted or printed directly onto a separate sheet of A4 paper that is white and opaque. The separate sheet of paper shall be used upright and shall not contain more than 25 reproductions.

(d) The reproductions accompanying an international application must be arranged in the orientation in which the applicant wishes them to be published. Where that application is filed on paper, a margin of at least 5 millimeters should be left around the representation of each industrial design.

(e) Each reproduction must fall within a right-angled quadrilateral containing no other reproduction or part of another reproduction and no numbering. The photographs or other graphic representations shall not be folded, stapled or marked in any way.

Hague Administrative Instructions Section 402:
Representation of the Industrial Design

(a) The photographs and other graphic representations shall represent the industrial design alone, or the product in relation to which the industrial design is to be used, to the exclusion of any other object, accessory, person or animal.

(b) The dimensions of the representation of each industrial design appearing in a photograph or other graphic representation may not exceed 16 x 16 centimeters, and in respect of at least one representation of each design, one of those dimensions must be at least 3 centimeters. With respect to the filing of international applications by electronic means, the International Bureau may establish a data format, the particulars of which shall be published on the web site of the Organization, to ensure compliance with these maximum and minimum dimensions.
(See page 196, Cropping Reproductions.)

(c) The following shall not be accepted:
    (i) technical drawings, particularly with axes and dimensions;
    (ii) explanatory text or legends in the representation.

Source: USPTO MPEP-9

Hague Administrative Instructions Section 403
Disclaimers and Matter That Does Not Form Part of the Industrial Design or the Product in Relation to Which the Industrial Design is to be Used

(a) Matter that is shown in a reproduction but for which protection is not sought may be indicated:

(i) in the description referred to in Rule 7(5)(a), and/or

(ii) by means of dotted or broken lines or coloring.

(b) Notwithstanding Section 402(a), matter that does not form part of the industrial design or the product in relation to which the industrial design is to be used may be shown in a reproduction if it is indicated in accordance with paragraph (a).

Hague Administrative Instructions Section 404
Requirements for Photographs and Other Graphic Representations

(a) The photographs supplied must be of professional standard and have all the edges cut at right angles. The industrial design must be shown against a neutral plain background. Photographs retouched with ink or correcting fluid shall not be allowed.

(b) Graphic representations must be of professional standard produced with drawing instruments or by electronic means and, where the application is filed on paper, must further be produced on good quality white, opaque paper, all of whose edges are cut at right angles. The industrial design represented may comprise shading and hatching to provide relief. Graphic representations executed by electronic means may be shown against a background, provided that it is neutral and plain and has only edges cut at right angles.

Source: USPTO MPEP-9

AUTHOR'S COMMENTS

Use a professional experienced in photographing products that are mostly studio shots that can capture the detail of the subject without shadows and other environmental objects that are not part of the design.

Use black & white or color, whichever is acceptable in your particular application.

Be prepared to give the photographer precise instructions of exactly what needs to be photographed for the various views, or better yet, you may want to act as art director on the photo shoot. It is your job, or the attorneys, to instruct the photographer on what is required in the way of views. It is the photographer's job to take good, clean, background-free photographs that are color, or gray-scale correct.

It is better to take too many pictures than too few.

Remember to have the photographer sign an *"assignment of copyright for the photographs"* so the inventor is the owner of the copyright on the patent application photographs. This would also apply to artists, if you have them do color drawings.

Hague Administrative Instructions Section 405
Numbering of Reproductions and Legends

(a) The numbering stipulated for multiple international applications shall appear in the margin of each photograph or other graphic representation. When the same industrial design is represented from different angles, the numbering shall consist of two separate figures separated by a dot (e.g., 1.1, 1.2, 1.3, etc. for the first design, 2.1, 2.2, 2.3, etc. for the second design, and so on).

(b) The reproductions shall be submitted in ascending numerical order.

(c) Legends to indicate a specific view of the product (e.g., "front view," "top view," etc.) may be indicated in association with the numbering of the reproduction. Reproductions in international design applications must comply with the requirements of Hague Agreement Rule 9 and Part Four of the Administrative Instructions. See 37 CFR 1.1026.

Pursuant to Rule 9, the reproductions of the industrial design shall, at the option of the applicant, be in the form of photographs or other graphic representations of the industrial design itself or of the product or products that constitute the industrial design. The same product may be shown from different angles; views from different angles shall be included in different photographs or other graphic representations. Pursuant to Administrative Instruction 401, only a single copy of each reproduction should be submitted.

The reproductions must be of a quality permitting all the details of the industrial design to be clearly distinguished and permitting publication. See Rule 9(2). The reproductions should represent the industrial design alone, or the product in relation to which the industrial design is to be used, without any other object, accessory, person, or animal. However, the reproduction may show matter for which protection is not sought if such matter is indicated as provided for in Administrative Instruction 403.

Pursuant to Rule 9(3)(a), a Contracting Party may require certain specified views of the product or products that constitute the industrial design or in relation to which the industrial design is to be used, if the Contracting Party has appropriately notified the International Bureau of the required views and the circumstances under which they are required. Information concerning specified views required by a Contracting Party pursuant to Rule 9(3)(a) is set forth in the section "Specific Requirements Concerning Views" of WIPO form DM/1.INF, "How to file an international application" currently available at WIPO's website at www.wipo.int/hague/en/forms/. Additional formal requirements for the reproductions (e.g., margins, paper, backgrounds, etc.) are set forth in the Administrative Instructions. In addition, technical requirements regarding image files, such as resolution, minimum and maximum image size, border width, etc., are set forth on the website of the International Bureau at www.wipo.int/ hague/en/ how_to/file/ prepare.html. Reproductions may be filed through the USPTO as an office of indirect filing via EFS-Web as PDF or JPEG files in accordance with the EFS-Web Legal Framework. See MPEP §§ 502.05 and 2909.02(a).

2909.02(a)   Reproductions Submitted Through EFS-Web [R-07.2015]

Reproductions of industrial designs are required in international design applications and may be submitted as drawings, photographs, or a combination thereof, and may be in black & white or in color. See Rule 9 and Part Four of the Administrative Instructions for the Application of the Hague Agreement. Reproductions may be submitted through EFS-Web as PDF or JPEG files as set forth below. Technical requirements regarding image files, such as resolution, minimum and maximum image size, border width, etc., are also set forth on the website of the International Bureau at www.wipo.int/hague/en/how_to/file/ prepare.html.

Reproductions may be submitted as single page PDF or JPEG files by attaching the file(s) using the "Attach Reproductions" section of the "Attach Documents" screen. Alternatively, applicants may attach reproductions as PDFs (including multi-page PDFs) using the "Attach Documents other than Reproductions" section of the "Attach Documents" screen. Attaching compliant reproductions via the "Attach Reproductions" section, rather than the "Attach Documents other than Reproductions" section, may help to avoid incurring additional per page publication fees that might otherwise be required by the International Bureau. Each image file attached through the "Attach Reproductions" section should contain only one view of the design. The "Attach Reproductions" section will prompt the user to assign a design and view number to each file attached under this section.

In accordance with the technical requirements set forth by the International Bureau, EFS-Web will not permit submission of any PDF or JPEG file via the "Attach Reproductions" section that exceeds a file size of two megabytes. For JPEG submissions, EFS-Web will provide warnings where requirements pertaining to image resolution and minimum and maximum dimensions have not been satisfied; EFS-Web does not check color mode or border size for JPEG images. For PDF submissions via the "Attach Reproductions" section, EFS-Web will not permit submission of any PDF file that is more than one page. In addition, EFS-Web does not check color mode, border size, resolution, or maximum or minimum dimensions of the reproduction (other than certain minimum and maximum page size dimensions) for PDF images. It is the responsibility of applicants to ensure that reproductions satisfy all applicable requirements.

Users attaching reproductions under either the "Attach Reproductions" section or the "Attach Documents other than Reproductions" section should use the document description "drawings – only black & white line drawings" or "drawing – other than black & white line drawings," as appropriate. EFS-Web will provide a warning to users about the possibility of incurring additional per page publication fees where reproductions are attached via the "Attach Documents other than Reproductions" section. EFS-Web will also provide a warning to users where a new international design application does not contain an indication that at least one reproduction is attached. See MPEP § 502.05 for additional information on using EFS-Web.

194

Locarno Classification (10th Edition) – List of Classes
(As of January 1, 2014)

Class 1 Foodstuffs

Class 2 Articles of Clothing and Haberdashery

Class 3 Travel Goods, **Cases, Parasols** and Personal Belongings, not elsewhere specified

Class 4 Brushware

Class 5 Textile **Piecegoods, Artificial** and **Natural** Sheet Material

Class 6 Furnishing

Class 7 Household Goods, not Elsewhere Specified

Class 8 Tools and Hardware

Class 9 Packages and Containers for the **Transport or Handling** of Goods

Class 10 **Clocks and Watches** and other Measuring Instruments, **Checking** and Signaling Instruments

Class 11 Articles of Adornment

Class 12 Means of Transport or **Hoisting**

Class 13 Equipment for Production, Distribution or Transformation of **Electricity**

Class 14 Recording, Communication or Information Retrieval Equipment

Class 15 Machines, not Elsewhere Specified

Class 16 Photographic, Cinematographic and Optical Apparatus

Class 17 Musical Instruments

Class 18 Printing and Office Machinery

Class 19 Stationery and Office Equipment, Artists' and Teaching Materials

Class 20 Sales and Advertising Equipment, **Signs**

Class 21 Games, Toys, **Tents** and Sports Goods

Class 22 Arms, Pyrotechnic Articles, Articles for Hunting, Fishing and **Pest Killing**

Class 23 Fluid Distribution Equipment, Sanitary, Heating, Ventilation and Air-conditioning Equipment, **Solid Fuel**

Class 24 Medical and Laboratory Equipment

Class 25 Building Units and Construction Elements

Class 26 Lighting Apparatus

Class 27 Tobacco and Smokers' Supplies

Class 28 Pharmaceutical and Cosmetic Products, Toilet Articles and Apparatus

Class 29 Devices and Equipment against Fire Hazards, for Accident Prevention and for Rescue

Class 30 Articles for the Care and Handling of Animals

Class 31 Machines and Appliances for Preparing Food or Drink, not elsewhere specified

Class 32 Graphic Symbols and Logos, Surface Patterns, Ornamentation

Notes on differences between the U.S. Design and the Locarno Classification:

1) Class indicated in *Italic typeface* are the same with differences in semantics.

2) Class wording the same except for word(s) in **Bold typeface.**

3) Class indicated in **Bold typeface** are the same wording.

4) Class completely or mostly different are in Regular typeface.

5) Locarno Class 31 is basically the same as U.S. Class D7.

Cropping Reproductions (Drawings) for WIPO Hague E-Filing

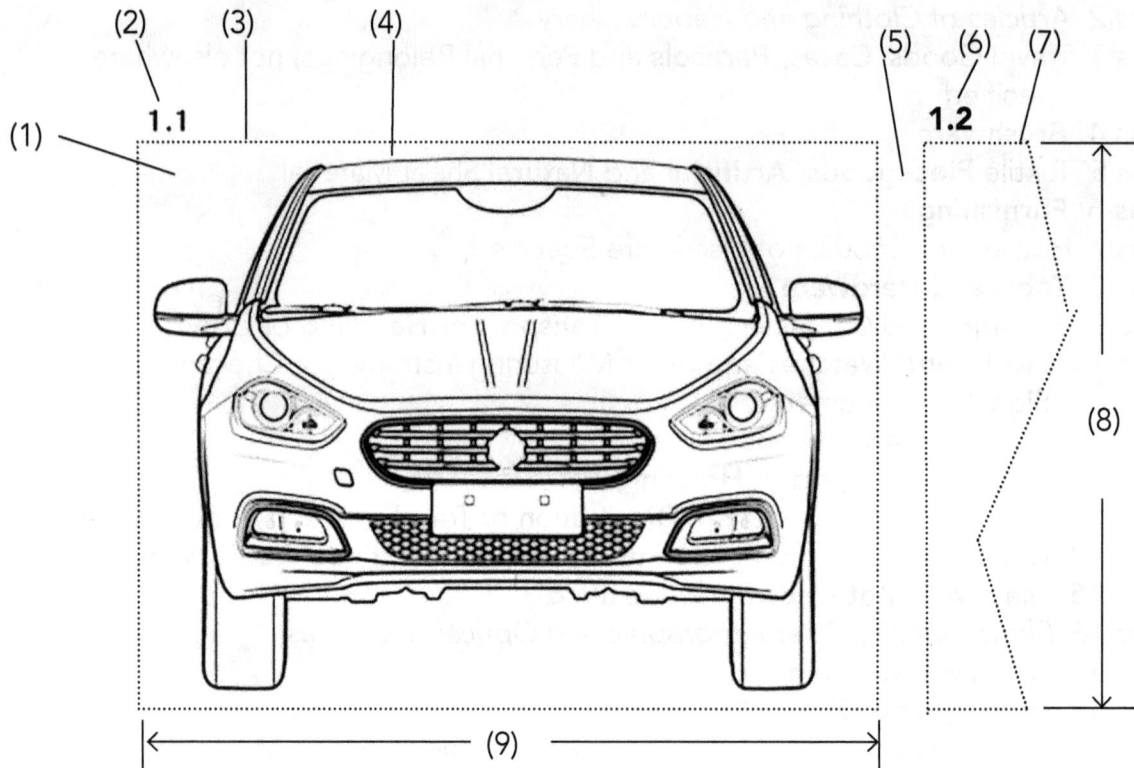

NOTES:

(1) - Anchor corner of all images submitted.

(2) - 1.1 applied by the Receiving Office (RO) automatically it signifies Design 1, Fig. 1
Applicant should identify JPEG image submitted as; [DRW_m001.001.jpg] and
indexed in the RO application form. If paper filing applicant applies the 1.1, 1.2

(3) - Cropped image border line.

(4) - Border/image area between 1 and 20 pixels.

(5) - Gap between separate reproduction images.

(6) - Design 1, Fig. 2.

(7) - Cropped Fig. 2 Reproduction, etc.

(8) - Maximum size 16cm (at 300 dpi); minimum size 3cm (at 300 dpi).

(9) - Maximum size 16cm (at 300 dpi); minimum size 3cm (at 300 dpi).

(10) - Image format: JPEG or TIFF (WIPO prefers JPEG); Line, Color: RGB or Grayscale
(if submitted); maximum file size (per file): 2 Megabytes.

Source: WIPO Hague Express Database, DM/078 221
Locarno Class: 12-08
Fiat Auto Design 24.04.2012
Automobile image property of: Fiat Group Automobiles S.P.A.
Corso Giovanni Agnelii, 200, 1-10135 Torino (IT)
Image instruction notes by: Studio 94 Publishing

Chapter Four

Section 3
Reproduction (Drawing) Rules under the
WIPO Hague Agreement for the
Registration of Industrial Designs

Guidance on Preparing and Providing Reproductions in Order to Forestall Possible Refusals on the Ground of Insufficient Disclosure of an Industrial Design by Examining Offices

August 2016

(Rule 9(4) of the Common Regulations under the 1999 Act and the 1960 Act of the Hague Agreement)

GENERAL DISCLAIMER:

This Guidance is prepared in consultation with the Examining Offices under the Hague System. The purpose of this guidance is neither to be self-sufficient nor all inclusive; each guidance focuses on a separate issue elaborating ways to help the applicant to avoid a possible refusal. A table at the end of this Guidance indicates whether a specific guidance is recommended by a given Examining Office.

CONTENTS

I. **NOT ENOUGH VIEWS**
GUIDANCE NO. 1
(a) Provide a sufficient number of views.
(b) Provide explanations on the omitted views.
(c) Provide views showing disclaimed part of the product.

II. **UNCLEAR REPRESENTATIONS OF THE CLAIMED DESIGN**
GUIDANCE NO. 2
Provide other specific views.

III. **UNCLEAR RELIEF OR CONTOURS OF SURFACES OF A THREE-DIMENSIONAL PRODUCT**
GUIDANCE NO. 3
Provide shading, hatching, dots or lines that may be used to indicate relief or contours of surfaces of a three-dimensional product.

IV. **DIFFERENCE IN FORM/COLOR BETWEEN THE REPRESENTATIONS OF THE CLAIMED DESIGN**
GUIDANCE NO. 4
No mixing of the reproductions in different forms; no mixing of the representations in black and white and in color.

Source: WIPO | Hague: Read full information notice (HAGUE/2016/9)
Author: This Guidance was published at time of book publication.
See Guidance table on page 208.

Roadmap to Reproduction (Drawing) Rules in the
Hague Agreement on the Registration of Industrial Designs

Geneva Act Legal Framework
Hague System Legal Framework

Articles
Articles 1 - 34
(No reference to Drawings & Reproductions)

Common Regulations
Rules 1 - 37
(Rule 9 Reproductions (Drawings), Rule 10 Specimens)

Administrative Instructions (A.I.)
Nine Parts
Sections 101 - 902
(Part Four Requirements Concerning Reproductions)
....
How to file a Hague Agreement:
http://www.wipo.int/hague/en/how_to/file/prepare.html

Laws & Regulations of Contracting Parties (member countries):

1) USPTO Rules on filing a Domestic (Chap. 16) Design Patent Application
   (See MPEP, Chapter 1500 Desgn Patents)

2) USPTO Rules on filing a Hague Agreement Application
   (See MPEP, Chapter 2900 International Design Applications)

3) Japan has made a declaration under Rule 9(3) requiring, where the product is three-dimensional, a front view, a back view, a top view, a bottom view, a left-side view and a right-side view, each made in compliance with the method of orthographic projection. It is recommended to indicate a legend for all views to avoid a possible refusal by the JPO on the grounds of insufficient disclosure of an industrial design pursuant to Rule 9(4).

4) The Republic of Korea has made a declaration under Rule 9(3) specifying that the following specific views are required, respectively:
   • for a design of a set of articles: one view of the coordinated whole and corresponding views of each of its components, and
   • for a design for typefaces: views of the given characters, a sample sentence and typical characters.

WIPO
WORLD INTELLECTUAL PROPERTY ORGANIZATION

| IP Services | Policy | Cooperation | Reference | About IP | Inside WIPO |

Home   IP Services   Hague System

Hague – The International Design System

The Hague System for the International Registration of Industrial Designs provides a practical business solution for registering up to 100 designs in over 65 territories through filing one single international application.

How to file your application: Overview
http://www.wipo.int/hague/en/how_to/file/index.html

This section shows how to file an industrial design application through the Hague System.

- Entitlement: Who can help you determine if you have the right to file an international application through the Hague System.

- Fees and payment: Helps you estimate the final cost and describes the payment options.

- **Preparing reproductions: Gives practical advice and helps you prepare your reproductions before filing.**

- Create user account: Walks you through the creation of a user account, which is mandatory to use the E-Filing.

- **File: Walks you through the filing of your application.**

- After filing: Describes what happens to your application once the International Bureau of WIPO receives it.

Source: WIPO-Hague

Locating the Drawing and Reproduction Rules for the Hague System.

How to file your application: Prepare reproductions
http://www.wipo.int/hague/en/how_to/file/prepare.html

The following instructions explain how to prepare your design(s) for electronic filing.

Terminology: A "design" refers to the subject matter for which protection is sought, and a "reproduction" refers to photographs or other graphic representations representing the design.

A design may be represented by several reproductions showing different views of the design.

Technical requirements regarding image files

These instructions help to ensure that your image files comply with the technical requirements under the Hague System. Moreover, they help to preserve the quality of the publication of your reproductions.

Summary of technical requirements for image files
used in the
Hague System E-Filing Portfolio Manager

Image format	JPEG or TIFF
Resolution	300 x 300 dpi
Minimum size	3 cm 3 cm (at 300 dpi)
Maximum size	16 cm x 16 cm (at 300 dpi)
Maximum file size (per file)	2 Megabytes)
Color	RGB or Grayscale
Borders	Between 1 and 20 pixels

NOTE: More on technical requirements regarding image files on the following page.

Providing quality image files

Image files with a low resolution (72 dpi or 150 dpi) will be scaled up to the minimum size of 3cm x 3cm 300 dpi. The result will be a blurry image where the details of the designs are not displayed. Images that are optimized for web, embedded in other documents or shot with smartphones are likely to have a low resolution. It is recommended to provide images with a native resolution of 300 dpi.

What is the resolution (or dpi) of my image?

The resolution corresponds to the density of information of your image. 300 x 300 dpi means that there are 300 pixels (or points) in a surface of one inch (2.54 cm). For optimal quality, your images should be between 250 x 250 dpi and 300 x 300 dpi. **Less or more than that, the system will resize automatically your images to a resolution of 266 x 266 dpi.**

How to keep proportions of your design consistent

To avoid undesired scaling and loss of proportions of you different images, ensure that all your reproductions have the same resolution, ideally 300 x 300 dpi. Providing image files in a resolution higher than 300 x 300 dpi shall not improve the quality of your publication, since the reproduction is automatically scaled down to 266 x 266 dpi.

Borders between 1 and 20 pixels

It is important to keep at least one pixel of border. This will avoid loosing information when your image is cropped for publication. Also, the image file must be trimmed to avoid having large borders. A trim between 1 and 20 pixels is suggested.

Source: WIPO-Hague

AUTHOR'S COMMENTS

1 – 300 dpi is the "sweet-spot" for all image resolution.

2 – No, you cannot file an application with your smartphone.

3 – Addressing the stubborn applicants out there who are going to do it their way and when there are problems blame it on the USPTO or WIPO – follow the guidelines!

4 – See page 47 for reference to large borders.

Common Regulations
Under the 1999 Act and the 1960 Act of the Hague Agreement
(as in force on January 1, 2015)

TABLE OF CONTENTS

• •

Rule 9
Reproductions of the Industrial Design

(1) *[Form and Number of Reproductions of the Industrial Design]*

(a) Reproductions of the industrial design shall, at the option of the applicant, be in the form of photographs or other graphic representations of the industrial design itself or of the product or products that constitute the industrial design. The same product may be shown from different angles; views from different angles shall be included in different photographs or other graphic representations.

(b) Any reproduction shall be submitted in the number of copies specified in the Administrative Instructions.

(2) *[Requirements Concerning Reproductions]*

(a) Reproductions shall be of a quality permitting all the details of the industrial design to be clearly distinguished and permitting publication.

(b) Matter which is shown in a reproduction but for which protection is not sought may be indicated as provided for in the Administrative Instructions.

(3) [Views Required]

(a) Subject to subparagraph (b), any Contracting Party bound by the 1999 Act that requires certain specified views of the product or products that constitute the industrial design or in relation to which the industrial design is to be used shall, in a declaration, so notify the Director General, specifying the views that are required and the circumstances in which they are required.

(b) No Contracting Party may require more than one view where the industrial design or product is two-dimensional, or more than six views where the product is three-dimensional.

(4) [Refusal on Grounds Relating to the Reproductions of the Industrial Design] A Contracting Party may not refuse the effects of the international registration on the ground that requirements relating to the form of the reproductions of the industrial design that are additional to, or different from, those notified by that Contracting Party in accordance with paragraph (3)(a) have not been satisfied under its law. A Contracting Party may however refuse the effects of the international registration on the ground that the reproductions contained in the international registration are not sufficient to disclose fully the industrial design.

Rule 10
Specimens of the Industrial Design
Where Deferment of Publication Is Requested

(1) [Number of Specimens] Where an international application governed exclusively by the 1999 Act contains a request for deferment of publication in respect of a two-dimensional industrial design and, instead of being accompanied by the reproductions referred to in Rule 9, is accompanied by specimens of the industrial design, the following number of specimens shall accompany the international application:

(i) one specimen for the International Bureau, and

(ii) one specimen for each designated Office that has notified the International Bureau under Article 10(5) of the 1999 Act that it wishes to receive copies of international registrations.

(2) [Specimens] All the specimens shall be contained in a single package. The specimens may be folded. The maximum dimensions and weight of the package shall be specified in the Administrative Instructions.

Administrative Instructions
for the Application of the Hague Agreement
(as in force on July 1, 2014)

TABLE OF CONTENTS

AUTHOR'S COMMENTS
In regard to two-dimensional designs such as Locarno Class 5 –
Textile Piecegoods; and Class 32 – Graphic Symbols and Logos, Surface
Patterns and Ornamentation, these Class subjects require only
one figure for submission to the Hague Agreement
on the registration of Industrial Designs.

There are occasions when these two-dimensional designs
are produced for the goods and you can use the same
graphic images for both the design registration
and the production of the goods (specimens),
as long as you follow the rules on disclosure.

NOTE:
**These two-dimensional designs are generally in color.
Sometimes you can scan the specimen and use it for registration.**

Part Four
Requirements Concerning Reproductions and Other Elements of the International Application

Section 401: Presentation of Reproductions

(a) One and the same international application may comprise both photographs and other graphic representations, in black & white or in color.

(b) Each reproduction accompanying an international application shall be submitted in a single copy.

(c) The photographs or other graphic representations accompanying an international application filed on paper shall be either pasted or printed directly onto a separate sheet of A4 paper which is white and opaque. The separate sheet of paper shall be used upright and shall not contain more than 25 reproductions.

(d) The reproductions accompanying an international application must be arranged in the orientation in which the applicant wishes them to be published. Where that application is filed on paper, a margin of at least 5 millimeters should be left around the representation of each industrial design.

(e) Each reproduction must fall within a right-angled quadrilateral containing no other reproduction or part of another reproduction and no numbering. The photographs or other graphic representations shall not be folded, stapled or marked in any way.

Section 402: Representation of the Industrial Design

(a) The photographs and other graphic representations shall represent the industrial design alone, or the product in relation to which the industrial design is to be used, to the exclusion of any other object, accessory, person or animal.

(b) The dimensions of the representation of each industrial design appearing in a photograph or other graphic representation may not exceed 16 x 16 centimeters, and in respect of at least one representation of each design, one of those dimensions must be at least 3 centimeters. With respect to the filing of international applications by electronic means, the International Bureau may establish a data format, the particulars of which shall be published on the website of the Organization, to ensure compliance with these maximum and minimum dimensions.

(c) The following shall not be accepted:
   1. (i) technical drawings, particularly with axes and dimensions;
   2. (ii) explanatory text or legends in the representation.

(Continued on next page).

Section 403: Disclaimers and Matter That Does Not Form Part of the Industrial Design or the Product in Relation to Which the Industrial Design is to be Used

(a) Matter that is shown in a reproduction but for which protection is not sought may be indicated

    1. (i) in the description referred to in Rule 7(5)(a), and/or

    2. (ii) by means of dotted or broken lines or coloring.

(b) Notwithstanding Section 402(a), matter that does not form part of the industrial design or the product in relation to which the industrial design is to be used may be shown in a reproduction if it is indicated in accordance with paragraph (a).

Section 404: Requirements for Photographs and Other Graphic Representations

(a) The photographs supplied must be of professional standard and have all the edges cut at right angles. The industrial design must be shown against a neutral, plain background. Photographs retouched with ink or correcting fluid shall not be allowed.

(b) Graphic representations must be of professional standard produced with drawing instruments or by electronic means and, where the application is filed on paper, must further be produced on good quality white, opaque paper, all of whose edges are cut at right angles. The industrial design represented may comprise shading and hatching to provide relief. Graphic representations executed by electronic means may be shown against a background, provided that it is neutral and plain and has only edges cut at right angles.

Section 405: Numbering of Reproductions and Legends

(a) The numbering stipulated for multiple international applications shall appear in the margin of each photograph or other graphic representation. When the same industrial design is represented from different angles, the numbering shall consist of two separate figures separated by a dot (e.g., 1.1, 1.2, 1.3, etc. for the first design, 2.1, 2.2, 2.3, etc. for the second design, and so on).

(b) The reproductions shall be submitted in ascending numerical order.

(c) Legends to indicate a specific view of the product (e.g., "front view," "top view," etc.) may be indicated in association with the numbering of the reproduction.

AUTHOR'S COMMENTS

A) Ref. Section 403 (a) Matter that is shown in reproduction: if it is a line drawing it can be illustrated with "broken lines. If it is a photograph and you use coloring, blue works better because it fades if copied in monotone, whereas red will print black. Better yet, remove the matter with image editing software.

B) Legends such as "front view," etc. are generally required by Contracting Parties that use them for translation into other languages. (See page 199.)

GUIDANCE	GUIDANCE to be taken into account/not taken into account when designating a given Contracting Party							
	HU	JP	KG	KR	MD	RO	SY	US
GUIDANCE NO. 1								
(a)(i) Submit six views of a three-dimensional product or two views of a two-dimensional product.		◎		O	O	◎	◎	*
(a)(ii) Submit perspective views instead of six views.	O			O	O	O	O	*
(a)(iii) Make views to be in the same scale		◎		O	◎	◎	◎	O
(a)(iv) Indicate the direction (angle) of each view.	X	◎		O	O	◎	◎	◎
(a)(v) Submit a sufficient number of views for each of the multiple designs	◎	◎		◎	O		O	◎
In a situation where an applicant wishes to omit a certain view(s):								
(b) Explain which view(s) are omitted and why they were omitted.	X	◎		◎	O	O	◎	*
In a situation where an applicant seeks protection of a certain part of the product:								
(c)(i) Submit view(s) of a part(s) of the product for which protection is not sought, showing it by means of a disclaimer.	◎	◎		◎	◎	◎	◎	*
(c)(ii.) Explain the means to indicate the disclaimed part.	O	◎		O	O	◎	◎	◎
GUIDANCE NO. 2								
(a) Submit another specific view at the time of filing for a clearer disclosure of the configuration of a certain part of the product where necessary to adequately disclose the design.	◎	◎		O	O	O	◎	◎
(b) Provide an appropriate legend/description of the other specific view.	X	◎		O	O	O	◎	◎
(c) Indicate which portion of the product is shown in a cross-sectional or enlarged view.	X	◎		O	◎	O	◎	◎
GUIDANCE NO. 3								
(a) Provide shading, hatching or lines that may be used to indicate relief or contours of the surface of the product.	O			O	O	O	O	◎
(b) Do not provide shading, hatching or lines on unclaimed subject matter where they lead to confusion as to the scope of the claimed design.	◎				◎		X	◎
(c) Explain the purpose of the shading, hatching or lines provided in the representation.	X	◎		O	O	O	◎	O
GUIDANCE NO. 4								
(a) No mixing of reproductions in different forms.	◎	O		O	O	O	O	◎
(b) No mixing of representations in black and white and in color.	◎	◎		O	◎	O	◎	◎

◎: Highly recommended   O: Recommended   X: Not recommended   * Appropriateness of use is dependent on circumstances. Refer to detailed guidance.

HU: Hungary; JP: Japan; KG: Kyrgyzstan; KR: Republic of Korea; MD: Republic of Moldova; RO: Romania; SY: Syrian Arab Republic; US: The United States of America

Guidance table for reproductions in choosing your designated Contracting Party.

Source: WIPO-Hague

Chapter Five

DRAWING CORRECTIONS

Section 1 - USPTO Drawing Corrections

Section 2 - WIPO PCT & Hague Drawing Corrections

Chapter Five

DRAWING CORRECTIONS

Section 1 - USPTO Drawing Corrections

Replacement, Modification, Corrections and Cancellation of Figures

608.02 - Drawing

Source: USPTO MPEP Chap.600 Contents with highlights by author.

1413   Drawings [R-11.2013]
37 CFR 1.173 Reissue specification, drawings, and amendments.

(a)

(2) Drawings. Applicant must submit a clean copy of each drawing sheet of the printed patent at the time the reissue application is filed. If such copy complies with § **1.84**, no further drawings will be required. Where a drawing of the reissue application is to include any changes relative to the patent being reissued, the changes to the drawing must be made in accordance with paragraph (b)(3) of this section. The Office will not transfer the drawings from the patent file to the reissue application.

A clean copy (e.g., good quality photocopies free of any extraneous markings) of each drawing sheet of the printed patent must be supplied by the applicant at the time of filing of the reissue application. If the copies meet the requirements of **37 CFR 1.84**, no further formal drawings will be required. New drawing sheets are not to be submitted, unless some change is made in the original patent drawings. Such changes must be made in accordance with **37 CFR 1.173(b)(3)**.

AMENDMENT OF DRAWINGS
37 CFR 1.173 Reissue specification, drawings, and amendments.

(b)

(3) Drawings. One or more patent drawings shall be amended in the following manner: Any changes to a patent drawing must be submitted as a replacement sheet of drawings that shall be an attachment to the amendment document. Any replacement sheet of drawings must be in compliance with § **1.84** and shall include all of the figures appearing on the original version of the sheet, even if only one figure is amended. Amended figures must be identified as "**Amended**," and any added figure must be identified as "**New**." In the event that a figure is canceled, the figure must be surrounded by brackets and identified as "**Canceled**." All changes to the drawing(s) shall be explained, in detail, beginning on a separate sheet accompanying the papers including the amendment to the drawings.

The provisions of **37 CFR 1.173(b)(3)** govern the manner of making amendments (changes) to the drawings in a reissue application. The following guidance is provided as to the procedure for amending drawings:

(A) Amending the original or printed patent drawing sheets by physically changing or altering them is not permitted. Any request to do so should be denied.

(Amendment of Drawings, continued)

(B) Where a change to the drawings is desired, applicant must submit a replacement sheet for each sheet of drawings containing a Figure to be revised. Any replacement sheet must comply with 37 CFR 1.84 and include all of the figures appearing on the original version of the sheet, even if only one figure is being amended. Each figure that is amended must be identified by placing the word "**Amended**" at the bottom of that figure. Any added figure must be identified as "**New**." In the event that a figure is canceled, the figure must be identified as "**Canceled**" and also surrounded by brackets. All changes to the figure(s) must be explained, in detail, beginning on a separate sheet that accompanies the papers including the amendment to the drawings.

(C) If desired, applicant may include a marked-up copy of any amended drawing figure, including annotations indicating the changes made. Such a marked-up copy must be clearly labeled as "**Annotated Marked-up Drawings**," and it must be presented in the amendment or remarks section that explains the change to the drawings. In addition, the examiner may desire a marked-up copy of any amended drawing figure, and so state in an Office action. A marked-up copy of any amended drawing figure, including annotations indicating the changes made, must be provided when required by the examiner.

(D) If any drawing change is not approved, or if any submitted sheet of drawings is not entered, the examiner will so inform the reissue applicant in the next Office action, and the examiner will set forth the reasons for same.

AUTHOR'S COMMENTS

In regard to drawing corrections, close collaboration between the patent illustrator and IP attorney is required to satisfy the patent examiner, especially if the patent will be a domestic and international filing. It is important to pay attention to the rules that govern placement of required **"identification of Amended, New, Canceled and/or Annotated Marked-up Drawings,"** as to their required location on the **drawings** and/or on the **drawing sheets**.

NOTE:

Elimination of PTO Form 948 Notice of Draftsperson's Patent Drawing Review. Effective on September 16, 2012, the Leahy-Smith America Invents Act (AIA) brought about the current procedure: the **"drawing formalities"** will be evaluated by the staff in the Office of Patent Application Processing (OPAP); drawings are reviewed for adequate reproduction for publication purposes only, this process occurs before the examiner begins examination of the application to determine if the drawings conform with 37 CFR § 1.83 and 37 CFR § 1.84. Referenced as the **"Substantive Examination"** (see page 153).

Chapter Five

DRAWING CORRECTIONS

Section 2 - WIPO PCT & Hague Drawing Corrections

PCT Newsletter 01/2005: Practical Advice

WARNING: Although the information that follows was correct at the time of original publication in the PCT Newsletter, some information may no longer be applicable; for example, amendments may have been made to the PCT Regulations and Administrative Instructions, as well as to PCT Forms, since the PCT Newsletter concerned was published; changes to certain fees and references to certain publications may no longer be valid. Wherever there is a reference to a PCT Rule, please check carefully whether the Rule in force at the date of publication of the advice has since been amended.

The importance of correcting defects in drawings

Q: *I recently filed a PCT application containing several pages of drawings. I have received an invitation from the receiving Office to correct certain defects in the drawings within a time limit set in the invitation. What would happen if I failed to respond within the time limit set by the receiving Office?*

A: Most international applications contain drawings since they provide an excellent means to better understand the invention. All drawings (including flow sheets and diagrams, which are considered drawings under PCT Rule 7(1)) must comply with the PCT standard for drawings contained in PCT Rules 11.10, 11.11 and, in particular, 11.13. Further details on the formality requirements for drawings can be found in paragraphs 143 to 178 of the PCT Applicant's Guide, Vol. I/A (www.wipo.int/pct/guide/en/index.html).

If a receiving Office finds that the submitted drawings do not comply with the PCT requirements, it will invite the applicant (Form PCT/RO/106) to correct any defects within a time limit set in the invitation. This could, for instance, be the case where the applicant, for the purposes of filing the PCT application, simply copied informal drawings that he or she had used for an earlier filed national application. If the applicant cannot meet the set time limit, the extension of that time limit will be at the discretion of the receiving Office (PCT Rule 26.2). Some receiving Offices (for example, RO/US) prefer, however, that the applicant does not file a separate request for an extension of the time limit, but simply furnishes the replacement pages of drawings as soon as possible. It is important that such replacement sheets reach the International Bureau before the technical preparations for publication are completed, therefore the closer it is to the scheduled international publication date, the less likely receiving Offices are to grant further extensions of time.

If an applicant fails to correct the defects in the drawings, the receiving Office is empowered under the Treaty to declare the international application to be considered withdrawn (Form PCT/RO/117) if it finds that, in accordance with PCT Rule 26.5, the international application does not meet the formal requirements of PCT Rule 11 to the extent necessary for the purposes of reasonably uniform international publication. If, however, the defects noted are not of such a nature that this standard of "reasonably uniform publication" would be affected, the international application should not be declared to be considered withdrawn and the International Bureau will proceed with the international publication of the application.

Even if the application continues to be processed in the international phase, examiners in the international search and preliminary examination procedures may experience problems if the quality of the drawings is very poor. It is understandable that receiving Offices do not want to consider the entire application withdrawn because of defects in the drawings, but allowing such applications to proceed can also have the effect of slowing examiners down in their work, both in performing the original search and in identifying whether the drawing is relevant for later searches, which may thus affect the quality of later searches.

If the original defective drawings are published, further difficulties could arise in the national phase if the defects in the drawings have not been corrected, and similarly, examiners in the national phase may have difficulties performing their search. In principle, under PCT Article 27(1), no national law shall require compliance with requirements relating to the form or contents of the international application different from or in addition to those that are provided for in the Treaty and the Regulations. That provision applies to the physical requirements of PCT Rule 11. However, if the requirements of PCT Rule 11 have not been complied with, any designated Office may, in accordance with PCT Rule 49.5(g), invite the applicant to correct the defects in the drawings during the national phase. Therefore, the fact that a receiving Office did not enforce the compliance with the requirements of PCT Rule 11.13 does not constitute protection against an invitation from a designated or elected Office to comply with those requirements after entry into the national phase. Moreover, the relatively high standard of PCT Rule 26.5 of "necessary for the purpose of the reasonably uniform international publication," does not bind designated or elected Offices to accept drawings as they are contained in international applications where the physical requirements provided in PCT Rule 11 have not been complied with.

Note that if essential elements of the invention are contained in a drawing, but that drawing has been so poorly executed that those essential elements did not properly appear in the publication, designated and elected Offices could also challenge that the invention has not been properly disclosed. This may happen, for example, where drawings that were initially executed in color have been scanned or copied by the applicant to produce black & white drawings that are inferior in quality.
(It is recalled that, according to PCT Rule 11.13(a), "drawings shall be executed in durable, black, sufficiently dense and dark, uniformly thick and well-defined, lines and strokes without colorings." A "practical advice" article was written on the requirement to file drawings in black & white in PCT Newsletter No. 04/2003.)

We therefore strongly recommend that invitations from receiving Offices to correct formal defects in drawings be taken seriously and be resolved within the set time limits. This will avoid any loss of rights and will avoid unnecessary additional work, effort and cost, for both applicants and designated/elected Offices, during the national phase. Further details on the correction of defects in drawings may also be found in the PCT Receiving Office Guidelines, paragraphs 153 to 159 (www.wipo.int/pct/en/texts/pdf/ro.pdf.)

It is important to note that when correcting formal defects in drawings, those drawings should not be modified. Should the applicant wish to correct an obvious error in a drawing, a request for rectification of an obvious error should be filed with the International Searching Authority (PCT Rule 91).

Source: WIPO

Areas where patent drawing irregularities can hold up a PCT application

Drawing and reproduction irregularities that require corrections can holdup a PCT patent application at various stages of the patent process: 1) In the National stage "pre-examination process," 2) the PCT filing formalities review, 3) the International search, 4) the International publication and, 5) a National "substantive examination."

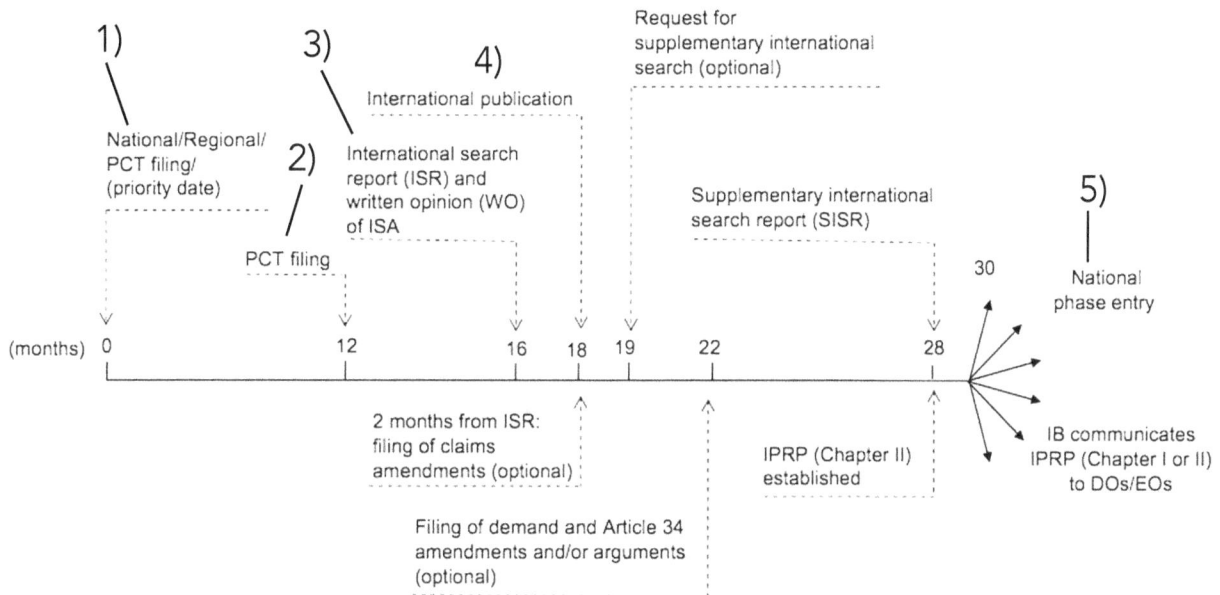

Source: Chart from WIPO-PCT Application Guide - International Phase.

AUTHOR'S COMMENTS
See author's chart on the differences between a
"Formalities" and a "Substantive Examination" on pages 152 and 153.

ANNEX

CONTENTS

SYMBOLS

Graphical drawing symbols, as indicated in 37 CFR 1.84(n), may be used for the conventional elements when appropriate. The elements for which such symbols and labeled representations are used must be adequately identified in the specification.

Known devices should be illustrated by symbols that have a universally recognized conventional meaning and are generally accepted in the art, provided no further detail is essential for understanding the subject matter of the claimed invention. Other symbols may be used on condition that they are not likely to be confused with existing conventional symbols, and that they are readily identifiable.

In general, in lieu of a symbol, a conventional element, combination, or circuit may be shown by an appropriately labeled rectangle, square, or circle; abbreviations should not be used unless their meanings are evident and not confusing with the abbreviations used in the suggested symbols. In electrical symbols, an arrow through an element indicates variability thereof; dotted-line connection of arrows indicates ganging thereof; and inherent property (as resistance) may be indicated by showing symbol (for resistor) in dotted lines.

The American National Standards Institute (ANSI) is a private nonprofit organization whose numerous publications include some that pertain to graphical symbols. Such publications for example, **Graphic Symbols for Fluid Power Diagrams, IEEE Standard Graphic Symbols for Logic Functions, Graphic Symbols for Electrical and Electronics Diagrams** are considered to be generally acceptable in patent drawings. ANSI headquarters are at 1899 L Street, NW, 11th Floor, Washington, DC 20036, with offices at 25 West 43rd Street, 4th Floor, New York, NY 10036. The organization's Internet address is **www.ansi.org.**

Although ANSI documents and other published sources may be used as guides during the selection of graphic symbols for patent drawings, the following should be kept in mind:
- The Office will not "approve" any published collection of symbols as a group, because the use and clarity of symbols must be decided on a case-by-case basis.
- Overly specific symbols should be avoided.
- Symbols with unclear meanings should be labeled for clarification.
- It is always necessary for the specification to include a complete description of the subject matter disclosed.

When the material is an important feature of the invention, the symbols shown on Pages 223 through 227 should be used.

USPTO MATERIAL SURFACE & SECTIONAL CODING

KEY

SURFACE	SECTION

ELEVATION IN SECTION

1 — Elevation | ALL METALS

2 — Transparent Material | CELLULOID, GLASS

3 — CONCRETE

4 — WOOD

5 — Refractory Material | PORCELAIN, CERAMIC QUARTZ, MICA

6 — CORK

7 — FIBRE, LEATHER

8 — THERMAL INSULATION

9 — Loose Packed | SECTION OF SAND SILICON OR THE LIKE

10 — SECTION OF SPONGE RUBBER

11 — Resilient Material | SECTION OF RUBBER OR ELECTRICAL INSULATION

12 — Small Large Surfaces | INSULATION | ELEVATION OF ELECTRICAL INSULATION

13 — PLASTIC

14 — LIQUID

15 — WIRE OR SCREENING

16 — CLOTH OR FABRIC-FELT

17 — ADHESIVE

18 — SUPER-CONDUCTOR

Sheet 1, Surface and Sectional Coding.

223

USPTO MATERIAL SURFACE & SECTIONAL CODING

KEY

SURFACE	SECTION

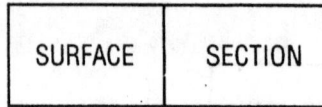

ELEVATION IN SECTION

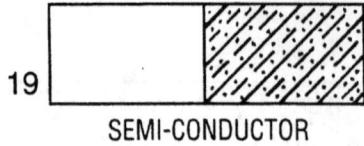

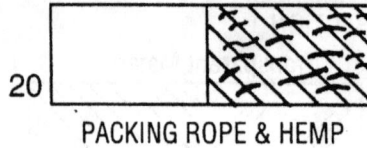

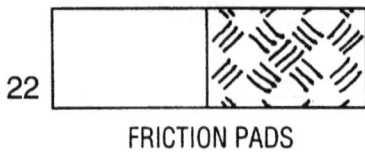

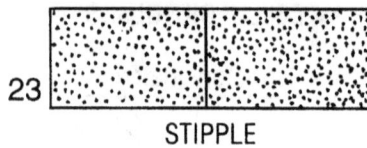

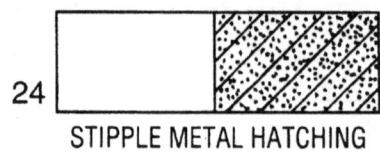

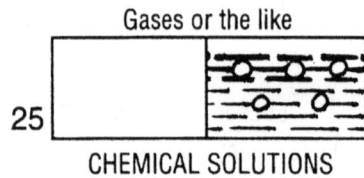

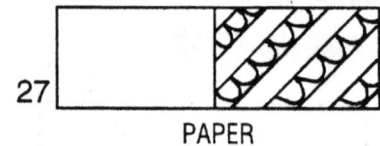

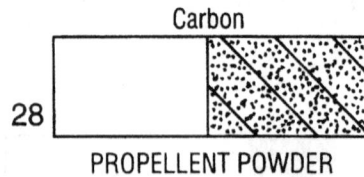

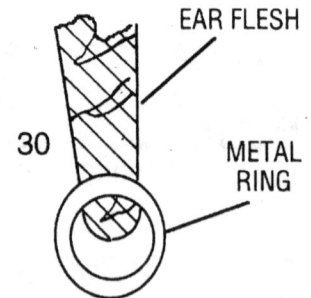

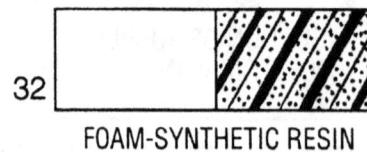

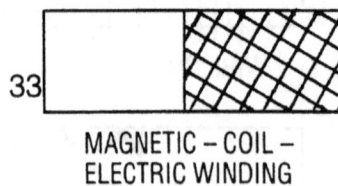

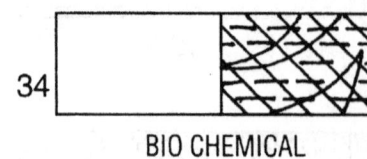

19 SEMI-CONDUCTOR

20 PACKING ROPE & HEMP

21 SYNTHETIC SPONGE

22 FRICTION PADS

23 STIPPLE

24 STIPPLE METAL HATCHING

Gases or the like

25 CHEMICAL SOLUTIONS

26 TAR & PITCH

27 PAPER

Carbon

28 PROPELLENT POWDER

29 CHEESE

30 EAR FLESH / METAL RING

31 EARTH

32 FOAM-SYNTHETIC RESIN

33 MAGNETIC – COIL – ELECTRIC WINDING

34 BIO CHEMICAL

35 HUMAN VEINS

NOTES:
1. Porous sintered metal: Powdered metal fused together-use stipple metal hatching.
2. Dielectric: is non conducting material, e.g., plastic, rubber, etc.
3. Abscissa: Horizontal line. ———
4. Ordinate: Vertical line. |

Sheet 2, Surface and Sectional Coding.

Electrical Symbols

RESISTOR	VARIABLE RESISTOR	POTENTIOMETER	RHEOSTATS	CONDENSERS	GANGED VARIABLE CONDENSERS
1	2	3	4	5	6
INDUCTORS	INDUCTOR ADJUSTABLE CORE	INDUCTOR OR REACTOR POWDERED MAGNETIC CORE	TRANSFORMER SATURABLE CORE	TRANSFORMER AIR CORE	VARIABLE TRANSFORMER
7	8	9	10	11	12
TRANSFORMER MAGNETIC CORE	AUTO-TRANSFORMER ADJUSTABLE	CROSSED AND JOINED WIRES	MAIN CIRCUITS / SHUNT OR CONTROL CIRCUITS	FUSE	COAXIAL CABLES
13	14	15	16	17	18
SHIELDING	BATTERY	THERMOELEMENT	BELL	AMMETER	MILLIAMMETER
19	20	21	22	23	24
VOLTMETER	GALVANOMETER	WATTMETER	SWITCH	DOUBLE POLE SWITCH	DOUBLE POLE DOUBLE THROW SWITCH
25	26	27	28	29	30
PUSH BUTTON TWO POINT MAKE	SELECTOR OR CONNECTOR OR FINDER SWITCH	CIRCUIT BREAKER OVERLOAD	RELAY	POLARIZED RELAY	DIFFERENTIAL RELAY
31	32	33	34	35	36
ANNUNCIATORS SIDE FRONT	DROP ANNUNCIATOR	DRUM TYPE SWITCH OR CONTROL	COMMUTATOR MOTOR OR GENERATOR	REPULSION MOTOR	INDUCTION MOTOR THREE PHASE SQUIRREL CAGE
37	38	39	40	41	42
INDUCTION MOTOR PHASE WOUND SECONDARY	SYNCHRONOUS MOTOR OR GEN. THREE PHASE	MOTOR GENERATOR	ROTARY CONVERTER THREE PHASE	FREQUENCY CHANGER THREE PHASE	TROLLEYS
43	44	45	46	47	48
THIRD RAIL SHOE	RECEIVERS	TRANSMITTER OR MICROPHONE	TELEPHONE HOOK	TELEGRAPH KEY	SWITCH BOARD PLUG AND JACK
49	50	51	52	53	54

Electrical Symbols.

Electrical Symbols – continued

PHONOGRAPH PICKUP 55	DYNAMIC SPEAKER 56	ANTENNA 57	LOOP ANTENNA 58	GROUND 59	SPARK GAP 60
LIGHTNING ARRESTER 61	DETECTOR OR RECTIFIER — Anode, Cathode — GENERIC 62	DETECTOR OR RECTIFIER — Anode, Cathode — CRYSTAL 63	PIEZOELECTRIC CRYSTAL 64	INCANDESCENT LAMP 65	MERCURY ARC RECTIFIER 66
ENVELOPE GAS FILLED 67	DIODE 68	TRIODE 69	PENTODE INDIRECTLY HEATED CATHODE 70	TRANSISTOR — EMITTER COLLECTOR BASE 71	TRANSISTOR — EMITTER COLLECTOR BASE 72
TRANSISTOR — NPN — JUNCTION TYPE 73	TRANSISTOR — PNP — JUNCTION TYPE 74	AMPLIFIER A 75	THERMIONIC FULL WAVE RECTIFIER 76	FULL WAVE RECTIFIER GAS FILLED 77	PHOTOELECTRIC CELL 78
GLOW DISCHARGE TUBE 79	X-RAY TUBE 80	CATHODE RAY TUBE 81	SPOT WELDING 82	DEPOSIT WELDING 83	

Mechanical Symbols

CONDUIT CROSSING AND INTERSECTING 1	SECTIONS LARGE ENDS — ROD — PIPE 2	SCREW THREAD 3	CLUTCH 4	FRICTION CLUTCH 5	BRAKE 6
FLEXIBLE COUPLING 7	FLUID COUPLING 8	SPROCKET AND CHAIN 9	SPUR GEARS 10	BEVEL GEARS 11	
WORM GEAR 12	SPUR GEARS SIDE VIEW 13	WELDS — PLAN — SECTION 14	SPOT WELD 15	INJECTOR NOZZLE 16	FIXED RESISTANCE 17

Electrical Symbols & Mechanical Symbols.

226

VARIABLE RESISTANCE 18	PUMP P 19	CONSTANT DELIVERY PUMP P CD 20	VARIABLE DELIVERY PUMP P VD 21	REVERSIBLE CONSTANT DELIVERY PUMP P RCD 22	REVERSIBLE VARIABLE DELIVERY PUMP P RVD 23
GEAR PUMP 24	ROTARY SLIDING VANE PUMP P RSV 25	CENTRIFUGAL PUMP P 26	LIFT PUMP P 27	FORCE PUMP P 28	PNEUMATIC DISCHARGE PUMP P 29
AIR LIFT PUMP 30	RAM 31	JET 32	STEAM ACCUMULATOR 33	MECHANICAL PRESSURE ACCUMULATOR 34	AIR PRESSURE ACCUMULATOR 35
RESERVOIR 36	MOTOR M 37	CONSTANT SPEED MOTOR M CS 38	VARIABLE SPEED MOTOR M VS 39	RECIPROCATING DIFFERENTIAL MOTOR 40	RECIPROCATING NON-DIFFERENTIAL MOTOR 41
GAS ENGINE TWO-CYCLE 42	GAS ENGINE FOUR-CYCLE 43	DIESEL ENGINE TWO-CYCLE 44	DIESEL ENGINE FOUR CYCLE 45	TURBINE 46	ROCKET MOTOR FLUID FUEL 47
ROCKET MOTOR SOLID FUEL 48	JET MOTOR 49	TURBO-JET 50	BOILER B 51	FIRE TUBE BOILER B FT 52	FLUE BOILER B FL 53
WATER TUBE BOILER B WT 54	JET CONDENSER C 55	SURFACE CONDENSER STEAM WATER C 56	JET HEATER H 57	SURFACE HEATER WATER STEAM H 58	VALVE V 59
THROTTLE VALVE V T 60	CHECK VALVE V CK 61	PRESSURE RELIEF VALVE V REL. 62	CONSTANT PRESSURE OUTLET VALVE V REG. CP 63	CONSTANT PRESSURE INLET VALVE CP V REG. 64	REDUCING VALVE V RED. 65
THREE-WAY VALVE 66	DISTRIBUTING VALVE V 67	THERMOSTATIC VALVE V THER. 68	BI-METALLIC THERMOSTAT 69	FILTER 70	HEAT EXCHANGER 71

Mechanical Symbols.

USPTO COLOR CODING

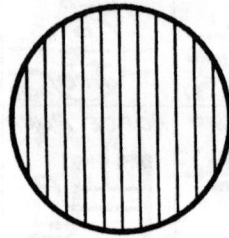

RED or PINK

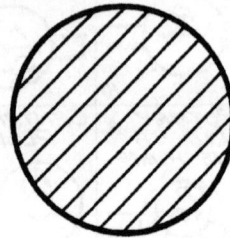

BROWN

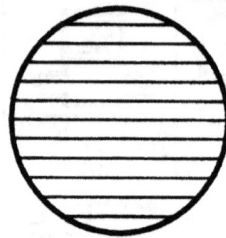

BLUE

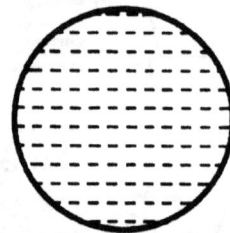

GREY or SILVER

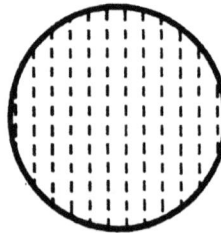

VIOLET or PURPLE

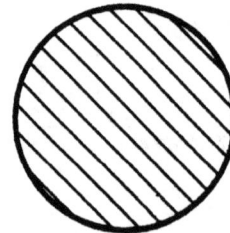

GREEN

ORANGE

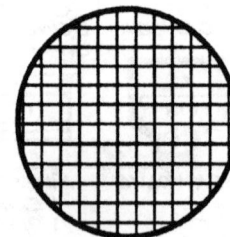

YELLOW or GOLD

Studio 94 Publishing 2001

Note: See following page for an example used in a Utility Patent.

Example: Color Coding Sheet.

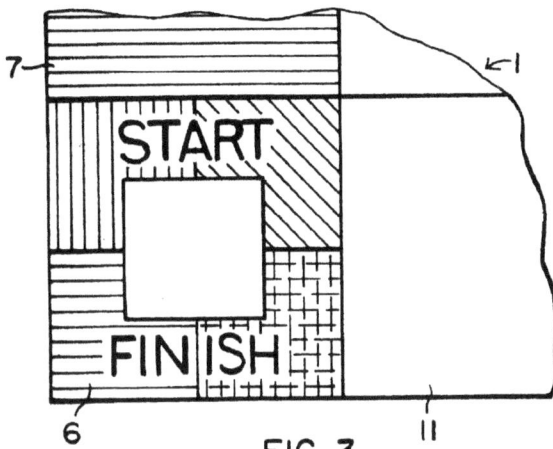

FIG. 3

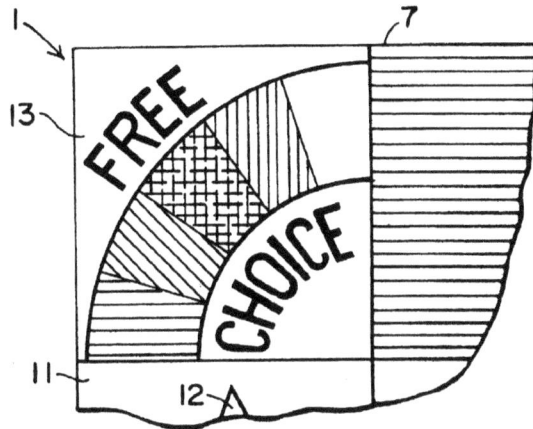

FIG. 4

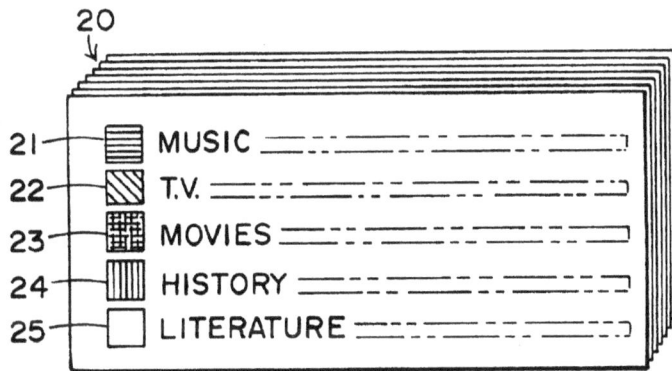

FIG. 5

EXAMPLE:
Used in a
utility patent
drawing.

AUTHOR'S NOTE

Color coding, or lining for color, is still used on some utility and
design patent drawings, but is no longer allowed on trademark drawings.
The advantage of black-ink lining for color is that all pages can be printed in black.
The disadvantage of it is that if you have, for example,
different shades of the same color, you cannot illustrate those shades with
this method. This *may* give you a reason to petition to use a color drawing.
**NOTE: At this time color drawings are not permitted
in international PCT applications.**

Examples of where I used lining for color:
Utility Patents: board games, outdoor games, toys and
medical packaging for safety.
Design Patents: packaging, tools, safety cones and vehicles.
Also **"Trade Dress"** used in design patents in conjunction with trademarks.

Example: Using Color Coding, or Lining, for Color on Patent Drawings.

Diagram of Page Showing Main Layout Requirements

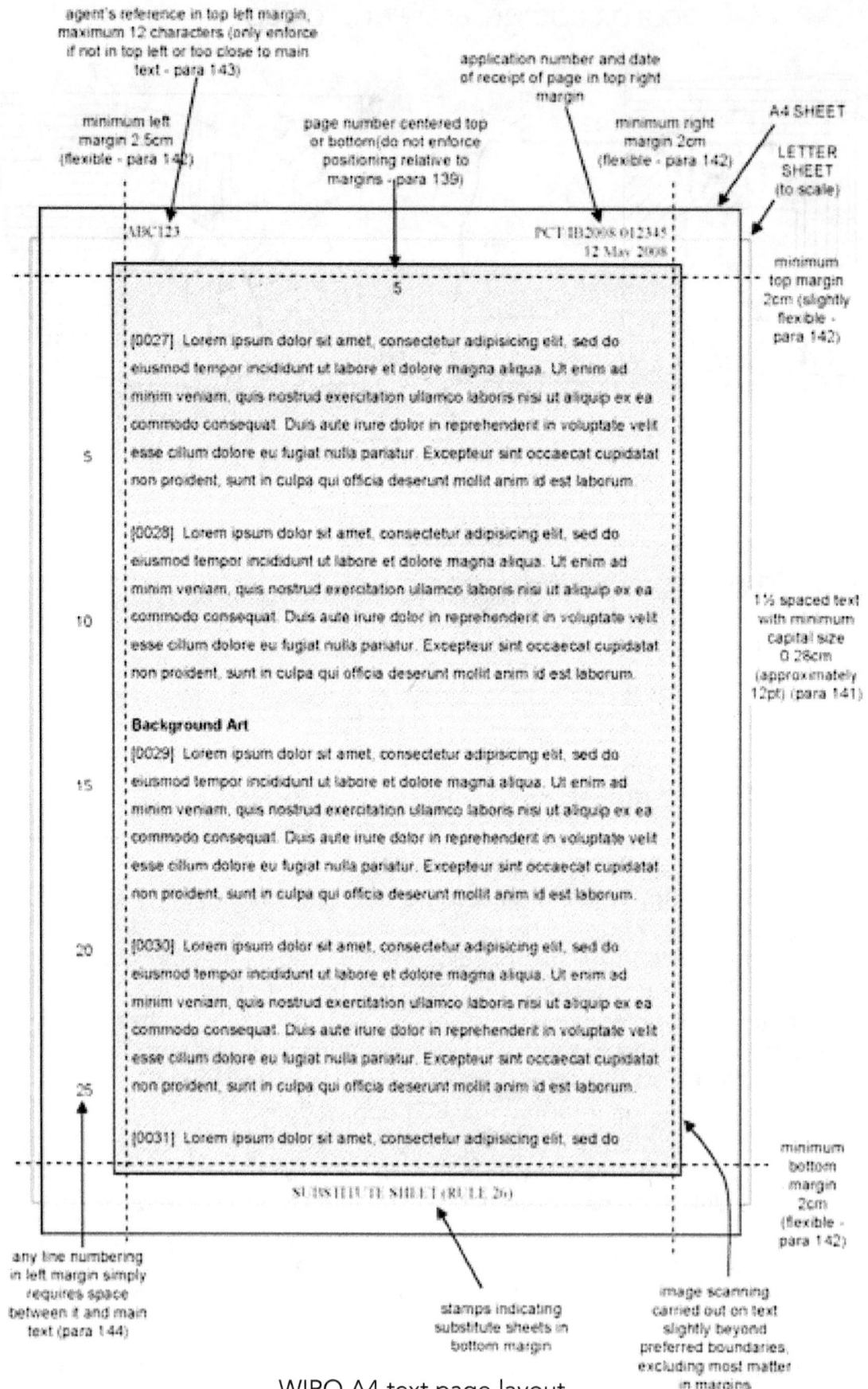

agent's reference in top left margin, maximum 12 characters (only enforce if not in top left or too close to main text - para 143)

application number and date of receipt of page in top right margin

minimum left margin 2.5cm (flexible - para 142)

page number centered top or bottom(do not enforce positioning relative to margins - para 139)

minimum right margin 2cm (flexible - para 142)

A4 SHEET

LETTER SHEET (to scale)

ABC123

PCT IB2008 012345
12 May 2008

minimum top margin 2cm (slightly flexible - para 142)

5

[0027] Lorem ipsum dolor sit amet, consectetur adipisicing elit, sed do eiusmod tempor incididunt ut labore et dolore magna aliqua. Ut enim ad minim veniam, quis nostrud exercitation ullamco laboris nisi ut aliquip ex ea commodo consequat. Duis aute irure dolor in reprehenderit in voluptate velit esse cillum dolore eu fugiat nulla pariatur. Excepteur sint occaecat cupidatat non proident, sunt in culpa qui officia deserunt mollit anim id est laborum.

5

[0028] Lorem ipsum dolor sit amet, consectetur adipisicing elit, sed do eiusmod tempor incididunt ut labore et dolore magna aliqua. Ut enim ad minim veniam, quis nostrud exercitation ullamco laboris nisi ut aliquip ex ea commodo consequat. Duis aute irure dolor in reprehenderit in voluptate velit esse cillum dolore eu fugiat nulla pariatur. Excepteur sint occaecat cupidatat non proident, sunt in culpa qui officia deserunt mollit anim id est laborum.

10

1½ spaced text with minimum capital size 0.28cm (approximately 12pt) (para 141)

Background Art

[0029] Lorem ipsum dolor sit amet, consectetur adipisicing elit, sed do eiusmod tempor incididunt ut labore et dolore magna aliqua. Ut enim ad minim veniam, quis nostrud exercitation ullamco laboris nisi ut aliquip ex ea commodo consequat. Duis aute irure dolor in reprehenderit in voluptate velit esse cillum dolore eu fugiat nulla pariatur. Excepteur sint occaecat cupidatat non proident, sunt in culpa qui officia deserunt mollit anim id est laborum.

15

[0030] Lorem ipsum dolor sit amet, consectetur adipisicing elit, sed do eiusmod tempor incididunt ut labore et dolore magna aliqua. Ut enim ad minim veniam, quis nostrud exercitation ullamco laboris nisi ut aliquip ex ea commodo consequat. Duis aute irure dolor in reprehenderit in voluptate velit esse cillum dolore eu fugiat nulla pariatur. Excepteur sint occaecat cupidatat non proident, sunt in culpa qui officia deserunt mollit anim id est laborum.

20

25

[0031] Lorem ipsum dolor sit amet, consectetur adipisicing elit, sed do

SUBSTITUTE SHEET (RULE 26)

minimum bottom margin 2cm (flexible - para 142)

any line numbering in left margin simply requires space between it and main text (para 144)

stamps indicating substitute sheets in bottom margin

image scanning carried out on text slightly beyond preferred boundaries, excluding most matter in margins

WIPO A4 text page layout.

230

Acronyms

DEFINITIONS OF USPTO & WIPO ACRONYMS
http://www.uspto.gov/learning-and-resources/glossary

ABSS	Automated Biotechnology Sequence Search System
ACRS	Application Capture and Review System
ACTS	Appeals Case Tracking System
ADS	Application Data Sheet
AIA	America Invents Act
BPAI	Board of Patent Appeals and Interferences
CCITT	Consultative Committee of International Telegraph and Telephone
CD-ROM	Compact Disc-Read Only Memory
CD-R	Compact Disc-Recordable
CDS	Classification Data System
CFR	Code of Federal Regulations
CIP	Continuation-In-Part
ConOps	Concept of Operations
CSIR	Classified Search & Image Retrieval
CSS	Cascading Style Sheet
CSS	Computer Search System
DO	Designated Office
Doc-Prep	A step in the Pre-Exam application process conducted by OIPE
DTD	Document Type Definition
EAR	Electronic Application Review
EAST	Examiner Automated Search Tool
EFS	Electronic Filing System (EFS-Web US)
EMR	Electronic Mail Room
EPAP	Electronic Patent Application Processing
EPAVE	Electronic Packaging and Validation Engine
EPO	European Patent Office
EU	European Union
FDC	Final Data Capture
FPAS	Foreign Patent Access System
FTP	File Transfer Protocol
FTS	File Tracking System
GAU	Group Art Unit, a subset of a Technology Center
GI	Geographical Indications
GPI	Global Patent Information
IA	International Application
IB	International Bureau (WIPO)
IDA	International Design Application
IDC	Initial Data Capture
IDS	Information Disclosure Statement
IFW	Image File Wrapper

231

Definitions of USPTO Acronyms [continued]:
http://www.uspto.gov/learning-and-resources/glossary

IPC	International Patent Classification
IPO	Intellectual Property Offices
IPSS	Integrated Patent Search System
ISA	International Searching Authority
IS&R	Image Search and Retrieval System
JPO	Japanese Patent Office
MPEP	Manual of Patent Examination Procedure
OACS	Office Action Correspondence Subsystem
OCR	Optical Character Recognition
OIPE	Office of Initial Pre-Examination
OPR	Office of Public Records
PAC	Patent Assistance Center
PACE	Patent Application Capture and Entry
PACR	Patent Application Capture and Review
PAIR	Patent Application Information Retrieval
PALM	Patent Application Locating and Monitoring
PCT	Patent Cooperation Treaty
PCT-Ops	PCT Operations
PGPUB	Pre-Grant Publication
PICS	Patent Image Capture System
PIRS	Patent Image Retrieval Systems
POWER	PCT Operations Workflow and Electronic Review
PTDLs	Patent and Trademark Depository Libraries
PREP	Patents Re-Engineering Prototype
RAM	Revenue Accounting & Management System
RO	Receiving Office
ROIB	Receiving Office International Bureau
SDF	Subclass Data File
SPE	Supervisory Patent Examiner
SPRE	Special Program Examiner
TAF	Technology Assessment and Forecast Program
TC	Technology Center
TEAM	Tools for Electronic Application Management
WEST	Web-based Examiner Search Tool
WIPO	World Intellectual Property Organization
XML	eXtensible Markup Language

INDEX

A

A4 drawing sheet size, 17, 19, 145, 230
Acknowledgements, ii
acronyms, 231, 232
actions, patent examiner, 5
allowance, 52
Annex, 221 - 232
arrows, 130
axonometric projection, 92
    dimetric projection, 92
    isometric projection, 92
    oblique projection, 92
    trimetric projection, 92
Author, about the, iii

B

broken lines, 170, 179, 207
browsers, supported, 41, 45

C

CAD/CAM, 26, 27
character of lines, numbers and letters, 107 - 109
chemical formulae, 74, 82
claim, design patent, 157, 167, 172, 173
classification, design patents, 185, 195
coding, 223, 224
coding for color, 228, 229
color drawings, 56, 77, 174, 175
color, lining for, 175, 228, 229
computer-generated icons, 163 - 166
content, tables of, iv - ix, 76, 158, 162, 170, 189, 212, 221
copyright, i, 131, 132, 168, 175, 192
cropping Hague reproductions, 196
corrections, patent drawings, 136, 209 - 219

D

data conversion, 54
description of design figures, 173
Design patent drawings, 157 - 159, 177 - 184
dimetric projection, 92
drawing, contents, 75
drawing, engineering, 67
drawing, graphic forms, 82, 83
drawing, identification of, 81, 145
drawing sheet, 15, 16, 19, 86, 87
drawing, words in, 15, 146, 147
drawings, color, 77, 157, 174, 175
drawings, design patent, 177 - 184
drawings, how made, 24, 25
drawings, informal, 65
drawings, processing of, 24, 25
drawings, production of, 24, 25
drawings, required, 74, 75

E

EFS-Web, USPTO, 40, 42 - 45, 62, 194
electrical symbols, 225, 226
examination of drawings, formalities and substantive, 153, 214, 219
Extensible markup language, 15, 48, 49, 54

F

Figure: Amended, Canceled, Correction, Modified, New, Reissue, 81, 212 - 214
fonts, 35, 127, 128, 134, 165
Foreign patent applications, see WIPO
formulae, chemical and mathematical, 74, 82, 146

G

graphic forms, 82, 83
graphic symbols, 222, 225 - 227
guidance, reproductions, 198, 208
Guides, patent drawing, 40, 57 - 63, 170, 185